COLOR CORRECTION FOR DIGITAL VIDEO

Using Desktop Tools to Perfect Your Image

*Steve Hullfish and
Jaime Fowler*

San Francisco, CA • New York, NY • Lawrence, KS

Published by CMP Books
an imprint of CMP Media LLC
Main office: 600 Harrison Street, San Francisco, CA 94107 USA
Tel: 415-947-6615; fax: 415-947-6015
Editorial office: 1601 West 23rd Street, Suite 200, Lawrence, KS 66046 USA
www.cmpbooks.com
email: books@cmp.com

Senior editor: Dorothy Cox
Managing editor: Michelle O'Neal
Copyeditor: Madeleine Reardon Dimond
Layout design: Michelle O'Neal and Madeleine Reardon Dimond
Graphics work: Justin Fulmer
Cover layout design: Damien Castaneda

Distributed to the book trade in the U.S. by: Distributed in Canada by:
Publishers Group West   Jaguar Book Group
1700 Fourth Street   100 Armstrong Avenue
Berkeley, CA 94710   Georgetown, Ontario M6K 3E7 Canada
1-800-788-3123   905-877-4483

For individual orders and for information on special discounts for quantity orders, please contact:
CMP Books Distribution Center, 6600 Silacci Way, Gilroy, CA 95020
Tel: 1-800-500-6875 or 408-848-3854; fax: 408-848-5784
email: cmp@rushorder.com; Web: www.cmpbooks.com

Printed in the United States of America
03 04 05 06 07   5 4 3 2 1

ISBN: 1-57820-201-9

CMP Books

Reviewers' Comments

"A great reference for all digital artists, from the diligent freelancer to the top colorist."
— Van Ling, VFX supervisor and DVD producer

"The book looks amazing! All those great color illustrations, wow. And the Tutorial section! I've always found color correction to be a daunting and impossible task, but *Color Correction for Digital Video* presents the subject in easy-to-understand language and offers very helpful sample images to help reinforce the concepts. This book should be required reading for every digital artist working in video today."
— Wes Plate, president, Automatic Duck, Inc.

"Color correction has gotten much more sophisticated over the years and learning about how and why it's done has gotten more complicated as a result. Fowler and Hullfish's book, *Color Correction for Digital Video*, demystifies the art of color correction, and shows you how to use the latest software to give your video and film work a unique look that's all your own. With interviews with master colorists, extensive tutorials using almost every current digital video editing application and plugin, and tips from every corner of the video and film industries, the book lets you in on the secrets of top professionals in the art of color correction in an accessible and interesting way. Now that color correction tools present themselves to you on just about every nonlinear editing system, this book is indispensable in showing you how to get the most out of these new capabilities. Highly recommended."
— Charlie White, digital video author and columnist, DigitalVideoEditing.com

"You have done an amazing job. Short of apprenticing with a colorist, the is the best guide I've ever seen. It's complete and detailed and I learned a great deal from it even though I've been color correcting for years. In fact, being mostly a self-taught colorist, I was happy to see that I was doing so much right. I think you've really hit an area that has a great need for this type of info. It could well become the text-book for color correction for years to come."
— Alan Miller, VP Postproduction, Moving Pictures. Editing credits include "Adoption" for the Hallmark Channel, "Soldiers in the Army of God" for HBO's America Undercover, a season of "Between the Lions" for WGBH, the opening for "The District" on CBS, and "Sesame English" for Sesame Workshop. Finish and color correction credits include the seven-part series "The Blues."

"This is the best book on video color correction I've ever seen. It is a *must-read* for any serious online Avid editor and needs to be in the bay alongside the tapes for reference when needed. This book does what the Avid user manuals can't—it teaches color correction, step-by-step, from theory to practice."
— Susan Perla, editor-producer, NBC Network News, *Today* show (formerly NBC *Dateline* and Discovery News)

Table of Contents

Chapter 8   Common Corrections Tutorials 123

Chapter 9   Advanced Corrections............................ 149

Appendix A   Software and Plugin Capabilities 163

Acknowledgments

Although writing is a fairly solitary task, the production of a book is not. Many people need to be acknowledged for their contributions to bringing this book to print.

Many experts from around the world generously offered their knowledge and wisdom, in particular Roy Wagner, Tal at Chainsaw, Thomas Madden at Kodak, Stephen Nakamura at Technique, Bob Sliga at Film and Tape, Randy Starnes, Mike Most, Peter Mavromates, Ed Colman of SuperDailies, Craig Leffel at Optimus, Alex Scudiero at I^3, Robert Lovejoy at Shooters, Rob Currier of Synthetic Aperture, Andre Brunger of 3-Prong, and Karl Sims of GenArts. For clarifying the finer points of waveforms and vectorscopes, thanks to Jonathan Giunchedi and Rick Hollowbush of VideoTek. My neighbor and friend, Greg "Tech Support" Gillis provided invaluable support and guidance. I'd also like to thank Thomas Madden, from Kodak, for his careful review of the theoretical aspects of the book and providing invaluable technical expertise and guidance.

I'd like to thank my editor at *DV* magazine, Jim Feeley, for buying the original pitch that a series of articles on color correction would be something that would interest his readers. That original series was the impetus for CMP Publications to begin discussions for this book.

I would like to thank Dorothy Cox for providing a guiding hand through the process of creating this book. Also at CMP Books, Michelle O'Neal, Justin Fulmer, Paul Temme, and Madeleine Reardon Dimond took on the task of turning lots of words and images into a final, marketable product.

I would like to thank my parents, William and Suzanne Hullfish, for instilling in me the importance of writing and creative thought. They also taught me that any journey begins with a single step and that the journey itself is often more wondrous and fulfilling than the destination. Those were important lessons to have tucked into my belt during the making of this book.

My co-author, Jaime Fowler, was a constant source of support and a great sounding board and cheerleader. Jaime's experience as both an author, editor, and teacher are evident throughout the book. In a field where being a storyteller is one of the hottest compliments to be paid to someone, Jaime is one of the best storytellers I know.

Finally, my wife, Jody, was the greatest force behind this book. She endured many months of being a *de facto* single parent to our two children, and she was more sympathetic to the strains and struggles that this book placed on our family than I had a right to expect. Without her patience, love, and understanding, I would not have been able to complete this book. Thank you, Jody.

–Steve Hullfish

My wife Peggy and children Lauren, Brendan, and Joshua all helped by leaving me be during the crunch stage of the book, feeding me leftovers, and basically letting me take over the dining room table *again* for a few crucial months.

My colleague and co-author Steven Hullfish managed to motivate and occasionally talked me down from writing "theory" into writing in the "real world." Steve's also been great for our first-time collaboration. It was kind of fun—in an evil sort of way—to watch him go through the same pain as I did during the writing of my first book. More importantly, I hope his wife Jody and the kids will let me borrow him for a few other concepts that are in the hopper.

Dorothy Cox was amazingly patient. She knew we had the right stuff and just waited for it to come out. Also I must thank Trish Meyer for quietly championing this book. Trish was our behind-the-scenes promoter—I can't thank her enough for that.

The colorists in this book are amazing. My special thanks to Jim Barrett and Julius Friede for shining light on the black art, and to my friend and fellow editor Lisa Day, who has always been very kind and helpful to me. Also thanks to DK and the Buda Bunch for occasionally bringing some "colorful" memories to light. Special thanks to Steve Bayes, whose cat analogy was borrowed for this book.

Joel Fowler (no relation) has been a teacher and mentor who never gave up and was always inspiring. Dave and Bettie Fowler (yes, they're my parents) have always been a guiding light to me by telling me to do what I want and have fun, pretty much what I've always done since Day One.

–Jaime Fowler

Introduction

As technology brings more and more innovations into the edit suite, editors are expected to perform a much broader spectrum of postproduction tasks, including audio sweetening, compositing, graphics, compression, and 3D animation—not to mention editing. Now you can add to this list the daunting responsibility of color correction. Not simply making an image brighter or darker or "legal," but manipulating the picture with a vast palette of tools that have only recently become available on the desktop.

In a traditional high-end postproduction workflow, a skilled colorist with dedicated, powerful equipment performs the color correction. The colorist is often one of the highest paid in the ranks of postproduction. And now, the humble editor is increasingly being called upon to perform the colorist's responsibilities, thanks to color correction engines that have been incorporated into many of the higher-end NLEs, like Avid's Symphony and DS, Discreet's Smoke, and Editbox from Quantel. Even on the lower end of the cost spectrum, powerful color correction tools are becoming widely available. Most prominent is the introduction of color correction capabilities in Apple's Final Cut Pro and in Avid's Xpress DV. The third-party plugin market is also providing color correction tools with products like Synthetic Aperture's Color Finesse and 3Prong's ColorFiX AVX plugin.

Many editors have used the basic video level adjustments for decades—hue, saturation, luminance, and black level—but are now discovering the astounding and confusing amount of control they can have to alter the quality and look of their images. Other editors still have not realized the scope of the control that they could have or how to harness the power of the tools at their disposal. Although professional colorists spend a lifetime perfecting their craft, this book will provide you with the important concepts and power-user tips that will allow you to improve the look of all your projects.

While many people have sought to mystify the talents of color correction—turning it into some form of unattainable black magic—this book seeks to demonstrate that the fundamentals can be learned and used by anyone with the proper tools at their disposal. As with anything, practice and experience will help transform the fundamental knowledge into a valuable skill.

This knowledge can have a fantastic impact on your career. Often clients don't see the difference that a well-paced montage or a perfectly timed cut can make in a project, but when you start using color correction to add polish to the images themselves, clients never fail to notice what you're adding to their project.

A note about the color images in this book

Color video is additive. As a result, some of the images in this book—which is printed subtractively with color inks—may not reproduce accurately on the printed page. For a more complete explanation of this issue, please refer to the "Additive and Subtractive Color" section beginning on page 16 in Chapter 2. Many of the book's images are also included on the companion CD-ROM.

Chapter 1

The Role of The Colorist

Almost every nonlinear editing system has a color correction tool. These range from built-in interfaces (such as Apple's Final Cut Pro and Avid's Symphony) to plugin effects. The difference for the editors is that in addition to cutting and effects, they are now required to have some experience with color correction. This doesn't mean that all editors should be great colorists, but the ability to at least correct color problems is a must.

Video-to-Video Color Correction

Twenty years ago, the term *colorist* did not exist. We lived in a world where what you shot was pretty much what you got. The only methods of adjusting color were primitive and coarse.

Video had a unique set of issues. Cameras in the 1970s had indoor and outdoor filters and white balancing. All too often, the person behind the lens would use the wrong filter and forget to do a white balance. Some color cameras had monochrome viewfinders. Other viewfinders had color, but you never trusted a viewfinder anyway. As a result, the filter mismatch was a common issue. And fixing the problem was, as they say, like taking glue off of a cat. No matter what you did—fix it or leave it alone—you got a bad result.

The only common means of correcting video in a postproduction suite was with a time base corrector. The TBC controlled video brightness, black levels, hue, and saturation. There were no settings for mid-tones, individual color channels, or any other commonly used color correction parameters that we see today.

For those postproduction facilities that served the more expensive clientele, video color correction was made available in the mid-1970s. These controls, by today's standards, were quite primitive, and yet they had the ability to adjust the picture enough to correct for improper camera filtering. There was individual control over each color channel. And that was it. The systems that were available at that time were considered revolutionary and at the same time, basic.

Video-to-video color correction wasn't particularly common or practical in the mid-1970s. The video signals were analog, measured by variable voltage. Creating a corrected master meant the loss of one generation of your original master. In most cases, the color correction was done during editing to prevent any further generational loss. The early correctional tools often generated more noise. There were no noise-canceling filters, no video-safe filters to regulate output, and the only analysis tools were a waveform, a vectorscope, and your eyes.

The biggest problem with early color correction was that it was not easy to recreate settings. Most, if not all, of the first-generation color correction systems had no memory or storage capacity. They could not use templates of previous setups. Although they used electronic manipulation, there was no computer control. As a result, one minor bump of a joystick could spell disaster.

Telecine Color Correction

The modern telecine started out as what is now known as a *film chain*. The film chain was a camera pointed at a film projector, usually 16mm. The film was projected directly into the camera lens. The signal from the camera was sent directly to a transmitter and was broadcast, or in some cases, transferred to videotape for later broadcast in one continuous pass. The camera on the film chain had some control over the amount of primary colors—red, green, and blue—as well as luminance and set-up values.

Aged film is hard to watch. The color and contrast fade. Much of the color has a magenta tone. As a result, film chain engineers could adjust the camera to compensate for these issues. By adjusting the color on the cameras, these engineers were the first colorists.

Years later, the telecine developed. The telecine actually is different from film chains in two key aspects. First, it has the ability to scan an image with a gas electron beam rather than by shining light through it. Because this beam does not generate the intense heat that old film chain lamps did, it was impossible to melt or burn the film with a telecine. Combined with a capstan-driven transport, the film in a telecine is handled gently enough so that even original negatives can be used in a transfer session. Another important development was that telecines use a method of synchronization to video so that the film passes through at a regular interval. Because film is 24 fps and NTSC video is (approximately) 30 fps, the telecine would hold each frame for a number of fields, based on a 2:3 ratio. This 2:3 pulldown enabled a precise synchronization of the video images to the film. A film chain was not that precise; whatever passed through the projector went to the camera. There was no synchronization of the two devices.

Roy Wagner, ASC, remembers the early days of experimentation:

> My initial involvement with this was in the sixties with the EBR—electron beam recorder. I was in the Air Force, and we were doing studies with the electron beam recorder. We were doing it way before Rank was involved, at least commercially involved. When the C5 bomber came out

we shot the first flight of the C5 with the electron beam recorder and also with 16mm. I was, at that time, pretty ignorant about the process, and I was startled at the quality of the image. Then years later, when I was doing the very first Showtime project, which was called *The Family Tree*, we transferred on the Rank, which was a baby. It was the first one that I'm aware of in Los Angeles, which was at Compact Video. And I looked at the beam that they were using and said, "This looks awfully, awfully much like an electron beam recorder." And they started laughing and said, "This is (very much) like an electron beam recorder." It was a horrific experience, but what was exciting for me was that what I was seeing was significantly better going from the negative to tape than what I was seeing going with a film chain, which was what had been done before.

Jim Barrett, Senior Colorist at Downstream Digital, has some similar recollections:

I entered into video postproduction while attending film school at Long Beach State University during the early 1980s. My first job was in mastering feature films for a company that made laserdiscs, the predecessor to the DVD format. We transferred films to video using the first device made at that time to create high-resolution video, a flying spot scanner by a company from England, Rank Cintel.

The Rank, as it was called, would evolve during the next few years to find a permanent place in the process of how film shot for commercials would be transferred to broadcast quality video. I found myself in the unique situation of just starting a career path in video postproduction at the same time as a new technology was emerging. It wasn't long before I was threading film onto the Rank and sitting at the remote controls to set the brightness and color settings for a particular film. The controls at the time were very rudimentary, allowing an operator to merely brighten and darken a scene, add or subtract the overall chroma levels, and set a basic white balance. The goal was to merely make a positive video print from a film internegative. It was nothing more than an elaborate and sophisticated film chain.

The Rank made film transfers to video possible. But one of its biggest features was its ability to handle film. The Rank was a scanner that was capstan driven, so it didn't have the jerky motion of a projector, which frequently could cause film breaks and burned film from hot projector bulbs. Jim Barrett remembers how it felt to be at the forefront of a revolution:

Up to this time, 1985, there was no device that would safely handle camera original negative film. You always had a print made by a film lab. Now that we could create the positive intermediate from the original film, video postproduction companies started the film to tape transfer process.

From Color Corrector to Colorist

Over time, the controls for color correction, particularly with telecine, became more elaborate (see Figure 1.1). As a result, the people associated with the task of correcting color—many of whom were video engineers—began to experiment with the controls, developing different looks or styles with film.

1.1   At the controls: A colorist manipulates a film with the Da Vinci Renaissance 8:8:8 Color Correction System, a state-of-the-art tool.

At first, it was more experimental, something to do between sessions. But in San Francisco, a director named Leslie Dektor had a novel idea.

Jim Barrett recalls one of the first telecine sessions that produced a style rather than just correction:

> Once the film was threaded up and you sat at the controls, it wasn't long before the more artistic commercial and music video directors figured out that they could have a multitude of "looks" and "treatments" from the same piece of film. I got to see this early on when I watched a colorist work with the commercial director Leslie Dektor. They took film footage from the streets of New York, put it on a Rank, made it dark with a heavy blue wash and created the Levi's 501 Blues campaign. Why would you take beautiful photography and mess it up? It seemed like a mistake. Weren't we supposed to be "color correcting?" That was the beauty of that moment. I finally understood what a colorist is and how pliable a piece of film can be.

When it became clear that elements of style could be implemented through the use of modern color correction, the use of style became more widespread. Today, everything—television commercials, programs, and feature films reflect the use of this modern technology. The role of colorist had clearly changed to color stylist.

A modern colorist has some tools to help affect the style of a transfer. These tools (shown on the left in Figure 1.2) are put through the gate of the telecine (shown on the right in Figure 1.2) to produce dazzling effects (see Figure 1.3).

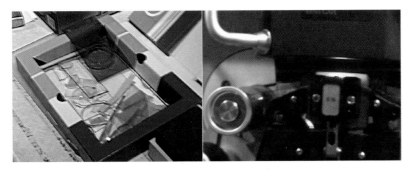

1.2 Gate tools. Jim Barrett uses a variety of tools for manipulation in the telecine gate. Glass slides, rubber bands, colored filters, plastic swizzle sticks, and a variety of small lenses produce a variety of effects.

Roy Wagner, ASC, discusses his use of telecine technology in the production of *CSI: Crime Scene Investigation*, produced by Jerry Bruckheimer:

It was originally my intent to create a surreal abstraction visually. Mr. Bruckheimer wanted a more dynamic, more hip style. I did not wish to incur the cost of weekly bleach-bypass lab bills. I chose to pursue the look in the negative to tape transfer. The series is filmed Super 35mm, transferred to High Definition. I steepened the gamma, concealing most of the middle values. I also pushed the pedestal until the grain structure was more visible. By making the gamma steeper, the color palette became more limited and more surreal. By overlighting the highlights and by not using fill light, the film didn't have a chance of ever appearing normal. The color choices were based upon the golden tones of the hot Las Vegas desert and the Technicolor saturation of Las Vegas nightlife. The murder scenes were cold and green, making the event grizzlier, uncomfortable for the viewer. Frankly, the other intention was to create a look that was so striking that it would halt channel surfers. Surfers don't stop on a channel because they hear a word that lures them. They are halted because something striking catches their eye. This is becoming a more prevalent requirement when creating a visual language for a new television series.

With the advent of artistry in the editing and telecine suite, some colorists feel awkward with the term *color correction* because it lacks the essence of the artistry that every colorist must employ.

1.3 Jim Barrett of Downstream Digital manipulates a rubber band in the gate *(left)* to create a dazzling transition effect *(right)*.

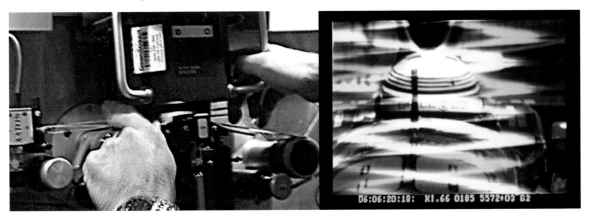

Jim Barrett discusses the creative process of the colorist at LucasFilm on **The Young Indiana Jones Chronicles**

The most demanding job I ever had as a colorist was in taking over the colorist duties for the television series of *Young Indiana Jones* produced by George Lucas. I spent three years on this project, and to this day it was the most rewarding. The typical episode would have many layers that need to blend together. But it is the Lucas approach to the colorist's duties that was unusual. A normal session with a colorist will occur in real time. The colorist will manipulate the look of a film image and through a process of comparison and elimination get an approval from the client who is sitting with him. Not so with George Lucas. I was asked to spend some hours on an episode, unsupervised, for about a month's time with all of the layers and then sit for a screening. The screening would take place in a small living room set-ting with myself, George Lucas, an editor and a pro-ducer or two seated on couches in front of a large screen television. We would watch the edited show that I had done color correction and scene-to-scene matching on. And with a yellow pad of paper and pen I would scribble notes in the darkened room whenever George Lucas would comment. "Too yellow." "Make that scene look like The Godfather." "That looks a little red." I remember thinking "This guy knows a thing or two about technology, and here I am writing notes on a yellow pad." I would leave this screening with my notes and spend an additional two weeks on the changes, and we would have another screening. It was an unusual way to work but satisfying in that he didn't need to rush things. It was a very traditional approach in film where a "timed" trial print would be screened from the original negative. A film lab tech-nician would take notes on the desired changes and make a new "answer" print that would incorporate those changes.

Jim Barrett stresses the need for stylized skills for the successful colorist.

> I like to look at fashion magazines for inspiration. Sometimes the style that they use is more important than the actual clothing. That's important to remember when you're working as a colorist.
>
> You don't wait for someone to suggest something when they come into the suite. You have to come up with a few ideas to get a reaction from the client. That way you can determine the direction they want to go. The image itself suggests what you might want to try to do with it. First I take a look at the image the way it was originally exposed. I store that in memory. You'll hear comments right away. Maybe they want to see more detail. So I'll adjust the detail. I'll try to introduce new looks. It's a great way to keep the session moving by getting a decision from the client. I'll show them something, and they'll say, "Hmmm." Then I'll change it, and they'll say, "Hey, that looks great!" So we'll run it that way. A lot of it is intuitive, based on your experience and exposure to different styles. With each film, it's a different approach. Even the same clients will approach each film differently.

Datacine

Today, telecines have expanded their capability to what is known as a datacine. A datacine works much the same as telecine, with one major exception: it has the ability to create large image files that are suitable for transfer to film. While previous telecines expanded their capability to high-definition television standards, a datacine can go beyond the HDTV standards, producing a 2K file (2,000×2,000 pixel image) Some datacines go beyond the 2K standard and produce 4K files. The datacine scans the film image and transfers it through a high-speed parallel protocol interface (HIPPI) which records the scan in an image file. The images can be stored on drive arrays for transfer to a film recorder, which reads the image file and scans it back onto film via a film recorder.

Datacines are very popular these days, and as a result, colorists are busier than ever. The reason that filmmakers love datacines is simple: using a datacine to create an IP (interpositive) of a film allows more flexibility and latitude for the director. An interpositive created by datacine is frequently referred to as a digital interpositive or digital IP.

The older method of creating the interpositive was done chemically by a person called a color timer. The color timer would adjust colors and exposure of a film. These adjustments are referred to as *points*. For example, a director would tell the color timer, "Increase brightness scene 53 by two points," which meant that the exposure was to go up by a set amount. Or, "Make it two points redder." The director would not see the results until the film positive was graded again. Once done, the new print was shown, and the director could readjust the film. The process was time consuming.

Film editor Lisa Day recalls the process of color timing:

> The first time through I would sit with the director, the DP, and the timer in the lab, and we would just run the film straight through, mostly commenting as we went. From that point, the timer knew where we were going, so the DP usually wouldn't have to come back to look at the answer print until we were finished.

Peter Mavromates, postproduction supervisor, Panic Room, *speaks about DataCine*

One of my roles is discussing with the director and the DP what it is we're doing on this movie and how we're going to get there. And can we get it done with the time and money that we have? With *Panic Room*, David (Director David Fincher) wanted to do this digital intermediate process. So "Is that doable?" That's the first question. In building a comfort level that it is doable, one of the things I have to do is—at different parts of the process—say, "Well, let's do a test." Then I have to design that test. And to make it a valid test, we need to take it from point A to point B.

In the case of this digital intermediate process it means, "Let's take some shots." In this case, we took some hair and makeup tests, which are going to begin to reflect the conditions of the movie, and did a film-out test. "Let's do a film-out test at different places and see what we think about it." But the film-out test is only partially valid. That only tells us that in theory the process works. But is this process robust enough to take it to a release print? So then we go to the next step, and we take this negative and go do a release print on it. We'll do an IP and then take a release print. And then let's take it one more step and say is this photochemical IP as good as if we filmed out a digital IP? And then we did that test, and we said, "It does look like we actually do improve quality by doing a digital IP instead of doing a digital negative and going photochemical from that point." So my point is that part of my contribution is designing and executing testing. Again, this is where David sort of gets what he wants by having a post supervisor around.

In other movies the DPs have to coordinate those tests on their own. By my doing it, I take some of the burden off the camera department so that their energies are not going to coordinating these things and the follow-through issues. So they can concentrate on the artistic part of their job and not get bogged down by having somebody produce those things for them.

[Color correction is] one of those things that is valuable so that when the person sitting down watching the movie is watching the movie. They are not distracted by things that they shouldn't be distracted by.

For the second run, I would look at the answer print and make notes with the timer without the director. We had to go over and over it again to get a good mix. For example, on *White Fang* it took several prints to get the snow the right color. Once the DP was happy with the snow color, the rest of the color sort of fell into place. Usually once the initial notes were made, the director and DP wouldn't screen the print until the timer got it to a point where I thought it was right. But that often took several prints.

With datacine, the director sees the results on the screen. Once the film is electronically graded, the disk images are scanned back to 35mm and projected. For the colorist, who works with the director to achieve the proper grading, it can be exciting. Julius Friede, Senior Colorist for *O Brother, Where Art Thou*, confirms:

> Working on commercials or music videos, you often get to work with the director, but in traditional film mastering, the grading usually happens farther down the line, and the director (and DP) too often, unfortunately, have moved on to other projects. When they are involved, you get immediate feedback on what is desired by the people that are most intimately involved.
>
> Joel and Ethan Coen, along with Roger Deakins (the DP), knew what they wanted to see on screen, and I was the one that had to technically figure how to best achieve that. The closest I can claim to development is in preproduction discussions whereby it was determined that it was best to shoot without filtration or other production techniques so as to give the widest palette possible during grading.

Phantom Telecine

One of the issues with datacine transfer is the lack of real-time capability. Some datacines transfer at somewhat slower rates than the 24 fps norm. It is crucial for the colorist to see the film as it will appear when projected.

After the film is transferred to a datacine, it is possible to play back the created files from the disk array to a coloring station. This is known as phantom datacine, because the scanner is not used. The colorist can play back from the disk array in real time with a phantom telecine and adjust the levels properly.

Whether it be a telecine, datacine, phantom telecine, or a plugin on a nonlinear editing system, the person in charge of such equipment today can be called a colorist. A colorist is defined as one who adjusts color in pictures on a daily basis and has more than enough experience in dealing with all aspects of color. Colorists understand range, contrast, gamut, chromaticity, and luminance. They understand how much latitude they can expect from a given source, be it a particular film stock or a video camera. To the professional colorist, analysis of pictures is a common, everyday occurrence.

As most professions, there are many different types of colorists, ranging from the more technically minded who work to attain proper signal-to-noise ratio and an accurate representation of the original color of a film, to the stylists, who will tweak the controls of their systems to create a different look through manipulation and an understanding of stylish trends.

This book is intended to help you understand color and will enable you to correct color. Throughout the chapters, you'll find a lot of information about both technical and creative aspects of being a colorist. Sometimes, two interview sources might not agree. It's a very subjective topic.

Diplomacy

An often forgotten but most important trait of both colorists and editors is the art of diplomacy. Julius Friede comments:

> About the best tip I can give is to listen to your client and don't always assume that you know best (as hard as that is to imagine.) Of course, you know your equipment better (I hope), but you can always learn something new. I can't even begin to list the times I scoffed (to myself) when I was asked by a client to try something, only to discover that he/she was right. Even if you prefer one setting or look over the client's preference, that is not necessarily better, just different. The big trick, in my opinion, is not to try and impose your own POV over the client's, but to enhance what the client is looking for, even if you would do it differently.

The Future

With the popularity of color correction on nonlinear systems, color correction—like video editing and desktop publishing—has truly become democratized. Consumers and professionals alike can benefit from the tools and skills of the colorist.

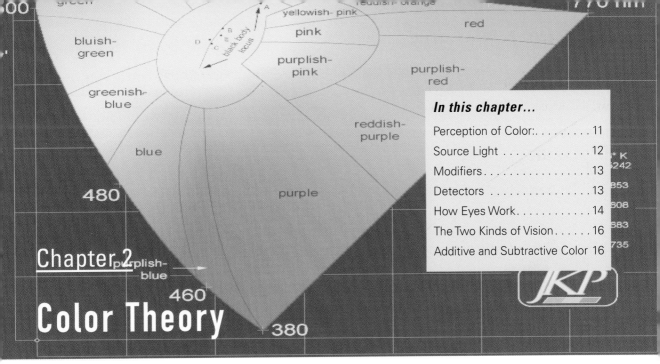

Chapter 2

Color Theory

Perception of Color:

It's All in Your Head[1]

There is a giant nuclear reaction of apocalyptic proportions taking place next door. This nuclear reaction, a continuing eruption of nuclear energy and the emission of electromagnetic waves, comes from the sun. Some of these electromagnetic waves are visible light and are perceived as color by human beings and animals. To the sun, they're just another form of electromagnetic energy, emitted in waves. These waves represent what we know as the visible wavelength spectrum.

Light is emitted at different wavelengths, each one corresponding to a different color. The visible portion of the electromagnetic spectrum starts at wavelengths of around 380 nm (nanometers) generally perceived as violet, and continues to wavelengths generally perceived as red (700 nm). Any waves above and below that spectrum are unseen by the human eye. Still, they exist.

In the model shown in Figure 2.1, the visible portion of the spectrum and adjacent waves are shown, but the visible portion is actually a very small part of the entire EMS. It's easy to remember the color order of the visible spectrum by using a simple code: *Roy G. Biv.* Red, Orange Yellow, Green, Blue, Indigo, Violet. The code begins with the longer wavelengths and proceeds to the shorter, i.e., violet. Another simple way of remembering the spectrum is: *Richard Of York Gave Battle In Vain.*

Color is a sensation created by a combination of three factors: a source, a modifier, and a detector. Each one of these components must be properly working in concert in order to create the perception of color.

---

1. Chapter opening image courtesy of Joe Kane Productions.

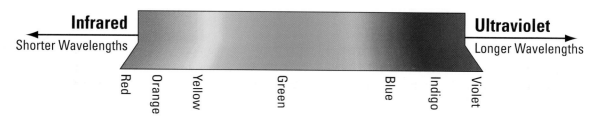

Infrared → Shorter Wavelengths

Ultraviolet → Longer Wavelengths

Red · Orange · Yellow · Green · Blue · Indigo · Violet

2.1   The Electromagnetic Spectrum.

Kelvin	Description
18000	Clear Blue Sky
16000	Average Blue Sky
13000	Blue Sky, Light Clouds
11000	Skylight–Indirect Sun
9000	Hazy Sky, Light Shade
8000	Cloudy Sky, Light Shade
7000	Overcast Sky
6500	D85–Sun and Sky Average Electronic Flash
6000	Blue Flashbulb
5500	Photo Daylight, Midday Sun
5000	Fluorescent
4500	2 Hours After Sunrise
4000	Moonlight
3500	Clear Flashbulb Photoflood
3000	Warm Fluorescent Studio Tungsten Light
2500	1000 Watt Light Bulb
2000	Sunrise
1400	Candle Light
1200	Molten Lava

2.2   Scale of light in degrees Kelvin.

Source Light

The source of light can come from any light-emitting object. That is, any object that emits electromagnetic energy at 400–700 nm. The sun, a lightbulb, a flashlight, or a firefly—these are all sources of light. The color of light emitted from the source will vary, which will affect the way that you see objects, which are illuminated by the source. Sometimes the color of light is altered by the medium through which it travels. For example, the light of the sun is refracted somewhat as it travels through our atmosphere.

Color temperature

Any source that emits light has a color temperature. Color temperatures are measured in degrees Kelvin. The Kelvin scale is derived from astronomy. The observation of light emitted from a black body when heated determines its color temperature. As the black body is heated to varying temperatures, the color of light emitted changes. Figure 2.2 illustrates the different color temperatures of light.

At the lower end of the Kelvin spectrum is red. The higher degrees of Kelvin temperatures emit blue. Lava emits a very red light at 1,200 K. Incandescent light, usually emitted by tungsten light bulbs, is a warm yellow at 2,850–3,200 K. The sun emits about 6,504 K.The light of the sun is bluish.

There is no perfect, uniform, untainted, white source of light in the universe. The sun, which is used as a reference when adjusting images, is known to radiate at a certain color temperature. The average color temperature of the sun is 6,504 K. But even this constant fluctuates, depending on variants including the earth's atmosphere which can affect the color temperature of the sun before it reaches our eyes.

The color temperature of light can alter our perception of modifiers. Consider diamonds, which are best seen in whiter light. In most jewelry stores, you will see special light bulbs, usually halogen, which emit light of higher color temperatures than tungsten indoor bulbs. If diamonds were to be viewed in orange tungsten light, their impression would be less favorable. An orange diamond is not a highly coveted possession. Merchants know this and often manipulate light so that shoppers can see their merchandise "in the best possible light."

When we express the color temperature of light in degrees Kelvin, the most accurate representation of a "pure" light source, aside from the sun, is any light source that radiates 6,500 K, or D_{65}. When adjusting computer monitors, it's important to be sure their white points are set to correspond to this color temperature, or else all other factors of color correction will be inaccurate. Broadcast video systems are defined for D_{65} white point chromaticity.

Modifiers

When light is emitted, it illuminates objects that can reflect (or transmit) and absorb different wavelengths of that light to varying degrees. These objects are called modifiers. When a modifier strongly reflects certain wavelengths of light, we perceive those reflected wavelengths to be the "color" of that object. For example, an orange tends to strongly reflect longer visible wavelengths and is generally seen as orange. A concord grape strongly reflects shorter visible wavelengths and is generally seen as purple. Modifiers can also reflect and even emit some electromagnetic waves that are not visible to the naked eye. For example, infrared sensors and "night vision" scopes can pick up emitted infrared heat or waves from people, animals, and plants.

Modifiers can also absorb different wavelengths of light. The orange mentioned previously reflects relatively more of the longer visible wavelengths of light, but when lluminated by wide spectrum light, it also absorbs much of the light of shorter wavelengths, generally seen as purple or indigo, which you normally wouldn't perceive when looking at an orange.

The spectral reflectance of modifiers is especially important to the colorist because the spectral reflection can cause a phenomenon known as a *color cast*. Color casts affect the immediate area surrounding the modifier. When an orange is illuminated, other objects near it that are capable of absorbing or reflecting orange-colored light, in addition to their normal spectral reflectance of a shared light source.

Detectors

The final component of color is the detector. In human beings, the detector is a combination of interaction between our eyes and our brains. While the eye might be in perfect condition, our brain must decipher the information received from the eye correctly. It is known that babies cannot process all of the information that their eyes give their brains; thus they can become overloaded visually with too much information. Parents are told that babies can decipher high-contrast black-and-white objects best. This is also true of many eye transplant recipients, who, even though given perfect eyes, are sometimes unable to decipher all of the information going to their brains. The color sensation is encoded in the eye and decoded in the brain. Without the proper elements to encode this sensation and the ability to decode it, we would be (and many are) color blind, or partially so.

How Eyes Work

Your eyes are the only true detectors of the sensation of color. Other means of color and light detection are artificial, derived from measuring electromagnetic waves. Eyes are a fairly sophisticated and accurate tool. They consist of two sensors that receive and encode the light reflected from or transmitted by the objects that you see. These sensors, located in the retina, are long in shape and are oriented so that they can determine pinpoint direction of a light source and adjust to different viewing conditions. Incoming electromagnetic waves are detected by these sensors and sent to your optic nerve, which takes them to the brain for deciphering.

Rods

The first of these detectors are the rods. Human beings have approximately 130,000,000 rods in each retina. Because they do not discriminate color, we could say that they detect brightness information only. The rods in your eye are located on the outside edge of an area of the retina, the center of which is populated by cones, which detect color. Because of this, you might notice that your perception of color detail in your peripheral vision is poorer than it is in your central field of view.

Cones

Cones come in three different varieties: red-, green-, and blue-light sensitive. But it isn't quite that simple, as you can see in Figure 2.3. Red cones (erythrolabe) can be achromatic, like rods, and also red-green and yellow sensitive. Blue cones (cyanolabe) can be achromatic and blue-yellow sensitive. Green cones (chlorolabe) can be achromatic, red-green, and yellow sensitive. You'll also notice that the yellow-only channel is a subchannel of the blue-yellow channel. Thus, electromagnetic waves that enter

2.3 A diagram of the human eye with the fovial region noted. Note that cones have both achromatic (luminance detection) abilities as well as color information. The two color channels are red-green and blue yellow, with an additional subchannel of yellows. Cones are in the fovial region of the eye, while rods are on the periphery, making color detection difficult within our peripheral vision. In darkness, when chromatic detection is near impossible, the rods and cones work together to try to compensate, making our peripheral vision somewhat better in darkness.

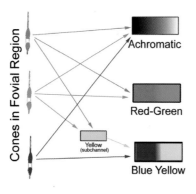

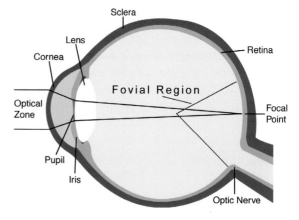

your eyes as continuous spectral energy are converted by the cones and rods to two channels of chrominance (blue-yellow and red-green) and one channel of luminance (achromatic). This method of visual perception is emulated in color video systems as we will see later on. Cones are located in the fovea, the center of your retina, adjacent to the optic nerve. The fovea is the region where highest resolution is perceived. Consequently, color detection is difficult within our peripheral vision. In darkness when chromatic detection is near impossible, the rods and cones work together to try to compensate, making our peripheral vision somewhat better in darkness.

Your eyes have many more rods than cones—there are only 7,000,000 cones in each retina compared to 130,000,000 rods. Thus we have far more sensitivity to luminance than we do chrominance. This comes into play when we determine the best methods of sampling color in video systems. Eyes are far more aware of variations in luminance than they are when it comes to chromatic differences.

Cone resolution

Eyes have different response to the varying wavelengths of color that we see. While our eyes are sensitive to all colors, some colors are not as resolved as others. The eye has little ability to detect high resolution in the color blue.

The reason for this is simple and related to the ratio of green and red cones to blue cones. Along the periphery of the fovea, the ratio of red and green cones to blue cones is 14:1. As we enter the center of the fovea, the ratio can increase by as much as 20:1. Thus our eyes do not perceive enough blue physically to obtain as much resolution from it, as opposed to green and red receptors.

As a result, we have a tendency to see blues as less resolved, or even fuzzy. In order to prevent this phenomenon from hindering our ability to perceive higher resolutions of red and green, the eye has a blue filter on top of the fovea called the macula lutea. The macula lutea blocks any blue light from green receptors in particular, which perceive some blue light. By blocking blue light in the center of the fovea, the macula lutea enables us to perceive high definition in reds and greens without blue interference.

Try focusing on the two blocks in Figure 2.4 for about 20 seconds. Note that after a while they both appear fuzzy. Our visual system cannot perceive higher resolution blue. As a result, it adapts and you perceive both blocks as fuzzy.

2.4 Blue and red blocks.

The Two Kinds of Vision

Our eyes, like most organs in our bodies, have the ability to adapt. Significant changes take place in our visual system when adapting from light to dark situations. These two different kinds of conditions result in physiological responses from our visual system. The two types of vision are referred to as:

- *photopic* (where light is plentiful)
- *scotopic* (where light is scarce)

Photopic vision

Under well-lit conditions, our eyes use cones as primary receptors. As mentioned previously, cones have the ability to detect brightness as well as color information. With photopic vision, the cones receive plentiful color information. We have excellent visual acuity because these cones, located in the fovea, are at the center of our retinas.

Scotopic vision

Scotopic vision, or night vision, uses rods as our primary receptors. During these dark or near-dark conditions, our ability to see color is absent. Cones are not used in scotopic vision, which prevents the perception of color. Another interesting fact is that scotopic vision is less *defined* because the foveal region of the retina is unused, thus the center receptors are not active, preventing visual acuity.

Additive and Subtractive Color

There are two methods of reproducing colors: additive and subtractive. Color produced by video monitors and projectors are generated using three additive primary colors of red, green, and blue (or *RGB*) light. In some cases, these devices use optic splitting devices—prisms—that create separate images corresponding to each channel of red, green, and blue light in the picture. As a result, a separate monochromatic image of each of these primary colors is generated. The light of the combined generated image is detected by your eye and the colors are recreated in your brain. When we use additive methods, we start with black, combining light of the primary colors red, green, and blue. When added in the right combination, these three colors can create white.

Inks, dyes, or pigments subtract light by using three subtractive primary colors. These colors are cyan, magenta, and yellow. Subtractive color works on the principle that a support material (a white piece of paper, for example) has colorants combined with it which absorb light of different wavelengths. Thus it could be said that subtractive color starts with white which is selectively filtered by the subtractive colorants. When combined in the right formulation, the subtractive primaries can create black. A problem with subtractive inks, dyes, and pigments is that they are inherently impure, i.e., they do not absorb light of only one primary color. Instead of a black, they can sometimes create a murky dark brown when combined. To remedy this, an additional black colorant is sometimes added to the subtractive process, and the colors are referred to as CMYK, where K represents black.

Although it may seem strange, the medium of film is actually a subtractive process. By combining different dyes, the print is created. One of Kodak's color scientist, Thomas Madden, explains the advantages and disadvantages of video and film gamuts:

> Since a video display works additively, it can do a good job of making certain saturated colors of high lightness because as more primary-colored light is added, the lightness of the color increases. Film, on the other hand, is good at producing dark, saturated colors because as more colored dye is added, the lightness of the color decreases. Depending on the particular video and film systems, there, of course, will be a volume of colors where the video display and film gamuts intersect, and there are other regions of color where one gamut may exceed the other.

Color spaces

How do we define a specific color or group of color? Scientists have been working on this problem for years. In 1633, Sir Isaac Newton was quarantined at home and could not return to Cambridge for the entire year because the plague was sweeping across Europe. To cure his boredom, he cut holes in his curtains and conducted experiments with light, using a prism. Newton discovered that white light was comprised of a spectrum of colors at pure wavelengths. His experiments resulted in the invention of the color wheel, which is much like the color picker used on some computers. The color wheel defined the spectrum of light as a continuous 360° circle with complementary colors opposed at 180° difference from each other. While this may seem common knowledge today, remember that in Newton's day, scientists were working more through observation and nature and had less proven facts. Note that rainbows have no magenta color in them. They are composed only of those colors found in the spectrum. The combination of red and violet, which are at opposite ends of the rainbow, are not displayed. Thus, Newton had to find the missing link to complete the color wheel (see Figure 2.5). He completed the wheel with the addition of magenta.

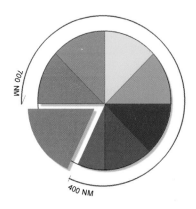

2.5 Newton's Color Wheel. Note that magenta, which bridges the spectrum boundaries of red and violet, is inserted.

Space vs. gamut—What's the difference?

A color space is a universally agreed upon description of color. There are two different kinds of color spaces: device dependent and stimulus dependent. But these color spaces only define the descriptions of the space, not the color variations within.

A lot of people use the term *color space* when referring to a color gamut and *color gamut* when referring to a color space. The two are ideologically different, but can be easily confused. When we say that a color space is a universally agreed upon description of color, we mean that it is just that—a description, usually mathematical. Color gamuts, however, are the actual colors or variations of color contained in that space.

A color space can be defined as a three-dimensional representation of a theoretical space defining the color coordinates of that space. It can be defined in density, units of measurement, headroom and footroom parameters, and so on. It broadly represents all of the colors within a given space. What it does not show are the color differences within the space. That is the definition of the gamut. When referring to color, nine times out of ten, we are referring to the range of color variation within the space, or gamut.

Stimulus-specific color space

In 1931, the CIE, an organization responsible for international recommendations for photometry and colorimetry, recommended a mathematically defined Standard Colorimetric Observer for characterizing the trichromatic characteristics of color stimuli. It should be noted that the CIE color spaces do not emulate adaptive states of our visual system or take into account any psychological processes.

The CIE Standard Observer resulted from a survey of human observers who were given sample colors and asked to match them with red, green, and blue light sources. As a result, the XYZ color space was derived where colors are described in terms of the amounts of the three primaries—denoted X, Y, and Z—that would combine additively to produce a visual match.

Device-dependent color space

A device-dependent color space is determined by any device that reproduces color within a predefined color gamut. The color space determined by a device in theory would be the same as any other similar device. Although we could say that in today's world, many devices reproduce color accurately, many factors relating to each individual device determine how accurate the reproduction will be.

Perhaps you have attempted to create an image on your computer screen which, when printed, looked entirely different than when it was previewed on your monitor. This is a common problem with device dependent color. The color variations and specific gamut that can be reproduced by the device are entirely dependent on the device itself.

To solve this problem, device vendors have created color management modules, or color profiles. Many of these modules are in use on computers without the user being aware of it. What the modules do is provide information between peripheral devices to ensure some accuracies in color reproduction between those devices. These can include video cameras, printers, scanners, and monitors.

Video color spaces

Video cameras are all device specific. A film camera is not device specific, but the medium, a certain film stock, is specific in terms of its spectral sensitivity and other imaging characteristics. So, for example, when we color correct YCbCr-component digital video in an RGB nonlinear editing system, some complicated processes are taking place. The camera, not the monitor, dictates the gamut of the image. The monitor must reproduce it as faithfully as possible. But when switching between color spaces, the gamut is remapped from one to the other, based upon their predefined equivalents. In some cases, one color space may have the exact same color in its gamut, but it will not necessarily be remapped to that color. So when you switch from one color space to another (in this case, YCbCr to RGB), what happens?

Thomas Madden explains:

> Well, strange things can happen if you're not careful. Artifacts such as changes in hue or objectionable lightness or chroma can occur. If the color gamut of your starting colors is much greater than that of your output device or medium, you must decide what to do with the starting colors your output device is not capable of reproducing. That technique is called *gamut mapping*. There's quite a bit of research going on, trying to find preferred ways of doing this. It boils down to what trade-offs are you willing to make in choosing an achievable output color to substitute for the original out-of-gamut color. If it is desirable, for example, to maintain the original color's hue, then compromises in chroma and lightness must be determined, which result in a least-objectionable substitute color displayable by the smaller gamut. The exact trade-offs in hue, lightness, and chroma will likely depend on the disparity between the two gamuts. There may well be different trade-off mappings in different areas of the gamuts, depending on the disparity in each area. The topic of gamut mapping is as at least as much art as it is science.

> Some color information generally is irretrievably lost when mapping colors from a larger gamut into a smaller gamut. Once colors are brought into the smaller gamut space, there is no way of knowing, without some form of tagging, whether a color value was originally in the intersection of the two gamuts (brought in without alteration), of if the color value is a substitute for an original color that was beyond the smaller gamut.

The Y factor

Video signals generally come in two flavors:

- *composite*, which consists of a single signal
- *component*, which consists of two or more individual components of the picture

When discussing the differences between device dependent color spaces, it's important to note that some terms used are general and others more specific.

The letter Y is used to denote the presence of luma, or a quantity of luminance in the picture. Because we're using additive colors, the Y signal is computed from a weighted sum of the red, green, and blue color primaries as follows:

$$Y = 0.3R + 0.59G + 0.11B$$

Now that we've defined luma or Y, let's take a look at some of the various color spaces used for video and discuss their differences.

Y, R-Y, B-Y

Y, R-Y, B-Y is an encoding and decoding signal used for PAL and NTSC component analog and digital video. The subcategories for this signal would be YPbPr and YCbCr, which are mentioned later in this section on page 20. The Y, R-Y, B-Y components are encoded by these formulae:

$$Y = 0.3R + 0.59G + 0.11B$$

$$R - Y = 0.7R - 0.59G - 0.11B$$

$$B - Y = 0.89B - 0.59G - 0.3R$$

Note that R-Y and B-Y are color-difference channels, where the difference of Y in the encoded signal is subtracted from each channel, and the rest of the R and B channels is added in each, respectively. The remaining 0.41 of the green signal is combined through a combination of the color-difference channels.

YUV (Y,U,V)

YUV consists of the luminance and color-difference channels used in PAL and NTSC systems. The components are actually Y, R-Y, and B-Y, the same as previously mentioned. But in composite NTSC, PAL, and S-video signals, the R-Y and B-Y are scaled down so that the combination of these signals is within the range of $-1/3$ to $+4/3$. These limits are due to limitations of composite signal recording and transmission. Note that YUV, while containing separate components, is actually an intermediary for composite signals, not a component signal. This is frequently misunderstood.

YCbCr

The International Telecommunications Union (ITU) makes recommendations for universally accepted standards for the video community. ITU's recommendation for encoding digital component video signals is ITU-R BT601-5. This document recommends use of YCbCr. YCbCr is essentially the same as the general term Y, R-Y, B-Y.

However, there are some differences. The specified range for YCbCr is based on values between 0 and 255, where 16 is the normal unit measure for video black and 235 is the normal unit measure for video white. So the range of the color and luminance channels is limited by headroom and footroom based on these values. Therefore, the excursion of this color space, defined in terms of steps or units from black to white, could be said to be 224. (255-16-15). But in the case of YCbCr, the excursion of the luminance channel, Y, is specified to be 219 rather than 224 units. As a result, the YCbCr specification differs somewhat from the more general Y, R-Y, B-Y color space.

YPbPr

YPbPr is very similar to the values expressed in YCbCr, with two major exceptions. The YPbPr color space is used for analog, not digital video. The other exception is that each channel of YPbPr has the same excursion. Because it is an analog signal, YPbPr is measured in millivolts (mV), where video black is 0mV and white is 700mV. Each color-difference channel has a signal between −350 and +350mV, half the bandwidth as the Y signal. YPbPr is also used in the ITU-R BY 709 standard for high-definition video, although different luma coefficients are used.

YIQ

The YIQ color space is very similar to YUV. It is an intermediary of components used to form a composite analog or digital signal. The YIQ space differs from YUV in that its color-difference channels lie in a different area than YUV. Scientists discovered that the human visual system has less visual acuity in magenta-to-green transitions than it does for red-to-cyan. As a result, when the U and V color channels from a YUV signal were shifted 123° on a vectorscope, the Q color channel could be more heavily filtered than the I channel, and the results would be almost imperceptible to a normal television viewer. YIQ was developed in 1953 for use in component analog video (CAV) using NTSC systems.

Bit depth

Now that we've analyzed color spaces used in encoding video signals, let's look at the concept of bit depth and how it can vastly improve the overall image. The quality of a video signal is determined by a number of factors. These can include the format, signal type (analog or digital), and whether the signal is divided into components. Contouring is affected by one significant factor called *bit depth*. Bit depth describes the number of bits used to encode each channel—luma and color differences—of the video signal. The higher the bit depth, the finer the definitions of color are encoded in the signal. Higher bit depth is almost always desirable.

The ITU-601-R BT recommends a bit depth of at least eight bits per channel, with the option of using ten. There is quite a difference between these two sampling rates, as we shall see.

For example, let's consider an NTSC component video signal digitized with 8-bit samples for each component channel of the video at 13.5 MHz, This is a fairly common video signal. In this case, a YCbCr image (digital component video) has each channel (Luma, R-Y, and B-Y) digitized at eight bits (256 levels per channel) and the reading of the luma or Y component is taken 13.5 million times per second.

Beyond the 8-bit standard

Some video production and postproduction equipment goes well beyond the 8-bit rate, allowing for a better overall picture. This is particularly good in cases where the signal is processed through several different sequential pieces of equipment and is switched from digital to analog frequently.

By maintaining, for example, a 10-bit sampling, there are 1,024 levels per channel—four times the number of levels using 8-bit sampling. Ten-bit sampling is also excellent for use as an intermediary in signal processing, where processing can reduce the number of signal levels. Starting with 10 bits of information, thus more values, makes it possible to process more information without compromising the quality of the signal.

Another advantage of 10-bit sampling is that the picture will always be better when it can be presented in a 10-bit mode. In some cases, such as multimedia presentations, 10-bit signals can be maintained and the color differences are spectacular.

The performance capabilities of 10-bit color are staggering when compared to 8-bit sampling. For example, use of tens bits can increase signal-to-noise ratios fourfold compared to that of an 8-bit signal because it has four times the number of discrete values. The number of discrete values is especially important in the darker regions of the picture, where most of the noise is generated. As a result, there is a potential increase in signal to noise of as much as 8–12db.

By virtue of the greater number of discrete values, 10-bit sampling reduces signal artifacts, particularly in areas that vary slightly in brightness. For example, a picture of a bright sky with a slight variation from left to right might cause *contouring*. Contouring occurs when quantized data is converted to an image that looks much like a contoured geographical map. The artifacts of contouring are frequently referred to as *quantizing errors*. In such cases, an 8-bit image displays rounding errors where the image data passes from one value to the next. But each value in a 10-bit signal is one-fourth as large as that of an 8-bit signal. Thus, the discrete steps are finer, resulting in a smoother-appearing image.

Figure 2.6 reveals some of these differences. The 8-bit picture on the left is exactly the same as the 10-bit picture to the right, with the exception of the sampling. There are more contours or *banding* visible in the 8-bit picture. Why is this so? Because there are more potential color values, i.e., more levels in a 10-bit picture. Thus the changes in color from pixel to pixel are finer in the 10-bit picture, making the image changes appear more gradual. Without 10-bit encoding, the picture might not be acceptable for use. This can also be said for situations where pixels in an image are so closely related in value that the image appears posterized. This can happen frequently in 8-bit images, depending on their subsampling ratios described later in this chapter. It is important for the colorist to remember that each tweak in color of images with lower bit depth produces greater change overall in the pixel values.

Perhaps the biggest advantage of 10-bit imaging (and beyond, when possible) is that the finer increments between discrete values allows for greater flexibility in contrast and gamma control for the

2.6   An 8-bit image vs. a 10-bit image. The 10-bit image appears smoother because it has four times the number of discrete values as the 8-bit image.

colorist. As a result, there is more control of the picture, with the possibility for greater contrast, brightness, and blacks in the picture. Because of the better quantization, the colorist need not worry much about producing artifacts and the picture can be corrected using a wider variety of tools.

Subsampling

One of the biggest challenges in the development of video formats has been the issue of bandwidth. The videotape revolution began with two-inch reels of videotape, which were loaded onto huge VTRs. Then came the portable camera and deck combinations of the 1970s. Now much of our footage can be captured with a DV camera onto a very small mini-DV cassette. With each evolutionary reduction in media size, issues of bandwidth continue to grow. How can you send a normal video signal to such a small medium without reducing some of the information originally recorded on the videotape?

The answer is that you cannot do this. As a result, subsampling was introduced into video signals. Subsampling defines the ratio of samples taken for each component in the video signal, i.e., Y, R-Y, and B-Y. As a result, subsampling is not available for composite systems using YIQ or YUV.

The reduction of samples in color-difference channels of component video was a result of the observation by scientists that the human visual system has much more luminance acuity than chrominance acuity. (As mentioned previously, there are many more rods in our retinas than cones.) By reducing the sampling rate in the chrominance components of the image, significant bandwidth can be saved. The result? To the human eye, there is very little difference.

Most professional video formats use a system of subsampling color in order to fit all of the picture information onto the relatively small video cassette. Each format of videotape uses a single subsampling method.

It's important to note that subsampling is not the same thing as compression. Compression works by averaging or consolidating pertinent information, throwing away unnecessary data that takes up space. Compression can be:

- lossy, where some original image information is lost, or
- lossless, where information is consolidated and the unnecessary data is thrown out, but the original image can be exactly reconstructed

So when someone refers to an image as "compressed," it isn't always a bad thing.

Subsampling works by sampling the luma channel and the two color-difference channels at a predefined ratio. For example, in expressing a subsampling ratio, we could say that for every four samples of luma, there will be two samples of chroma for each color channel. The sampling ratio is in direct relationship to a sampling frequency. Earlier in the chapter, we defined an 8-bit image as having a sampling frequency of 13.5MHz, which is the ITU-601-R BT recommendation. So in the case of a 4:2:2 sampling ratio, we could say that the color-difference channels are sampled at 6.75MHz, half that of the Y sampling ratio of 13.5MHz.

The notation used in the subsampling ratio is not only indicative of color difference to luma channel ratios, but also that of horizontal and vertical subsampling. Thus a 4:2:0 subsample would have four

2.7   Diagram of a subsampling ratio.

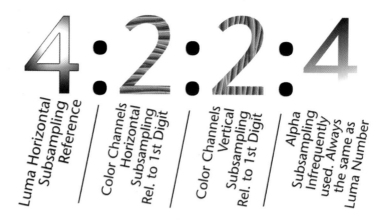

samples of luma, two horizontal samples of R-Y and R-B, and then 0 samples of R-Y and B-Y vertically. In other words, the color-difference channels would sample every other line, effectively.

Figure 2.7 shows a diagram of subsampling ratio. A subsampling ratio can consist of four numbers, with the fourth number indicating an alpha or key channel. The fourth number is always the same as the luma sample and is used infrequently. The ratio of the second and third coefficient is for both color channels, divided into horizontal, then vertical sampling of the image.

The most common professional subsample is 4:2:2, where for every four pixels of luma (with green signal encoded) we sample two pixels of red minus luma and two pixels of blue minus luma. The diagram in Figure 2.7 shows how this is done. Examples of formats that use 4:2:2 subsampling are: Digital-S, Beta SP, D-1, DVCPRO-50, Digital Betacam, and D-5.

Other formats use 4:1:1 subsampling, where for every four samples of luma, there is one pixel of R-Y and one pixel of B-Y both horizontally and vertically. Even at this rate of subsampling, the picture may be acceptable for broadcast in some regions. The only major limitation is that it is nearly impossible to chroma key with 4:1:1 color, because the subsampling limits the ability to consistently key out even the most evenly lit color background. Examples of formats that use 4:1:1 subsampling are: NTSC DV, DVCAM, and DVCPRO.

PAL DV uses 4:2:0 subsampling, where for every four samples of luma, two samples of each color-difference channel are sampled horizontally on every other line. Again the subsampling notation indicates horizontal and vertical sampling and not a ratio for each individual color-difference channel.

Now that we've explored the physical process of viewing color and the ways that we recreate colors electronically, let's dive into the often subjective yet fascinating world of color perception!

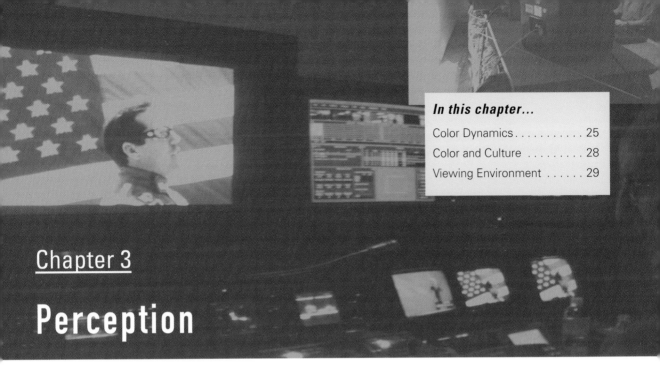

Chapter 3

Perception

It is impossible to discuss color without perception. Perceptual phenomena can alter the way in which we think and even feel about color images. For purposes of definition, we have divided perception into three categories:

- color dynamics
- cultural adaptation
- viewing environment

Color Dynamics

Colors can stimulate, excite, calm, depress, increase your appetite or thirst, and create an external feeling of warmness or coolness. The science of how color affects us is called color dynamics.

The Luscher Test

In 1947 Max Luscher, a Swiss psychologist, developed a color test using colored chips. The patient would lay the chips in order, depending on their preference. Luscher developed methods of interpreting the patient's state of mind (and thus, required therapies) by interpreting the chips.

Many of Luscher's observations were already commonly used (red and yellow are warm colors; blue and green are cool colors). This also opened the door to interpretation by corporate marketing and advertising executives, as well as the development of light and color therapies.

Although Luscher didn't envision his test to become a parlor game and insisted that results must be read by a qualified professional, practically anyone can take the test on the Internet and analyze their state of mind.

Color for advertising and marketing

For a marketer or advertiser, the Luscher test gives some insight into how our minds react to color. For example, red is widely known to excite or us agitate us, to keep us moving. Yellow, to which the human visual system is particularly sensitive, excites us. And what are the two most popular colors for fast food restaurants? Red and yellow, of course.

Black is considered sleek and sophisticated. Black is a common color for cars and fashion.

Luscher's interpretations can go beyond physical reactions to color and sometimes relate to personality type. Blue is considered a very conservative color. Red is daring and sometimes troubled. But again, we summarize Luscher's work here.

Hot and cold colors

There are some studies that relate to our reactions to color. Red can be dangerous and risk taking. It was proven that people take bigger risks when exposed to red light for a period of time. As a result, casinos are full of red light. It has also been proven that, when exposed to red light for long periods of time, our blood pressure rises.

Alfred Hitchcock knew this when he inserted frames of red into the motion picture *Marnie*. By adding the red frames, Hitchcock tried to excite the audience during key scenes. Other directors, such as David Lynch and Federico Fellini, use reds frequently to foreshadow tension. The viewer can be made to feel uncomfortable during a scene but not know why.

Hues of blue and green, on the other hand, tend to calm and relax us. Blood pressure drops when cooler colors bombard the visual system. Hospitals use greens and blues to calm us. Greens and blues have a tendency to relax us, make us stick around for a while. Blue can be a good color for bookstores and other places where we're encouraged to browse. Cool colors are also popular with corporate interiors, to keep the excitement to a minimum. These colors also have a tendency of making us feel colder physically.

One company had received complaints from employees that the temperature in the cafeteria was too cold. Employees were wearing sweaters and coats when going to lunch. The plant manager made temperature readings in various parts of the building and found no detectable difference in temperature between the cafeteria and any other office on the premises. A color expert was brought in to consult, and the walls of the cafeteria were repainted from the original mint green to peach. The employee complaints ceased.

Color could possibly even heal us. Dr. Francis Owens, a physician in Pinehurst, North Carolina, would routinely expose some of his burn patients to green light. The result was that the patients felt less pain and inexplicably healed faster.

Color and mental activity

In Munich researchers discovered that color can even affect our ability to think. Children placed in brightly colored rooms performed 12 points higher on average in their I.Q. tests. Children placed in black, white, and brown rooms scored 14 points lower than average.

Dr. Oscar Brunler, a Swedish researcher who studied the effects of color on animals, found that mice placed in slate blue boxes became listless and inactive, like couch potatoes. When these same mice were switched to yellow boxes, they became alert and active.

There are always exceptions to rules, especially when it comes to human behavior. Warm colors tend to arouse and cool colors, to calm, but sometimes the brightness and saturation of a color can cause changes in our perception. For example, a forest green room may help you relax, but a bright turquoise room could cause excitement.

Here's another oddity: blue used to be the primary color of many aircraft interiors. For some reason, it was discovered that blue increased anxiety among passengers with a fear of flying. Perhaps the passengers perceived that the blue was trying to calm them down. Maybe the blue signified the sky to those passengers, heightening their fears. The reason was never found. But the color of aircraft interiors has changed somewhat. While some still have blue colors, they also integrate earth tones, which, although not the best color scheme, tend to relax those with a fear of flying.

Color and depth perception

Warm colors always appear closer than cool colors. For example, using warm colors in the foreground of a picture and cool colors in the background enhances depth, a trick that many cinematographers and art directors use.

Figure 3.1 shows two pictures, one with a warm foreground and a cool background, the other with the same foreground but a warm background. Why does the picture with the cool background appear to have slightly more depth?

3.1 Depth determined by color.

Color and Culture

Color also has different meanings attributed by cultural. In fact, some cultures do not have words for all of the colors in Newton's Color Wheel.

Traditionally, the Japanese used a single word for the colors blue and green. Imagine sitting at a stoplight and being told that the light is blue! However, in recent years, more descriptive terms of color have been added to the language.

While some cultures don't use all the spectrum colors by name, many reserve certain colors for purposes of reverence, joy, sadness, and other emotions. In many cases, they differ from western tradition. For Roy Wagner, ASC, composition and color interact, and are interpreted differently by culture:

> Not only do colors have a symbolic meaning, but the composition of how the color space fits within the frame, where it sits within the frame, how we respond to that wherever it is. For example, because we read English, we read from left to right. Power streams from left to right, as far as how we see things. In relation to Asians who read in a different manner, their symbols display in a different way than the way our mind interprets images. There are significant arguments regarding which is the most powerful side of the frame, the left or right side of the frame. And so a strong contrast in the left side of the frame or a strong contrast in the right side of the frame; a spherical form in the right side of the frame or the left side of the frame; all of these have significant interpretive power

But even among Asians of different nationality, certain colors can symbolize significantly different emotions and events. In China, a bride will almost always wear a red dress. In Chinese culture, red signifies joy and happiness. It is reserved for festive occasions. But in Japan, red signifies danger or anger.

Egyptians consider blue a symbol of truth and virtue. Yellow signifies happiness and prosperity. But to the Cherokee, blue is a symbol of defeat. In Japanese theater, blue is the color for villains. In the 10th century, the French painted the doors of criminals' homes yellow to differentiate them from the public. But yellow is considered a symbol of holiness to Hindus.

When it comes to color, the many belief systems of different cultures are impossible to categorize and would take reams of paper to define. Wagner says:

> We are interpretive beings. Whether you believe that man has a soul or whether man is just an analytical being, we are interpretive beings. And colors have a very significant interpretive power and emotional response in a human being. Blues have a symbolic meaning, and reds have a symbolic meaning, and all of the variations in between.

There is a basic rule of thumb: when dealing with material where the content or potential viewing audience is of a different culture of your own, it is important to ask questions and do research.

Viewing Environment

Much of what we see is based upon the environment in which we see it. The relationship between colorimetry and the appearance of color in a viewing environment is affected by image luminance levels, surround types, and adaptive white points.

A first-run motion picture is normally viewed in a theater. Theaters have certain standards which, under ideal conditions, would offer the viewer the exact same viewing standards whether the viewer were to see a film in a London theater or a New York theater. While we know that these standards—which can include sound systems, lighting, screen size, projector type, and even room temperature—can be achieved, there are differences at individual locations which make each experience unique.

The viewing condition standards of theaters might be ideal, but they aren't always applicable. The colorist must determine the environment in which the audience will be viewing his or her work. If the finished program is going to be viewed on a computer or video monitor, there are many considerations to take into account. The colorist can be sure of two things:

- The finished program will not always be viewed in ideal conditions.
- No two viewing environments will be exactly the same.

Image luminance levels

The luminance of a finished program should be judged under the exact same conditions in which it will be viewed. Even though the program is created in an environment of ideal low surround light, with limited flare and neutral surrounding colors, it's important to remember that it will not necessarily be viewed under those same conditions.

Consider this example: You're creating a corporate program for employees of a huge insurance company. These employees will be viewing your work at their convenience on a CD-ROM that can be played in their computer workstations or at home. Most of the employees work in a large, boisterous room separated by light blue cubicles where fluorescent light looms overhead.

On the other hand, should these same employees determine that it would be easier to view the CD-ROM at home, the conditions will be completely different and ultimately unpredictable. Is the CD-ROM available for both Macs and PCs? The gamma level of the monitors of these two systems varies significantly. Mac monitors have higher gamma than PC monitors, so a perfectly acceptable picture on a Mac might look dark on a PC.

In order for the colorist to determine the best way to adjust for these settings, a number of test outputs should be run to see how the picture will look in different environments.

Image luminance levels are also affected by *flare*—extraneous light that reflects off of the monitor faceplate. If you've ever tried to work on a PC outside on a sunny day, you have experienced an intolerable amount of flare firsthand. While there are glare reflectors that can reduce flare, they also reduce the luminance of the viewed image. As a result, the picture will not be seen in the best possible manner.

3.2 Nonlinear editing suite with indirect lighting.

But flare can exist in most any environment. Where light and reflection are present, flare is present. So how can you adjust for flare when setting up your working environment?

Figure 3.2 shows an example of indirect light in a nonlinear suite that was designed in 1995. The indirect light came from a specialized dimmer of colored fluorescents that maintained a constant color temperature of 6,500K. The background used to reflect the indirect light was of textured neutral colored fabric, to disperse the light evenly but indirectly over the working area. The countertops, though semigloss, were gray and patterned to reduce flare on the monitors. Unfortunately, the trim was painted with black gloss, which, though low in reflectance, produced some specular reflections. The stair-stepped theatre ceiling prevented the source light from extending beyond the back of the console, which eliminated direct light, but the reflectance angles were such that some light would fall onto the working surfaces.

Although this was a good design, it had its flaws. Doors leading to the machine room had glass surfaces that caused some specular reflections. But the white point and luminance were balanced well enough to do some serious work in this environment.

Monitors

Computer monitors and televisions can be limited in their ability to display black. If you eliminate all surrounding light and view black on a monitor, you'll see that it is really sort of dark gray. Even with the monitor off, it appears to be somewhat gray. So the absence of phosphorous light in a monitor will rarely meet the same luminance as, say a black image projected on a theater screen. Nonetheless, our eyes adapt to this luminance and adjust so that we perceive the color as black. There are similar problems with white. As we discussed in Chapter 2, D_{65} light is bluish in color. At lower luminance levels, we rarely notice. But as the brightness increases, most monitors and televisions have a bluish tint to bright white. As a result, our eyes must again adapt.

Adaptive white points and chromatic adaptation

Look around you and determine what colors you see. If you're in a white room, take a look at the walls. Are they really white? Chances are, you've adapted from what *truly is* white to what *should be* white. If the room is illuminated by tungsten light, notice that the walls probably appear yellowish. If the light in the room is fluorescent, the walls may be tinted slightly green or green-yellow.

Our ability to adapt to different light sources is guided by what are known as *chromatic adaptation*. In a sense, the human visual system is "white balancing" itself to adjust your brain so that you can perceive correctness of color in most environments.

Whenever we are placed in a situation where the lighting doesn't provide correct white color, no matter how extreme, our visual system will adapt toward that color of light and try to determine which elements that surround us are achromatic. As a result, we mentally adapt and use that adaptive white point as a reference subconsciously, seeing it as an achromatic source.

If a viewer is surrounded by a light blue cubicle, the amount of reflected blue light would be significant. So much so that any references of white would probably have some colorcast of blue. This would ultimately lead to the viewer's eyes being somewhat desensitized to lower wavelength blues. As a result, a subtle blue color in the environment could appear to the viewer as neutral.

Thomas Madden, Eastman Kodak's color scientist, explains:

> A given color stimulus presented under different viewing conditions will likely result in different color appearances. In an imaging system, input devices are "looking" at these stimuli, not human observers. Devices are not subject to the adaptive effects our visual systems are. An instrument or device sensing a given color stimulus presented under different conditions would confirm the stimuli to be equivalent (which they are!). A human observer, on the other hand, would view those stimuli in each condition and perceive them to be different (which is their correct perception!).

The colorist's suite often has an item known as a reference spot. It can be framed on the wall or on a table. A source of light at 6,500 K is cast on the spot area. The reference spot is not only good for adapting to the right white point, it also serves as a tool to use for placing colored objects or swatches for reference. If the director shows you a color or a picture that he or she wants as an overall tone to a scene, you can place it on the reference spot and look at it while matching the colors on the screen.

Surround types

Another perception issue deals with the environment around the monitor. Perhaps the biggest advantage of going to the theater is that the image is so large that it is difficult to be distracted. In addition to the image size, a dark movie theater offers little if any visual references, so our visual adaptation is focused on the projected image, not surrounding stimuli.

But in the case of computers and televisions, we are bombarded with color and luminance information that surrounds the medium. The brightness and color of the image surround can affect our perception of the viewed image.

For example, a darker surround gives us the perception that the image has lower luminance contrast than would be perceived if the image were viewed under lighter surround conditions. Thomas Madden clarifies the point:

> The adaptive white point for dark-surround images will depend on a number of factors including the degree to which the image fills the observer's field of view, the luminance of the image, and the fact that an observer adapts somewhat to the image itself in this viewing condition.

In Figure 3.3 we see how surrounds interact with a neutral gray. In this figure, the gray dot is identical in every square, but the surrounds create an illusion that causes the viewer to believe that each dot is of a different luminance. As the surrounds grow darker, the dot appears to be brighter.

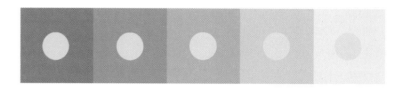

3.3 Gray surrounds.

Color can evoke psychological or physiological effects. A combination of adjacent colors can play tricks with our brain. When we place different colored backgrounds behind a given color, it sometimes appears to change. This illusion can cause problems for the colorist.

When doing a scene-by-scene color correction, the context of the image background can fool you (and your audience) into believing that one scene is not painted correctly when placed adjacent to another scene. In many cases, it is the image background that makes us believe this is so.

Also, placement of different colors with different backgrounds may actually cause the foreground colors to appear identical. When seen in context, colors are often not what they seem. This phenomenon is known as *simultaneous color contrast*. This is of particular importance when doing scene-by-scene corrections.

When two complementary colors are placed adjacent to each other without separation, they create a vibrating effect that most people find most disturbing. This sort of discomfort could easily be used to help the audience feel that something is wrong in the scene, even without actually enhancing the feeling with music, effects or other visual cues.

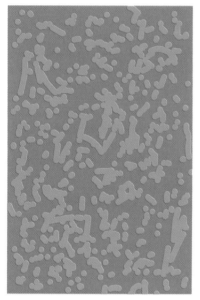

3.4 When complementaries attack!

When two complementaries are placed together, as in Figure 3.4, it results in a perceived vibration and can also cause some afterimage effects to your eyes. Afterimage is the effect of having colors "burned in" when looking away from the color stimulus.

Surround effects can affect the colorist's judgment and cause less than satisfactory results. In the next chapter, we'll take a close look at the more common issues with surrounds.

Chapter 4

Analyze This—Your Monitor

The first way for the desktop editor to analyze the video image is to simply view the image on his computer screen. This is not recommended, though, because the gamma response of a computer display is different from a TV set or video monitor. A properly adjusted video monitor is a much better way to look at your image unless your project is going to be delivered solely on computer monitors.

Monitor Environment

In the last chapter we saw that surrounding colors and adjacent colors affect our perception of color. Similarly, the colors surrounding our video or computer monitor affect the way we perceive the colors on the monitors. Most color correction suites are designed so that the colors and lighting that surround the monitors do not influence the way the colors on the monitor are perceived.

The color temperature of the lighting near the monitor and the paint colors near the monitor can affect the way the colorist sees the colors that are on the screen. Even the color temperature and amount of light reflected onto the face of the monitor from elsewhere in the room should be controlled as much as possible.

The color correction suite shown in Figure 4.1 was fairly brightly lit for this photograph to be taken, but during a session the lights would be dimmed to reduce flare light. And although the walls appear bluish in this publicity photograph, the monitor actually sits in front of a neutral gray field.

4.1   Color correction suite—not photographed under working conditions. (Image courtesy of The Film & Tape Works.)

Viewing conditions have evolved over the years. Randy Starnes, a veteran colorist who works on projects like *NYPD Blue*, remembers the comfortable surroundings of his first color correction suite:

> To relate how important the surround is, when I first started, we worked in a room that was designed to resemble the living room. The thought was: you're going to watch television in an environment similar to this, so let's color grade in this environment.

> The monitor was set in a bookcase. It was a warmly lit room with a desk lamp and overhead tungsten lights. It was a beautiful room. It was very comfortable, like a den or a gentlemen's smoking room.

> The longer you would color correct something in that room, the more red you would put into the pictures, because your eyes became desensitized. The color receptors became desensitized to the warm environment. At the start of the day, skin tones would look normal, but after six or eight hours, you were correcting skin tones oversaturated, like basketballs, because your perception has changed.

It is real-life experiences like Starnes' that create a strong case for understanding the principles of color theory when designing an ideal color correction suite, or simply adapting a basic edit suite to be suitable to the task of color correction.

According to Thomas Madden, an imaging scientist with Eastman Kodak Company, Starnes' anecdotal example of color surrounds has a strong foundation in scientific principle. The viewing conditions for an image profoundly affect the way the image is perceived. The viewing environment alters the adaptive state of the observer's visual system—the way they perceive color. This subject is addressed thoroughly in a book written by Madden and his colleague Edward Giorgianni called *Digital Color Management*.

4.2 This is a modern color correction suite that is more attuned to the need for a neutral color balance. The blue cast of the lights in this photograph is actually daylight balanced "white" light. (Image courtesy of Westwind Media.)

The eyes have it

Madden says:

> A given color stimulus, the light that reaches your eyes, presented to an observer under different viewing conditions may very well have different color appearances in each condition. So in the example where the same color stimulus is presented in two different viewing environments, an instrument would sense each stimulus and say, "These are the same," and a viewer may well look at each and say, "Well, no, they're not. They look entirely different to me." That result has to do with image luminance levels and surrounds as well as other factors. So, the viewing conditions have a big influence on color management.
>
> If you start with a live scene that was captured by a digital camera and the digital image was brought to a monitor on a workstation, and then the image was going out to film, and then to be projected in a dark theater, you've got three very different viewing conditions for the same image: the original scene, the monitor, and the theater conditions. An observer in each of those viewing conditions is going to be under different adaptive states. If I reproduce the same colorimetry in those three environments, the viewer will have a different impression of each presentation. So, the question I've got to ask is, "What colors do I need to produce in each viewing condition that will evoke in the observer the same visual impression of the original colors?"

For the colorist, this task is ultimately complicated further by the fact that we rarely have control over the final viewing environment. This would not seem to be very significant, but consider the fact that some video monitors have been tested to have contrast ratios as high as 1,000:1 when tested with contact instruments, unaffected by the viewing environment. Yet that same monitor would be perceived to have only a 100:1 contrast ratio under poor viewing conditions. According to Madden, even flare light as low as 0.5% of a white image displayed on the screen can have a significant impact on the quality of the image.

In the previous example, *flare light*, or the light that falls on the face of the screen from various lights and sources in the room, effectively lowers the contrast ratio of the image. But that's not the only effect. In addition, the colors on the monitor appear desaturated because of the addition of white light to the colors being transmitted from the monitor itself. The problem of flare light polluting the saturation and contrast of an image is especially evident and damaging in the darker portions of the picture.

For many color critical applications, people work in near total darkness. This is not always practical for those working with clients, but many video professionals, when they do not worry about entertaining clients during the creative process, work completely in the dark. This even extends to the 3D lighters on animated films. After the modeling and animation are completed, the lighting specialists step in to really determine the final look of the images by determining how much light bounces off the characters and sets from various directions. This lighting process is carried out almost entirely in the dark, similar to the environment where the footage will eventually be shown: a darkened movie theater.

Another interesting phenomenon that applies to the perception of video images is that softness in image detail is also perceived by the viewer as lowered contrast and even decreased saturation. This phenomenon is exploited by numerous graphics programs that offer the ability to sharpen a fuzzy image. Many of these programs rely on algorithms that increase contrast to create part of the perception that the picture is sharper.

Further complicating the reproduction of "correct" colors is that, in reality, nobody wants the true color of the scene most of the time! Madden explains:

> There are other factors that affect color reproduction. There's color memory and color preference. With regard to color memory, studies have shown that we don't remember colors exactly as they were if we're removed from the original scene. We tend to remember colors as being somewhat more saturated than they originally were. So when we design a system that reproduces original scene colors, they tend to be reproduced at a higher saturation level because that's what people remember. We also have preferences for the reproduction of certain colors, particularly skies and grass. Grass and foliage we tend to prefer being reproduced a little cooler—more cyan than they really are. If we reproduced grass accurately, people would tend to think it was yellow and pale looking.

Colorists often exploit this human preference; the colors we *want* to see may not be the colors that are actually there. Therefore, the job of finding the right color is not a completely technical exercise.

 Note _____

For an example of how this preference can be exploited, check out Randy Starnes' use of secondary color correction on page 118.

Let's take a look at some real-world visual examples and how they can affect our perception of color. The phenomenon of surrounding color can be demonstrated with simple blocks of color.

In Figure 4.3 notice that the gray square in the black border seems brighter than the exact same shade of gray with the light gray border. The black surround in Figure 4.4 increases the perceived luminance of both reddish blocks compared to the lighter surround. Notice in Figure 4.5 the shift in hue of the two

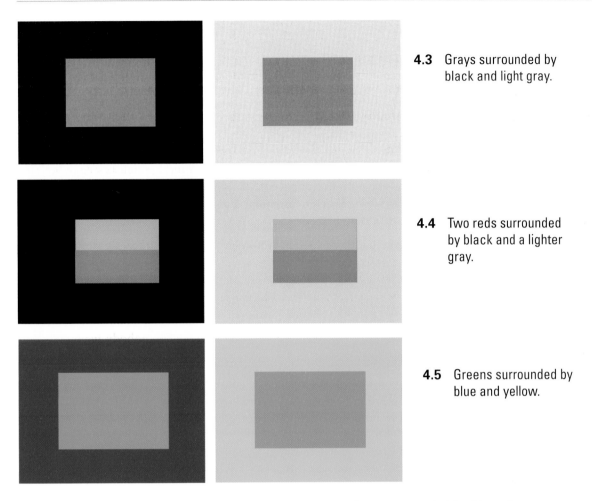

4.3 Grays surrounded by black and light gray.

4.4 Two reds surrounded by black and a lighter gray.

4.5 Greens surrounded by blue and yellow.

identical blocks of green when surrounded by blue and yellow. Surrounded by blue, the green seems more yellow and surrounded by yellow, it appears more blue.

Understanding what these surround colors can do to your perception of the color within them explains the care that most colorists, or a least the care of the people who designed their rooms, take in eliminating any false perception of color. Lighting in a colorist's suite is carefully chosen and monitored. Specialized lamps are ordered to emit a smooth, consistent light in the 6,000 K range, which is considered daylight—or even a little beyond daylight. Most colorists agree on a Kelvin temperature of 6,500 K. But some color professionals use white references as low as 5,000 K. Walls surrounding the main monitor the colorist uses are painted a specific neutral gray. The care taken in eliminating surrounding colors even extends in many cases to using waveform and vectorscopes that do not have the traditional green trace color, but a white or neutral color instead.

These surrounds affect the colorist day in and day out. Randy Starnes explains:

> The reason you have the neutral background is that you keep the same perception all along. You refer to something that is neutral. Otherwise, if you bathe the area in blue, you're going to

compensate for that. You're going to lose your sensitivity to blue and then you become desensitized to that. If you sit in a yellow room, your pictures are going to end up yellow. Or you're going to be constantly fighting what you perceive. So the easiest way to compensate for that is to surround the monitor with something that is neutral and daylight.

You can also take your monitor to black and white to refresh your perspective. Or sometimes I'll use the switcher to put a gray border or a white border around my image to judge what pure white should look like or pure gray. Sometimes that helps the colorist and sometimes that helps the client, whose perception is just as important to the process. Because they might feel like a white shirt needs to be whiter, looks dingy. Doing commercial work, selling laundry soap, sometimes you might add a little blue to the whites to make them whiter than white. Depending on how the set is designed. If you have an environment that is not neutral, the hardest thing to get right is going to be the white scenes.

Colorists who are working on green screen or blue screen color corrections that are destined to be keyed over another background are well aware of how the large amount of background color floods their eyes and can affect the way they correct the foreground images. That is why many colorists will key out the backing color to black or a neutral gray before attempting their correction.

The real and the ideal

For many people working in established rooms or even improvised spaces, these surround issues will not be easy to resolve. But at least you should understand the consequences of color correcting next to a warm table lamp, under fluorescents, or adjacent to a huge red movie poster. Try to limit flares, lights, and distracting surrounding colors in order to assist your eyes in presenting your brain with the most accurate colors.

Setting Up Your Monitors

Before viewing any images on a computer monitor, you'll need to set it up. Usually, your monitor will come with some sort of set-up procedure from the manufacturer that creates a *profile* for your monitor. These profiles attempt to ensure that the colors on the image in your monitor match the colors of the image that is sent from your computer. Even if you are monitoring your main output color on a video monitor, the computer monitor should be set up as accurately as possible.

Print retouchers and graphic artists who must deal with computer images matching print images on a daily basis have very carefully created profiles of their scanners, monitors, and printers so that they have a consistent reference throughout the process. We'll focus our efforts on creating usable video images; that means that the real reference tool is your video monitor, sometimes called an NTSC monitor for those in the U.S.

Making sure that your viewing monitor properly represents the image you're correcting is critical. Since this book is aimed at a wide range of editors, we should point out that using a consumer-grade TV set as a monitoring device is far from optimal. One reason is that broadcast video monitors have a better picture than most consumer TV sets, and the color of consumer sets is often skewed—most often going bluish. These consumer sets are also set up very specifically to hide certain errors in the picture that you need to see. They are also generally tweaked to provide a much more colorful picture than the signal fed to them is actually delivering. Studies show that this is how people remember color and prefer color to be portrayed, whether it's accurate or not.

Broadcast or professional monitors more accurately represent the image the camera sees. They have tighter tolerances than a regular TV set. Monitors usually have less overscan (usually 2–5%), allowing you to see more of the picture. In addition, most monitors have underscan functions to allow you to see all of the picture area for critical analysis of the entire frame.

Professional monitors also conform to color standards. Color temperature is preset to 6,500 or 9,300 K. (6,500 K is the broadcast standard.) Also the phosphors used on these CRTs conform to either SMPTE (Broadcast Standard = SMPTE C), EIA, or P22 standards while consumer tubes do not.

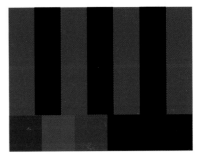

4.6 Simulated image of SMPTE bars viewed as Blue Only.

In addition to color and tonal accuracy and sharpness, one of the advantages of a professional quality video monitor is the presence of the **Blue Only** button. The purpose of **Blue Only** is to allow the correct adjustment of the color, hue, and brightness controls on the monitor using a SMPTE color bar signal (see Figure 4.6). On some monitors **Blue Only** is also called **Blue Check**. With still other monitors, you achieve this by pressing buttons that disable the red and green guns. Viewing an image as **Blue Only** allows you to easily see phase errors or video signal level errors. **Blue Only** mode turns off the red and green signals feeding the CRT displaying only the blue signal. On some monitors the blue signal is fed to the red, green, and blue guns on the CRT in **Blue Only** mode, giving you a black-and-white representation of the blue signal.

If you don't have a monitor that allows you to select only the blue channel in some manner, you can also view the monitor through a dark blue filter, like those used by veteran lighting directors to check for contrast differences. A Tiffen or Wratten 47B dark blue photographic filter would work as well.

The blue photographic filter or blue filter button on the monitor have the same effect, which is that a SMPTE color bar pattern viewed as Blue Only shows a series of bars that alternate in brightness.

Attempting to adjust chroma and hue with the full spectrum of colors is a very subjective judgment, but adjusting chroma and hue while monitoring only the blue channel becomes "black and white."

How does this work? The order of the colors in the color bars signal is not random. These color bars (SMPTE color bars) have certain features that some other color bar signals do not (see Figure 4.7). The order of the colors is always the same, though some other color bar signals include a black bar to the right of the blue bar. They are arranged by brightness with the brightest to the left and the darkest to the right. (White, yellow, cyan, green, magenta, red, and blue).

There are also some other interesting arrangements of the bars that are evident only when viewing specific color channels. If you have a monitor that can turn off individual channels, check it out on your monitor. Otherwise, refer to the Figure 4.8. Notice that the bars alternate from 100% blue to 0% blue

4.7   This pattern is known as SMPTE bars—a color bar test signal recommended as a standard by the Society of Motion Picture and Television Engineers.

with every bar. The red and green values show similar patterns. The red values alternate in pairs, and the green values are all grouped together.

If you look at the blue channel only, SMPTE color bars are essentially black and white bars (actually, black and bright blue) that appear as white, black, white, black, white, black, and white. Why? Because the first bar in color bars is white. Pure white in video in made by having all three channels—red, green, and blue—at full level. For the sake of simplicity let's use a scale from 0 to 100 for this discussion, so white has 100 Red, 100 Blue, and 100 Green. (For most computers and color levels, this is usually described with a scale from 0 to 255, but a scale based on 100 makes it easier to understand the math.) If you are only looking at the blue channel, that means you are looking at 100 brightness.

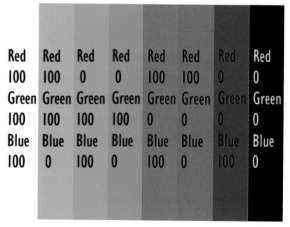

4.8   Read the blue values of the color bars from left to right.

4.9   EBU bars have an extra bar of black on the right side, making the patterns in the RGB values a little clearer.

The next bar in color bars is yellow. Yellow is made up of 100 Red, 0 Blue, and 100 Green. Monitoring Blue Only means that you are looking at a bar with 0 brightness. Cyan is a combination of 0 Red, 100 Blue, and 100 Green. This means the bar should have 100 brightness. The green bar is 0 Red, 0 Blue, and 100 Green. This gives this bar a 0 brightness if set up properly. Magenta is 100 Red, 100 Blue, and 0 Green, giving the green bar a 100 brightness when viewed as blue only. The red bar is comprised of 100 Red, 0 Blue, and 0 Green. That makes this bar appear as 0 brightness. Finally, the blue bar is made from 0 Red, 100 Blue, and 0 Green. That means that, when viewed as Blue Only, this bar appears at 100 brightness. EBU bars and some other color bars have a final bar of black to the right of the blue bar. That bar has no amount of red, green, or blue, so it would also appear as black, or 0 brightness, as shown in Figure 4.9.

If you only look at the numbers in the blue row across the bottom of the color bars, you can see that whether the blue channel is on or not alternates from one color bar to the next. There are also patterns in the red and green channels. With red, the first two colors bars have 100 Red, and the second pair of bars have 0 Red. The third pair of bars have 100 Red, and the final bar has 0 Red. With the green channel, the first four bars have 100 Green, and the last three have 0 Green. (Note that if you are looking at EBU bars, there is a final bar of black on the far right. That means that with the red channel, there are even pairs of bars that are on or off. With green, the first four bars are on and the last four are off, grouping the green values together.)

So what do these patterns in the bars have to do with properly calibrating your monitor? A lot. To explain it, let's look at the RGB readings as we move along a color wheel. The color wheel in Corel's Painter makes it easy to visualize (see Figure 4.10).

As we rotate along the color wheel while monitoring the RGB levels of the colors on the wheel, the amount of blue increases or decreases. Similarly, as we rotate the hue of the video monitor, the amount of blue in each bar increases or decreases. The object is to match the brightness of each bar that should have 100 Blue (white, cyan, magenta, and blue) and to match the darkness of the bars that should have 0 Blue (yellow, green, and red). This is much less subjective than trying to determine if the yellow bar is a little too green or a little too red. In addition to being less subjective, our eyes are much better conditioned to notice variations in brightness than they are in hue.

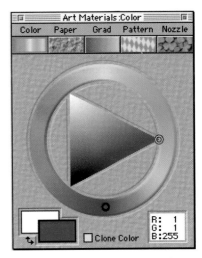

4.10 As hue rotates around the wheel, the blue values rise and fall similarly to the values in the bars in Figure 4.8 and Figure 4.9.

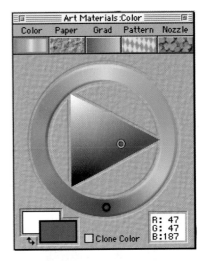

4.11 Saturation changes also affect the amount of blue in a color.

4.12 Match the brightness of the small rectangles indicated by the arrows with the longer color bars above them.

4.13 A properly calibrated monitor's SMPTE bars when viewed with Blue Only.

4.14 SMPTE bars in Blue Only with the hue rotated only 10° off.

4.15 In full spectrum, 10° doesn't change the hue very much.

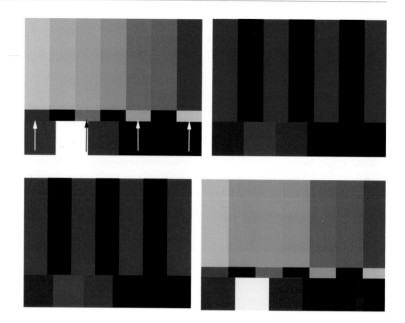

One trick to the Blue Only system is that **Chroma** controls also adjust how much blue is in each bar. To see this, let's go back to Corel Painter in Figure 4.11 and watch the blue level as we slide the amount of chroma down. Even though the color wheel indicates a pure blue hue, adjusting the intensity of the saturation changes the amount of blue in the pure blue hue. (Try saying that three times fast!)

So chroma and hue interact with each other in determining the brightness of each bar. The key to figuring out which control is affecting the blue hue and which is affecting the blue saturation is to match the brightness of the smaller rectangles in SMPTE color bars with the longer bright bars above them, as shown in Figure 4.12 (page 42). Notice that these smaller rectangles are the same colors that contained 100% blue in the longer bars. They are just in the reverse order from the regular full-length bars.

The **Hue** controls on the monitor will mostly affect the middle bright bars, and the **Chroma** will mostly affect the outer bright bars. Look at the following figures to see how bars look in Blue Only when correctly set up (see Figure 4.13) and on an improperly set-up monitor (see Figures 4.14–4.17).

Figures 4.14 and 4.15 have with the hue rotated 10° off. To the untrained eye, 10° does not change the hue of the full spectrum bars that much, but it is quite noticeable when viewed as Blue Only. Notice the third dark bar from the left is brighter than the others. Also, the tall, top bars vary in brightness from the shorter bars below them.

Figures 4.16 and 4.17 show chroma lowered by 10%. Once again, to the untrained eye, they look pretty good, but viewed as Blue Only, you can see the difference in the luminance levels between the top set of long bars and the shorter bars below them. Compare this to Figure 4.12 where you cannot see where the long bars end and the short bars begin.

With the **Hue** and **Saturation** controls set properly, we can now adjust the **Brightness and Contrast** controls. Brightness should be adjusted first. To do this, watch the three small black bars under the red color bar. This is called the *pluge* (rhymes with "huge" or "luge," depending on whom you ask). The goal is to adjust the contrast so that the middle bar is just barely distinguishable from the bar to the right, and then tweak it a bit more so that the two bars to the right just merge, while the third bar to the left is just a bit brighter than the two to the right. When tweaking **Contrast**, the key is to look at the only rectangle that is truly 100% white. That rectangle is at the bottom, under the yellow and cyan bars. Set the contrast so that this bar appears very white, but not annoyingly bright or glowing. Also, there should be a difference in brightness between the small bottom square, which is 100% white, and the other white rectangles, which are only 75% white.

4.16 Chroma lowered by 10%, Blue Only.

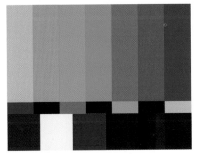

4.17 Full spectrum with chroma lowered by 10%.

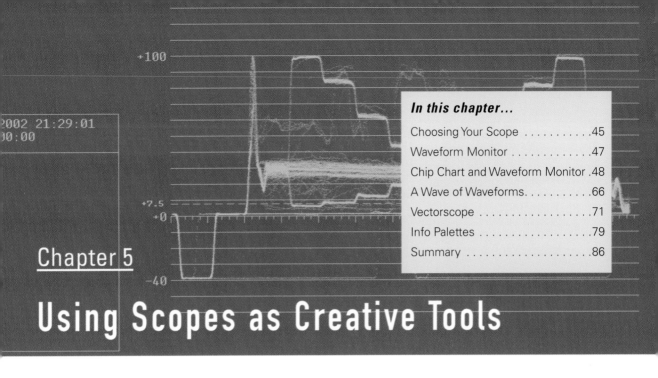

Chapter 5

Using Scopes as Creative Tools

The next two important tools in analyzing a video image are a waveform and vectorscope. There are three general categories of scopes available. The first type is completely hardware based, with the waveform and vectorscope trace presented on a cathode ray tube face built into the scope. The second type is software-based, with the resulting image of the scope displayed on your computer monitor. The third type uses hardware to display the scopes on its own computer monitor or as an overlay on your video monitor (see Figures 5.1–5.3).[1]

Choosing Your Scope

One of the main aspects that distinguish good scopes from bad is the resolution of the trace. The trace, which is the scope's visual representation of the video signal on the monitor, has a much higher resolution in hardware-based scopes and hybrids. The resolution of the trace is particularly important when analyzing the video signal to be color corrected. This is where almost all software scopes—and even some hybrid scopes that are displayed on the video monitor—suffer. Hybrid scopes presented on a computer monitor are preferable to those presented on a video monitor because of the increased resolution possible with computer CRTs. Many CRTs are switchable between two inputs so that an extra monitor is not needed. You can have your editing computer displayed on the A side and the scopes on the B side. This saves lots of monitor real estate that would be taken up by software-based scopes displaying simultaneously with your editing interface.

---

1. Figures 5.1–5.3 are courtesy of VideoTek.

5.1 Rackmount hybrid with monitor.

5.2 Rackmounted hardware vectorscope.

5.3 Rackmounted hardware waveform monitor.

Another factor to consider is that most external scopes and hybrids offer a broader range of variables that can be controlled or monitored, while many software scopes are set to a default configuration that cannot be changed. Often these software scopes are not designed to measure all of the elements of the video signal, such as blanking. Some of the analyses in this book are best performed on scopes that can be deliberately set out of calibration or that require specific settings. So users of software scopes will be somewhat limited in these examples.

Many people cannot afford the cost of these hardware-based scopes or the hybrid scopes. Fortunately for them, there are several software scopes—like the Scopo Gigio scopes from META/DMA (Figure 5.4)—that allow you to see a waveform and vectorscope on your computer monitor.

However, an important and often hidden problem with many software scopes is that they may not present information on all of the lines of the video raster. Some scopes present just a single line, which is virtually useless. This is like trying to determine what a scene looks like through a paper-thin slit in a wall. Other scopes may *appear* to give you all of the lines, but are in fact only presenting a quarter or a sixteenth of the number of possible lines, similar to viewing a scene through a set of half-closed Venetian blinds. This is very dangerous for trying to establish broadcast limits because you could have illegal areas—like a bright specular point—that sneak in between the lines that are being analyzed by the scope. Software scopes are constantly evolving and being updated with greater capabilities, so we won't point out specific deficient scopes here, because as computers increase in speed, they may increase their number of scanned lines. Be sure to read you user's manuals carefully for this information.

Whatever style of scopes you choose, having access to the information that the waveform and vectorscopes provide is essential for proper color correction. The main reason is that, as an analytical tool, the scopes provide critical information that can guide you in fixing color correction problems. Scopes also provide a fixed, objective reference as you work and compare shots. Imagine trying to maintain a consistent audio level throughout a program if you didn't have audio meters. Each audio edit may sound okay next to the one beside it, but over the course of a program, the levels could easily slip a substantial amount as you progress farther and farther from your initial point of reference. Or imagine completing a mix without audio meters, only to discover that the monitors were turned up very loud, making your mix much too low.

Scopes also help you to provide a legal output of your creative product. Part of the responsibility of the colorist is to insure that the luma and chroma signals are within certain technical limits. Being a brilliant editor and colorist doesn't mean much if no one will air your product or if the dubs are not viewable. *Legal limits* are set by broadcasters and cablecasters and vary from one to the next. But even if your product isn't being broadcast, the regularly stated limits in the setup, luma, and chroma levels of the signal affect dubbing and monitoring of the signal by consumer TV sets.

Let's take a look at how the waveform and vectorscopes can help us as we analyze the images we are attempting to correct. There are probably two groups who are about to roll their eyes and flip ahead a few pages. The first group is experienced online videotape editors: crusty veterans who've been using scopes forever. They know all about sync pulse, blanking, back porches, and breezeways, and they aren't interested in sitting through the basics. The second group is the new wave of digital whiz kids who have no interest in all the hard-core video engineering stuff that is largely obsolete since the death of the quad machine. Well, we're not going to be discussing all that video engineering stuff, with the exception of a brief discussion on keeping levels legal. We want to show how these two pieces of engineering equipment can be put to good use as creative tools.

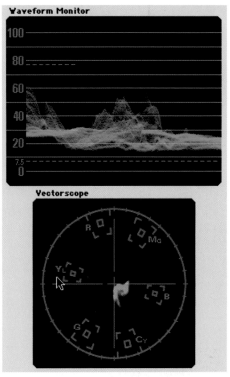

Waveform Monitor

First, let's explore the waveform monitor. To many, the waveform is simply a way to look at the luminance or brightness of the video signal, but it can also display the chrominance levels of the signal as well. This chrominance information can be used to minimize color casts in your images.

5.4 Screenshot of software scopes.

One of the most basic uses of the waveform monitor is to allow you to see that your luminance and setup levels are legal. This means that the brightest part of the luminance signal does not extend beyond the 100IRE mark—with occasional specular highlights allowed to reach 108IRE, more or less, depending on individual broadcaster's specs—and that the darkest part of the picture does not drop below either the 7.5IRE mark for NTSC video with setup, or below 0IRE for NTSC video without setup.

So how do you know if your video should be with or without setup? Well, with virtually all analog NTSC video, you need to have setup with blacks at 7.5IRE. However, no digital format has setup. From DV to HDCAM, setup is not used anywhere in the world.

In analog formats, only the U.S. still uses setup (broadcast specification RS170A). NTSC in other parts of the world may or may not have setup. PAL and SECAM do not use setup. Component analog video has different standards also. The SMPTE/EBU (N10) standard does not have setup. Betacam and MII standards in the U.S. use setup. Other parts of the world do not use setup on the component Betacam or MII signal. So what do you do if you have a digital VTR and are using the analog in/out connectors? You need to know what standards are being used by the other analog machines. Then match the **In/Out** settings for **Add/Remove Setup** to match the rest of the system.

Allowing your video to extend outside of the range defined by whatever form of video you are using can cause broadcasters to refuse to air your finished tape until corrections are made, or for dubs to have quality issues, like sparkling, bleeding, bearding, and buzzing. Sometimes, if video levels are far enough astray, they can even cause buzzing in the audio channels.

There are also legal chrominance levels and other technical specifications regarding timing of the signals and other signal amplitudes and relationships. These all vary slightly from broadcaster to broadcaster. But let's leave this technical stuff aside and concentrate on how to use the waveform monitor for the fun stuff.

Chip Chart and Waveform Monitor

 Note _____

EIA Grey Scale Chart. This specific chart is designed to have a logarithmic reflectance that does not form a perfect, diagonal X shape. Accuchart also has charts that do deliver a perfect X shape. We chose this because it is an industry standard with many technical directors and because of its special low-reflectance black patch in the center of the chart.)

One of the important skills that is necessary to acquire, is to understand what part of an image corresponds to a particular part of the trace on the waveform monitor. Since the waveform primarily is used to display luminance information, we will use an image that provides a full range of luma values, but little chroma information, to limit the confusion. The source image we will use is commonly referred to as a *chip chart*, in particular, an EIA Logarithmic reflectance Grey Scale Chart, The charts are manufactured by Vertex Video and are distributed by NalPak Sales of El Cajon, California. (part # AC-GSE).

On multicamera programs—like sports, soaps, talk shows, specials, concerts, and news—the cameras must be *matched* so that the colors from each camera angle match all of the other angles. To do this, usually all cameras are pointed at a chip chart comprised entirely of black, gray, and white chips. The process of setting up a camera to properly reproduce the chip chart is an excellent introduction to many principles of both color correction and the use of a waveform monitor.

First, notice the side-by-side images of Figure 5.5. Figure 5.5 shows a waveform monitor and a chip chart. Notice the unique pattern that the chip chart forms on the waveform monitor. When properly lit and set up—or *shaded*—the pattern is clean and uniform in shape. The ultimate goal is that each gray square—or *chip*—is the same level on each camera.

Before we try to correct or color balance this image, let's examine it and figure out which parts of the image are represented by specific portions of the trace on the waveform. The trace shows an X shape with a thick band running horizontally through the center and a small straight line on the bottom of the waveform monitor, centered horizontally. The X is created by the two strips of chips. The top set of chips, which starts with dark chips to the left, creates the diagonal steps of the X that start in the lower left corner and ends in the upper right. The bottom set of chips is shown on the waveform as the diagonal series of steps that starts in the upper left and descends to the lower right. Remember: there is no way to see the vertical position of any source element on a waveform monitor, since the vertical axis is used to display luminance.

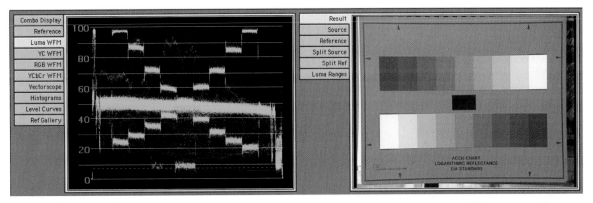

5.5 On the left, a waveform monitor displaying the chip chart. Both images captured in a screenshot from the Color Finesse UI and on the right, a reproduction of a NalPak EIA Logarithmic Reflectance Grey Scale Chart or chip chart.

The background gray color that makes up most of the chart surface is represented on the waveform by the thick horizontal line that runs around the 50IRE level. And the small black patch in the middle of the chip chart is represented on the waveform by the small horizontal line in the center at around 7.5IRE.

When trying to analyze an image on the waveform monitor, it is important to remember that the horizontal positions of items in the image will correspond to the horizontal position on the trace, but that vertical positioning in the image is inconsequential. The vertical positioning on the waveform monitor is completely determined by the brightness of the object. So an image with a gradation from black at the bottom and white at the top (or vice versa) will create a waveform with an even spread of the trace across its entire raster. A gradation from black on one side to white on the other side will create a diagonal line across the waveform monitor.

Figure 5.6 shows what a side-to-side gradation looks like on a waveform. The gradation goes from black on the left to white on the right. Figure 5.7 shows how a gradation from top to bottom is represented. Whether the image was gradated from black to white or white to black would not matter, since vertical positions of images are not represented on a waveform.

For fun, let's look at an image of a simple title page with gradated text. This causes a distinct pattern on the waveform monitor (see Figure 5.8). This waveform was generated by typing the word "Wave" in a titling program and gradating the image with white at the top of the word and black at the bottom. Switching the gradation with white on the bottom would have caused the word to appear upside down in the waveform monitor.

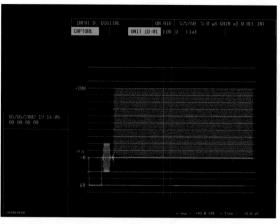

5.6 Waveform of a side-to-side gradation (captured using a VideoTek VM330E).

5.7 Waveform of a gradation from top to bottom.

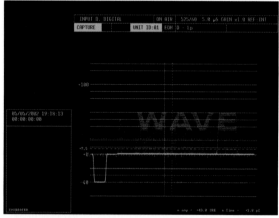

5.8 Title page with gradated text.

Although the primary point in monitoring the waveform is to match the gain and setup (brightness and blackness) of the signal, we can also use it to get important information on the chrominance of the signal, which would allow for the proper white balance and black balance of a live camera or a videotaped image. Most people do white balancing on their cameras using the automatic **White Balance** button while pointing the camera at a white target. Then they do a black balance by capping their camera and using the auto **Black Balance** button. It is also possible to manually do these corrections with the proper camera controls and the proper monitoring tools. Knowing how to accomplish this can help you understand a lot about color correction.

In a studio or in a remote truck, each camera control unit allows for individual control of the RGB channels of the camera for gain, gamma, and setup. Because you are reading this book for the purpose of color correction in the postproduction process, you can try these same experiments with color correction software and some footage of a chip chart or even a white sheet of paper that has bad white balance. The CD has several files that can be imported and manipulated.

The important thing to remember when attempting to manually white balance or black balance a camera (or preexisting footage) is that black and white should be as achromatic as possible. Figures 5.9 shows what a white piece of paper at 90IRE should look like on a waveform—with a **Flat** filter setting—and a vectorscope.

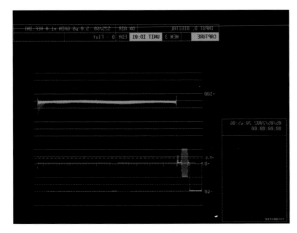

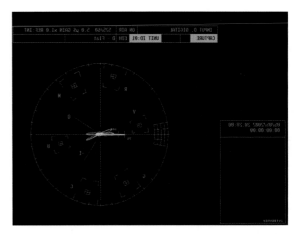

5.9 Waveform of white balanced paper at 90IRE.

5.10 Vectorscope of white balanced paper at 90IRE.

The image was shot with the luminance set at 90IRE instead of 100IRE because it's possible to destroy chrominance information by clipping the video levels. So, even a poorly white balanced piece of white paper could look white if the luminance levels are cranked up high enough so that the chroma information is clipped completely. At 90IRE, there are obviously no clipped signals. Notice that the vectorscope in Figure 5.10 shows a single, fuzzy dot in its center, while the waveform monitor—set to **Flat**—shows a clean, thin white line. Both of these are indications that the balance is good. We're primarily focusing on waveform monitors in this chapter, but comparing indications on both a waveform monitor and vectorscope is an important skill. Vectorscopes will be discussed in further detail starting on page 71.

The waveform monitor is capable of many different displays which are used for different purposes. In order to see the chrominance information on the waveform monitor, there are several different displays that can be used, including several parade modes. On an older model waveform monitor with limited display options, the key to seeing chroma information is to set the waveform's IRE filter.

Note

Excursion is used to define the fact that something is causing the trace on the waveform monitor to deviate from a thin, straight line. Hue and saturation information is transmitted using NTSC color subcarrier, which is the high frequency, "fuzzy" part of a waveform in "Flat filter" mode. The amplitude of the subcarrier waves determines the intensity or saturation of the color.

The Flat filter on a waveform monitor allows all frequencies (luminance—low frequencies and chroma—high frequencies) to be displayed on the scope. The Low Pass filter only allows the low frequencies (luminance) to be displayed. –Rick Hollowbush, Vice President, Technical Services, VideoTek

Figure 5.11 shows SMPTE color bars in **Low Pass** filter mode. This only displays luminance information. With SMPTE bars, each bar is displayed in order of luminance, so you see an even stairstepping of levels from white on the left, down to blue on the right. Figure 5.12 is generated from the same SMPTE bar signal but the waveform is in **Flat** filter mode. This combines luminance with chrominance information. The thick vertical bars represent the chrominance of the color bars.

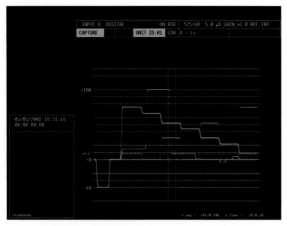

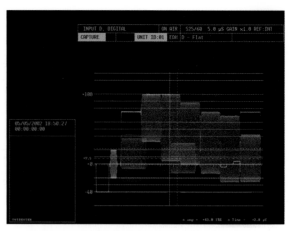

5.11 SMPTE color bars in Low Pass mode displaying only luminance information.

5.12 The same SMPTE bar signal but with the waveform in Flat filter mode, combining luminance with chrominance.

With the IRE filter on the waveform monitor set to **Low Pass**, only luminance information is displayed. Set to **High Pass**, you don't see any luminance information, only chroma. Set to **Flat**, the filter passes both luma and chroma information. Many people set their waveform monitor so that it displays both types of information. However, if you are trying to look for legal luminance values, it is difficult to read the display in this mode because the chroma information will make the levels seem higher than they should be.

Tutorial —Minimizing the chrominance of the chip chart

5.13 A video capture of a piece of white paper that was improperly white balanced.

For the following tutorial, set the waveform monitor filter to **Flat**. If the camera was not properly white balanced, the displays would look like they do in Figures 5.14 and 5.15. Figure 5.14 shows the waveform of a white piece of paper with a strong blue color cast. Notice the thickness of the excursion of the trace. This indicates the presence of chroma, though it doesn't indicate the specific hue. Compare this image with Figure 5.9. Figure 5.15 shows this same blue cast on a vectorscope. Notice the trace extending away from the center of the vectorscope, towards the blue target of the graticule. Compare this with the properly balanced white displayed on the vectorscope in Figure 5.24 (page 57).

The vectorscope now shows the fuzzier dot that is no longer in the center, but extends out toward the color box that matches the color cast of the camera. (In this case, the white paper is fairly blue and the vectorscope shows the dot approaching the blue target box on the vectorscope display.) The waveform also gives us clues that the paper is not white. Notice the difference in the thickness of the line between Figure 5.11 and Figure 5.14. (Your waveform needs to be set to the **Flat** filter to see the excursion of the chroma values.) The line has become fuzzy

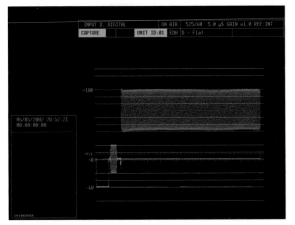
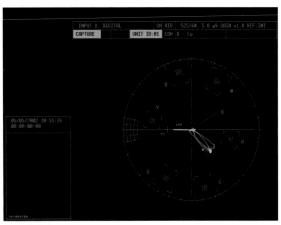

5.14 Waveform of white piece of paper with a strong blue color cast and thick excursion.

5.15 The same blue cast on a vectorscope.

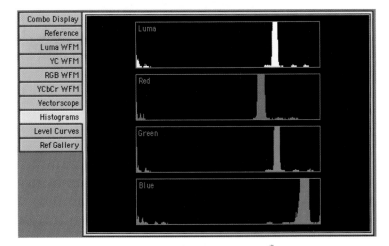

5.16 Histogram of the blue image (Figure 5.13).

as the excursion is greater, showing greater amplitude. This is the indication on a waveform that there is chroma information in the signal. Eliminating the chroma information can be accomplished by trying to focus the fuzzy line into a sharp line. The technical term for this is *minimizing the excursion*. It is possible to do this using just the RGB gain controls.

One of the tricks to understand is that adjusting the green gain also moves the overall luminance of the signal. Moving the luminance should not be done with the green gain because the green signal and the luminance are encoded together. Because we were setting only the white balance, which is exclusively a high luminance signal, we did not adjust the gamma or setup controls. Attempting to adjust the gamma and setup levels when looking only at what should be a white piece of paper is a recipe for disaster, because you will be making adjustments that you will only be able to see when you finally have an image that has some darker levels in it.

We used several different waveform modes and other analytical tools to check our work. Figures 5.14–5.20 are the readings on several of these tools or modes as they displayed the poorly white balanced image.

5.17 YC waveform (similar to a waveform set to the Flat IRE filter).

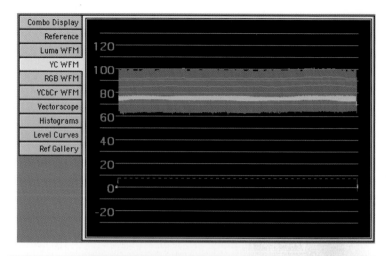

5.18 YCbCr waveform, difficult to use for this process.

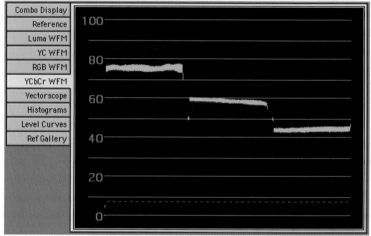

Figure 5.16[2] is a histogram of the blue image (Figure 5.13). The positions of the spikes on the right side show that the green channel is similar to the master luminance level, while the red channel is slightly below it and the blue channel is well above it.

Figure 5.17 is a YC waveform (similar to a waveform set to the **Flat** IRE filter) showing that there is quite a bit of chroma in the signal as indicated by the magnitude of the excursion surrounding the main luminance trace which is the bright part of the signal around 75IRE. But looking at this display, you can't tell what color the chroma information is.

Figure 5.18 is a YCbCr waveform, which is difficult to use for this process. It shows three signals across the scope in what is known as a *parade* display. The first portion is Y or luminance. You can see that this matches the position on the YC waveform. The middle portion shows the Cb or first color difference channel, and the final portion shows the Cr or second color difference channel.

2. The waveform monitor and vectorscope images in Figures 5.16–5.20 are from Synthetic Aperture's Color Finesse.

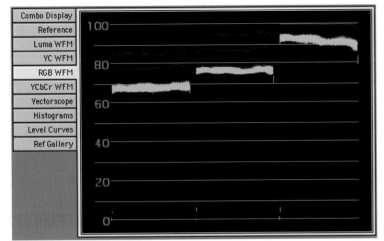

5.19 RGB waveform image with each color channel in the parade.

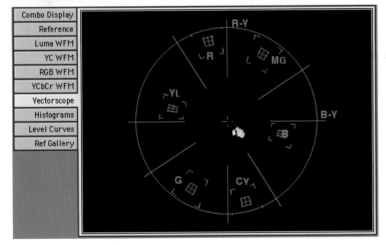

5.20 Vectorscope image with uncentered chroma.

Figure 5.19 is an RGB waveform image, similar to the YCbCr except that the parade shows each color channel in the parade. The left portion of the parade is red, the center portion is green, and the blue channel is on the right. This display shows that there is a deficiency of red and a surplus of blue in the image (assuming that we're trying to end up with white, which is the even distribution of the three color channels).

Figure 5.20 is a vectorscope image showing that the chroma information is not centered in the middle of the vectorscope as it should be if the image were white, but that the chroma is edging toward the blue target on the vectorscope graticule. Figures 5.15 and 5.20 are two different vectorscopes fed the same image of the mis-balanced piece of white paper. Notice the differences. Figure 5.15 is from a hybrid, dedicated device (the VideoTek VM330E) and 5.20 is a screen capture of the software vectorscope in Synthetic Aperture's Color Finesse. Notice the difference in resolution of the information.

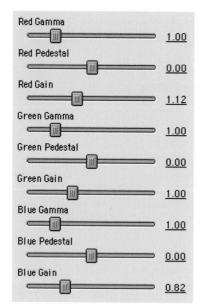

5.21 Color Finesse settings that fixed the white balance on the blue image.

In attempting to white balance this image, try not to even look at the color of the image itself—since we are just working on a purely technical level—and rely completely on the scopes. You wouldn't want to do that in a real-life situation, but this exercise is to build confidence in using the tools correctly.

The easiest way to do this task manually is probably to use the **Hue Offset** wheels for control while viewing the vectorscope. However, as a tutorial, try to do this with just the red and blue **Gain** controls while viewing the various waveform displays. This will be similar to trying to focus a camera with the main focus ring and the back focus ring without being able to set one before the other. Attempting to use the YC waveform monitor will be tricky because you are probably not able to twiddle the red and blue channels simultaneously as you would on the CCU in a remote truck or in a dedicated color corrector with a tactile interface.

This inability to control multiple parameters while doing corrections is one of the main complaints that experienced colorists have with desktop color correction systems. Because so many parameters affect others, they feel they need to have simultaneous control of these parameters.

To see the settings that fixed the white balance on the blue image, see Figure 5.21.

Figure 5.22 shows a YC waveform with very little excursion around the luma information (the brighter line). The information between 85 and 100IRE is an anomaly.

Figure 5.23 shows a YCbCr waveform display. While this is a little hard to understand, the parade displays the luma information first, which is identical to the position of the YC display. The Cb and Cr portions of the image show that the two color difference signals are of equal strength.

5.22 YC waveform display with very little excursion.

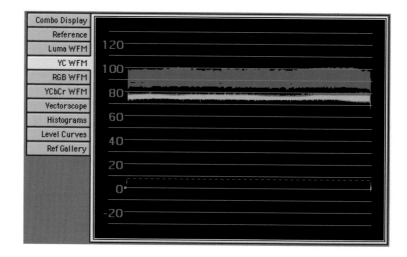

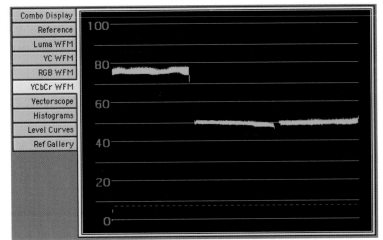

5.23 YCbCr waveform display.

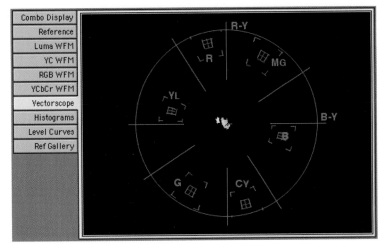

5.24 Vectorscope with the chroma information centered on the graticule.

Figure 5.24 shows a vectorscope display with the chroma information centered on the graticule as it should be, showing an image with very little chroma information. Figure 5.25 is an RGB waveform display showing that all three channels have equal video levels.

The same process is applicable to black balance. The vectorscope should show a slightly fuzzy black dot directly in the center and the waveform monitor should show a clean, fine line at either 7.5IRE or 0 IRE (See the "Waveform Monitor" section on page 47 for a refresher on the correct position for setup or black level for various video systems.). For our discussion, let's assume that you want the blacks to be at 0IRE.

The other important step in setting up a camera to a chip chart is in making sure that all of the whites are the same brightness from camera to camera and the blacks are the same blackness. Normally, in a remote truck this is checked by putting a vertical wipe between the signals of two cameras. The same trick can be applied in post, though it is rare that you'll have these chip charts shot on tape. You can use wipes to check and compare other images side-by-side.

5.25 RGB waveform display with all three channels with equal video levels.

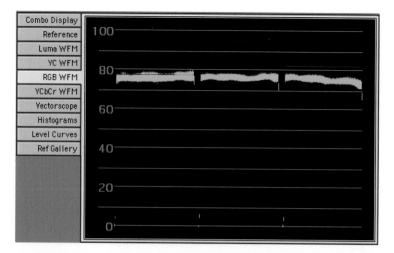

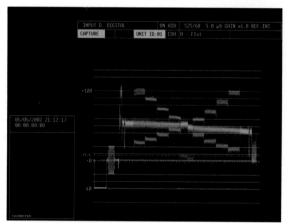

5.26 Waveform of two chip charts.

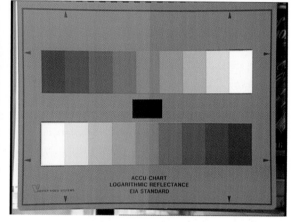

5.27 The chip charts with a split wipe between them.

Figure 5.26 shows a waveform of two chip charts with a split wipe between them. Figure 5.27 shows the chip charts themselves. They are identically balanced with identical levels, with the exception of gamma level which is higher on the left side of the image. You can see that the increase in gamma has also pulled the level of the blacks up noticeably, though the white levels appear to be identical between the two charts.

Gamma controls must be set so that the middle grays from one camera are the same as all other cameras. Merely insuring that the top and bottom levels are set is not enough to have the cameras match. Let's take a look at how some postproduction color correction controls can affect how the image looks—both on the waveform monitor and on the video monitor. Watching how the waveform monitor behaves and comparing it to the image on the video monitor while doing these adjustments will provide an excellent primer in how the various controls work as well as giving you experience in using the waveform monitor as a creative tool that will help guide your color corrections.

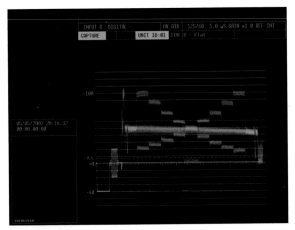 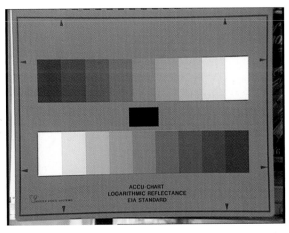

5.28 Waveform of chip chart in Flat filter, properly exposed and balanced. The chip chart that generated the image is on the left.

Try several different controls and several different analytical tools. Find what you are most comfortable with in certain situations. Until you gain experience, try several different approaches while watching several different displays. Not every person likes to use the same tools for the same job, but it is dangerous to settle on a "favorite" tool for correction or a way to analyze the picture without experimenting with all of the options thoroughly. You'll need experience with many different color issues to discover which tools and which methods of analysis best suit the task and your way of thinking. Some things will be harder to learn at first, but in the long run will provide faster corrections and better results. You may finally determine your favorite toolset, but be open to the idea that for some solutions, you're better off using a tool that is not in that toolset. Different problems are solved by different tools, and attempting to make one tool your all-purpose solution will limit your ability to solve all of the problems presented to you in the quickest or best way.

We have already discussed how to watch for color casts in the waveform monitor. This will also be discussed in more detail when we get to the vectorscope. Now, let's take color out of the mix and concentrate on an image that is supposed to be pure black and white. We'll use the waveform monitor and the chip chart to understand how the various controls affect the image and how some controls interact with others quite intimately, while other controls are designed to be more isolated in their affect on the image. While viewing the image of the chip chart on a waveform, let's try a few adjustments that are common to most color correction graphical user interfaces.

We'll stick with the **Master HSL** controls in this example. These controls are essentially the same as a TBC. When you are controlling the Master levels, you will affect all of the image, but some controls will isolate level changes a little more effectively to certain luminance ranges. Understanding how to isolate a portion of the picture you want to affect is very important.

Figure 5.28 is the proper exposure and balance for the chip chart. Notice the black—in the center —is set at 0. Midtones are around 50IRE, and whites are at 100IRE. Excursion is fairly minimal in **Flat** filter mode.

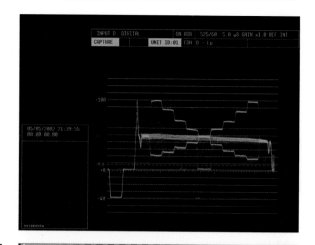

5.29 Waveform of same chip chart in Low Pass.

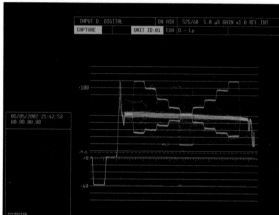

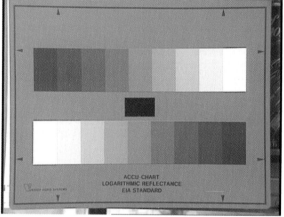

5.30 Waveform of same chip chart in Low Pass after increasing brightness.

Figure 5.29 is the same image with the same settings, except we are viewing the waveform in **Low Pass**. This eliminates the chrominance information, letting you concentrate on luminance levels. Notice the excursion of each line—how blurry or fat it is—is almost nothing.

Figure 5.30 is a **Low Pass** waveform of the chip chart after increasing the brightness control. Brightness is an additive function. If you have a 0IRE black and a 100IRE white and you increase brightness by 10, you now have a 10IRE black and a 110IRE white. The entire signal is brought up. You may want to do this sometimes, but usually you want more control than to affect the image so globally.

Figure 5.31 is a **Low Pass** waveform of the chip chart after decreasing contrast. Contrast adjustments control two parameters at the same time. When contrast is decreased, shadow levels are raised and highlights are lowered and when contrast is increased, shadow levels are lowered and highlights are raised. So decreasing contrast by 10 would make an adjustment of raising blacks by 10 and lowering whites by 10. (This will depend on the algorithm used by the color correction engine to calculate the moves. Some engines use linear equations, and some are graded on a curve or allow you to set a center

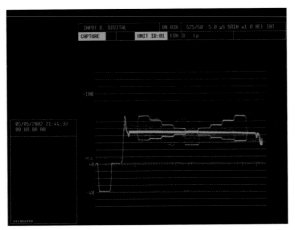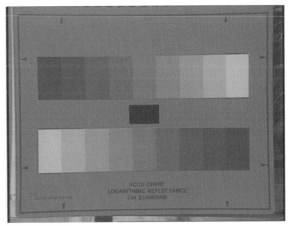

5.31 Waveform of same chip chart in Low Pass after decreasing contrast.

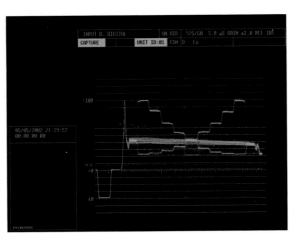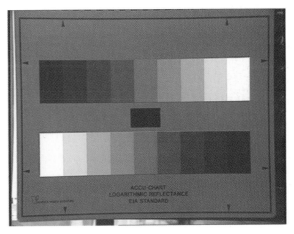

5.32 Waveform of same chip chart in Low Pass after raising blacks.

for contrast, so that the contrast move could affect brightness and darkness differently.) Like brightness, you might want to use this occasionally, but usually it is better to control these functions separately.

The Low Pass waveform in Figure 5.32 shows raised blacks. Note that all other levels remained virtually unchanged from proper levels. Gamma is still at 50IRE, and whites are at 100IRE. We did this by specifically correcting the shadow regions. A Master black level adjustment would probably isolate the blacks almost as well. But if you discover that you are affecting other portions of the picture more than you would like, attempt your corrections one range at a time instead of as Master adjustments.

The **Low Pass** waveform in Figure 5.33 shows lowered midtones. Black levels are only slightly changed and whites remain the same. Pulling down the midtones has two effects on the picture. It compresses the range between black and the input midtone level and it expands the level between the midtone level and the whites.

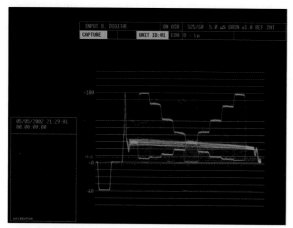
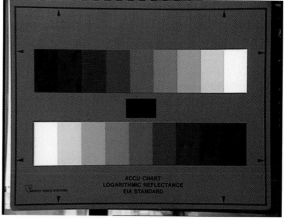

5.33 Waveform of same chip chart in Low Pass after lowering midtones.

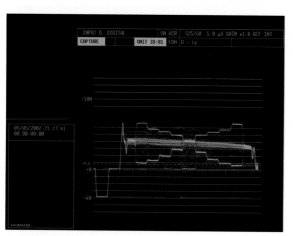
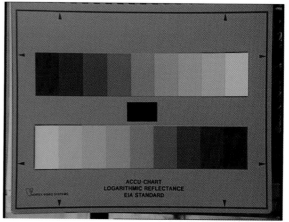

5.34 Waveform of same chip chart in Low Pass after lowering highlights.

The **Low Pass** waveform in Figure 5.34 shows lowered highlights. The isolation of the highlights was accomplished by only changing the gain of the highlight portion of the picture. This is an effective method of being able to keep illegal highlight levels in check while maintaining the overall image level.

The **Low Pass** waveforms in Figures 5.35 and 5.36 show a black level adjustment. The first image, Figure 5.35, shows illegal blacks, but they have not yet started to be crushed by the color correction engine. In Figure 5.36 the excursion in the black center chips has been crushed to a single tight, bright line. This indicates a loss of detail. Looking at the specific shape of a wave as it starts to compress into a thin line is a good indication that you are compressing or clipping your image. This may be an effect that you are trying for, or it may be an indication that you are doing something wrong.

Just as the previous example shows how the waveform can see loss of detail as blacks are crushed, it can also show the fine line between crisp, bright highlights and blown-out whites. Sometimes these blown-out whites are desirable as a look, but usually they just mean lost detail.

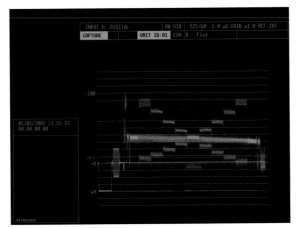

5.35 Black level adjustment. Note the thickness of the excursion in the center black chip.

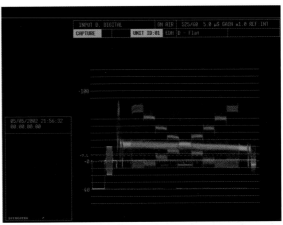

5.36 Black level adjustment with crushing. The excursion in the center black chip has been crushed to a thin line.

Figures 5.37 and 5.38 are very, very similar. They are meant to show one small thing that acted as a signal as the gain was being raised. Note the shape of the top left and right chips in Figure 5.37, then compare them to the same chips in Figure 5.38. In Figure 5.38, the shape of that portion of the trace has changed slightly—flattening out somewhat—and the excursion has been minimized. That shows that

 Note _____

This waveform also shows an important danger that should be guarded against. Many color correctors are capable of creating signals that are illegal. If you plan to do your color corrections, then send the signal through a limiter or legalizer, you may end up with a legal signal, but it might not be representative of the images you thought you had created. In this example, the illegal blacks, though they aren't crushed now, will be crushed later as this signal is brought into legal specs at some point down the road.

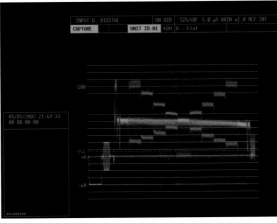

5.37 Note the shape of the top chips.

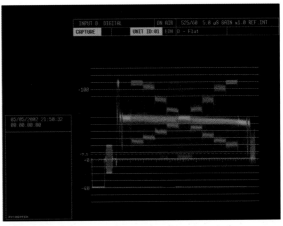

5.38 Now that gain has been raised, note the flattened trace for the top chips.

the detail in those brightest chips is starting to get lost. You can use this compression of the trace as a sign that your highlights are probably high enough.

5.39 From Artbeats' Kids of Summer Collection, shot KS109.

Now that we have shown how some basic adjustments appear on a waveform monitor, lets examine some real images and analyze them with the waveform monitor.

Figure 5.39 has nice, strong chroma values and a full range of luminance. Figure 5.40 is the **Low Pass** waveform view, showing only luma values. Figure 5.41 shows the **Flat** filter image, displaying chroma and luma information. The **Flat Pass** image is much harder to evaluate because of the large amount of chroma information. Since the horizontal orientation between the full raster image and the waveform always lines up, the trick is to assign the vertical position on the waveform to a luminance level in the image.

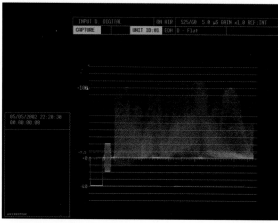

5.40 Waveform of Figure 5.39 with Low Pass filter (luma only).

5.41 Waveform with Flat filter (chroma and luma).

Figure 5.42 is another image from Artbeats' Kids of Summer Collection. Figure 5.44 is a **Low Pass** waveform showing that the image sits primarily in shadows with some midrange values. To analyze various portions of the image, black wipes or garbage mattes were used to mask portions of the picture to more definitively conclude what portions of the image were being represented by which portions of the waveform trace. Compare the original image and its waveform with the masked images and their waveforms.

Figure 5.43 masks out the boy to let you compare the waveforms of Figure 5.45 and Figure 5.44. With the boy masked out, you can see the sweep of the sky that continues and the darker shadows that compromise the rest of the image in that same horizontal space where the boy was.

Figure 5.46 (page 66) crudely masks the sky so that you can compare the waveforms in Figures 5.44 and 5.47. With the sky masked out, it becomes quite clear what part of the waveform in Figure 5.44 is sky.

In addition to the traditional waveform displays, other displays, such as parade displays of RGB or YCbCr, provide substantial data on chroma values in a very usable form. The RGB parade scopes are useful and widely used by professional colorists. They show you the same waveform

5.42 From Artbeats' Kids of Summer Collection, shot 121.

5.43 From Artbeats' Kids of Summer Collection, shot 121, with boy masked out.

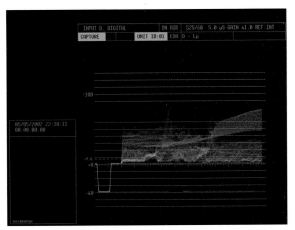

5.44 Low Pass waveform showing image from Figure 5.42 in shadows with some midrange values.

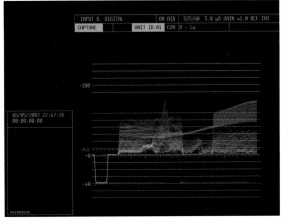

5.45 Waveform of Figure 5.43 revealing more sky and shadows.

information that usually presents luminance information, but they break it into three sequential images that show specific waveforms for each of the RGB channels. Because many of your corrections will be made using RGB controls, these scopes provide a very direct form of feedback.

Stephen Nakamura is a well-known colorist at Technique in LA. His latest project was color correcting David Fincher's *Panic Room* for its film release. *Panic Room* was one of the first features to be color corrected electronically. Nakamura swears by his RGB scope:

> I just look at the waveform, vectorscope, and RGB Parade. The RGB Parade shows you where your cells are. It lets you see what you're driving up too high or too low or balancing your RGB channels. That's how you correct, by controlling the RGBs, so you need to be able to see those and what level they are and see if that coincides with the picture you're looking at.

5.46 Artbeats' shot 121, sky masked.

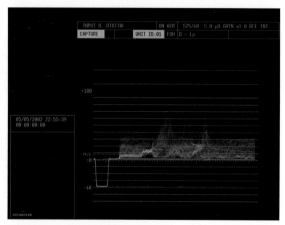

5.47 Waveform of Figure 5.46.

A Wave of Waveforms

Figure 5.48[3] (top of page 67) is comprised of three distinct levels of red, green, and blue images. There is the reddish color of the earth and some skin tones. There is the green of the trees and the swing supports. And there is the blue of the sky and the boy's shirt.

As you would guess from looking at the image, the red tones of the earth and the skin tones are fairly dark as seen in the red channel, indicated in the left image in Figure 5.49. The center image in Figure 5.49 is the green channel with its strong green midtones and a darker level of green for the shadowed portions of the leaves. The black, vertical lines running through the green channel represent one of the swing chains blocking the tree and the swing supports blocking the trees. The blue channel (the image on the right in Figure 5.49) displays the obvious bright blue luminance of the sky. The brightest part of the trace in the blue channel is broken up by the dark, vertical slices representing the chains of the swings and the swing supports.

Isolating luminance information is a little easier to do on moving images. See Figures 5.50–5.53 (page 68) for an example. It is quite apparent where the image of the boy is registering on the waveform when you see sequential images. Compare the waveforms in Figures 5.51 and 5.53 as the boy passes from one spot to another in horizontal space.

Another parade scope display shows YCbCr as individual waveforms. To explain this display, we'll go back to NalPak's EIA Logarithmic Reflectance Grey Scale Chart. The image we'll use is one that was captured after taking the straight chip chart image. We'll turn just the highlights blue, leaving the rest of the image untouched (see Figure 5.54, page 69).

In Figure 5.54, there is little or no chroma information in the midtones and blacks. Only the highlights have been adjusted to show blue. This is seen on the YCbCr Parade in Figure 5.55 (page 69). On the left is the luminance or Y value. This looks very similar to the standard wave display seen in Figure 5.28.

---

3. Figures 5.48, 5.50, and 5.52 are courtesy of Artbeats' Kids of Summer Collection, KS133.

5.48 Image with strong red tones.

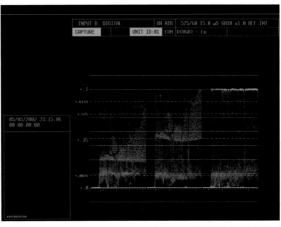

5.49 All three color channels in an RGB "parade" from left to right for the previous image (Figure 5.48).

The next two parade images are harder to understand (Figure 5.55, page 69). The middle image in the waveform is displaying Cb, which is the blue channel minus the luminance (gamma corrected). The trace shows that there are elevated blue levels. The right image on the waveform is showing Cr, which is red minus the luminance (gamma corrected). This display is showing that the red is deficient in portions of the image. If the image had no chroma values, the Cb and Cr traces would be centered on the line, showing no excursion as in Figure 5.56.

Figure 5.57 (page 69) shows a regular **Flat Pass** waveform. The trace shows a huge amount of excursion in the highlight chips while the midtones and the shadows show very little excursion from chroma information. Figure 5.58 shows an RGB Parade of the same chip chart. Because there should be no chroma information in this chart, all three portions of the parade should be identical. Because only the highlights were moved towards blue, note that all three portions are almost identical at the midtone line and below. But above the midtones, the red channel is very low, the green channel is close to being correct, and the blue channel is well above 0.7v.

To further explain the use of the YCbCr display, let's look at a display for a properly white balanced piece of paper and another for a paper with a blue cast to it.

 Tip

Trick of the Trade. With a good hardware or hybrid scope, it is possible to zoom in on a specific part of the waveform for a closer look. Film and Tape's Bob Sliga, a veteran Chicago colorist, often uses this feature to check for compression when he is raising whites or lowering blacks. This allows him to keep a closer eye on any clipping or crushing of detail.

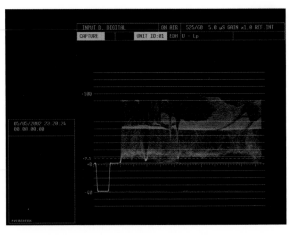

5.50 Swing shot in motion (image courtesy of Artbeats' Kids of Summer Collection, KS133).

5.51 Waveform of previous image (Figure 5.50).

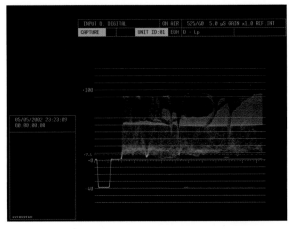

5.52 Subsequent swing shot (image courtesy of Artbeats' Kids of Summer Collection, KS133).

5.53 Waveform of previous image (Figure 5.52).

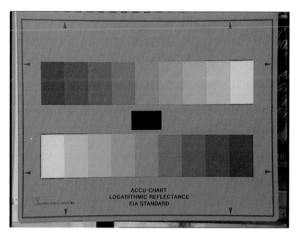

5.54 Chip Chart with a blue cast in the highlights only.

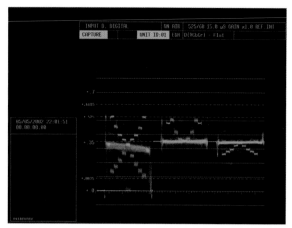

5.55 YCbCr Parade display of the chip chart in Figure 5.54.

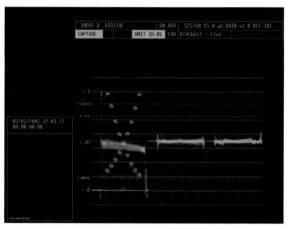

5.56 YCbCr Parade display of a correctly balanced chip chart.

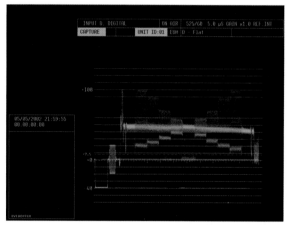

5.57 Flat Pass waveform displaying of the chip chart in Figure 5.54.

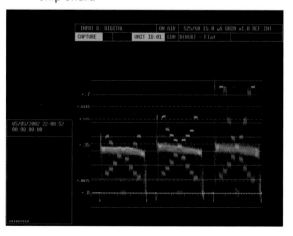

5.58 RGB Parade display of the chip chart in Figure 5.54.

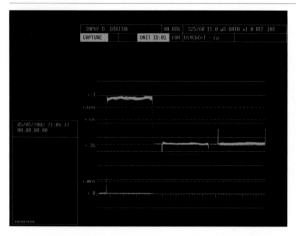

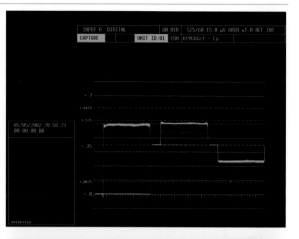

5.59 YCbCr of a piece of paper, properly white balanced *(upper left)*.

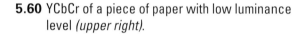

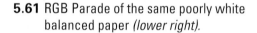

5.60 YCbCr of a piece of paper with low luminance level *(upper right)*.

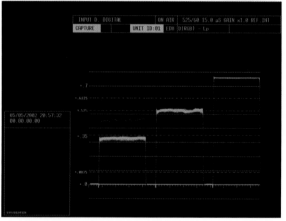

5.61 RGB Parade of the same poorly white balanced paper *(lower right)*.

Figure 5.59 is a YCbCr display of a properly white balanced piece of paper. Note that the luminance portion of the display on the left, shows a full 0.7v luminance level (100IRE). The Cb and Cr portions show no excursion at all. (The small spikes came from art behind the piece of white paper.) Figure 5.60 shows the YCbCr display from the poorly white balanced paper. Note the low luminance level, which is essentially the same as the Cb level. The Cb level—representing mostly blue—is elevated from the 0.35v line where it should be resting. The Cr portion is under the 0.35v line by almost exactly the same amount that the Cb trace is above the line. Figure 5.61 is an RGB Parade of the same image. This shows that the blue level is actually so high that it is clipping. Pulling an image back to proper balance would be tricky because there will be lost information in the highlights of the blue channel. All three channels should be at the 0.7v line. Obviously blues need to be pulled down a bit, and the green and red channels need to be brought up.

For many colorists, these parade displays are as important in obtaining chroma information as luminance information. But the most obvious evaluator of chroma information is the vectorscope.

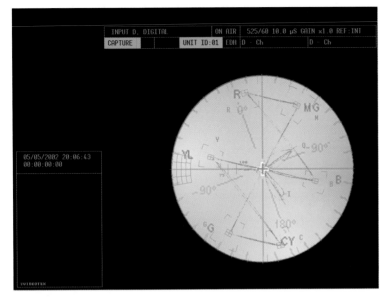

5.62 Color wheel over vectorscope.

Vectorscope

The vectorscope helps analyze hue and chroma levels, keeping colors legal and helping to eliminate unwanted color casts. We will get into some detail in this section of the book on how the vectorscope works. For more in-depth descriptions, see the bibliography of this book for other resources to explore.

With the gain, setup, and gamma corrections done while monitoring the waveform monitor primarily, the colorist's attention focuses on the vectorscope for the hue and chroma work. The chroma strength of the signal is indicated by its distance from the center of the vectorscope. The closer the trace is to the outer edge of the vectorscope, the greater the chrominance or the more vivid the color. The hue of the image is indicated by its rotational position around the circle compared to the burst position. (The little line sticking out towards the nine o'clock position.) The easiest way to imagine these relationships is to picture a color wheel superimposed over the face of the vectorscope, as in Figure 5.62.

One of the important relationships to understand is the position of the various colors around the periphery of the vectorscope (see Figure 5.62). The targets for red, blue, and green form a triangle. In between each of these primary colors are the colors formed by mixing those primaries. So the color between red and blue is magenta. The color between blue and green is cyan, and the color between red and green is yellow. These secondary colors form another triangle. The other interesting relationship that is formed on the vectorscope is that complementary colors are directly opposite each other. Red is opposite cyan, magenta is opposite green, and yellow is opposite blue. These relationships will play a pivotal role as you begin to manipulate colors.

For example, if you are trying to eliminate a magenta cast in an image, a glance at the vectorscope will tell you that you need to add green. Or you could reduce red and blue in equal amounts. If an image has yellows that are too green, then adding red will begin to solve the problem. Eventually, you should not

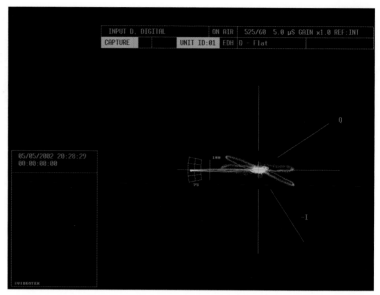

5.63 Vector display of a white signal on a VideoTek VM330E. The display has been zoomed in to magnify the center of the vectorscope.

even need the graticule (the graphic part of the vectorscope that identifies color targets) to know where the colors lie on the face of the vectorscope.

The chroma information presented on the vectorscope is instrumental in trying to eliminate color casts in images. As stated earlier, chroma strength is represented by its distance from the center of the vector-scope. Since white, black, and pure grays are devoid of chroma information, they all should sit neatly in the center of the vectorscope. While most video images will have a range of colors, they also usually have some amount of whites, blacks, and neutral grays. The key is to be able to see where these parts of the picture sit on the vectorscope and then use the color correction tools at your disposal to move them toward the center of the vectorscope.

One useful tip in trying to accomplish this task is to use the vectorscope's chroma gain controls to zoom in on the center of the signal. Increasing the gain allows you to better see exactly where the neutral chroma information is sitting. Most software-based scopes do not allow you to take this setting out of calibration like this. Many scopes, such as VideoTek's VM330E (see Figure 5.63), have magnifying functions that serve the same purpose. In Figure 5.63 the vectorscope was set to **Magnify** in order to better examine the very center of the vectorscope display. As you may guess by the clean trace with no chroma, the vectorscope was being fed a perfect white signal.

Let's take a look at some example images to see how these images appear on the vectorscope. Remember, luminance is not displayed on the vectorscope, so we only need to consider how the chroma and hue of an image are displayed.

Let's start with a white sheet of paper. Figure 5.64 shows the same white sheet of paper we saw earlier in Figures 5.9 and 5.10. This white sheet of paper has had a proper white balance. Notice how all of the trace is limited to a fairly tight circle around the center of the vectorscope. Figure 5.65 shows a white piece of paper that is not white balanced. Notice that the trace has begun to extend outward from the center, toward the yellow and red targets. This is the indication of the reddish cast of the image.

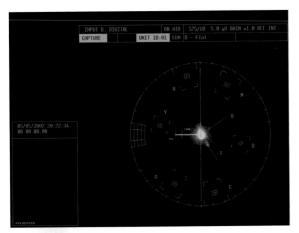
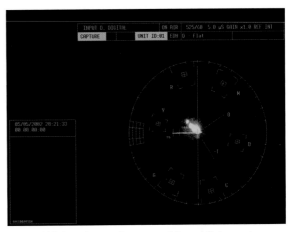

5.64 White sheet of paper after white balancing. **5.65** White sheet of paper with reddish cast.

Masking again

In order to simplify the task of understanding how a vectorscope displays a more complex image, we will use the same masking technique that we used in the waveform examples. We already analyzed this image in the waveform section (see Figures 5.39–5.41). Figure 5.67 is the resulting vectorscope display. Notice the large amounts of trace extending toward yellow, green, and blue.

Figure 5.68 shows the Artbeats' image with a small rectangular mask over the blue blanket in the background and a small corner of the girl's shoulder. Notice the difference between Figure 5.67 and Figure 5.69. In Figure 5.69, the small tangent of blue that was closer to the center of the vectorscope (a less intense blue) is missing. So is a small hook on the top of the tangent extending toward red. That hook was the highest chroma value of skin tone, coming from a highlight of skin on the girl's shoulder. The rest of the vectorscope is unchanged.

Figure 5.70 has the image with the mask over the intense blue of the dress. Figure 5.71 is the vectorscope reading for Figure 5.70. Notice that the large tangent that is just to the cyan side of the blue target is missing, while the smaller, less intense blue near the center is back. Compare Figure 5.67 and Figure 5.71. The portion of the trace that indicates the blue dress becomes very apparent.

We also analyzed Figure 5.72 in the waveform discussions (see Figures 5.42–5.47). In Figure 5.73, the vectorscope reading show an image without huge amounts of chroma. Skin tones and the blue of the sky are visible, but not really prominent. To make sure that the small area that extends out toward blue really is the sky, we used the same garbage matte for the sky that we used in Figure 5.46. Now, comparing Figures 5.73 and 5.74, you can see where the sky is being represented.

The most critical colors to reproduce accurately are flesh tones. Because everyone knows instinctively how these should look, there is little room for error. Regardless of the racial background of the subject, flesh tones are always indicated on the vectorscope within a few degrees of each other. There are, however, trends in reproducing skin tones and even a geographic bias towards certain skin tone hues depending on where the colorist works, according to some colorists. A veteran Chicago colorist, Bob Sliga,

5.66 From Artbeats' Kids of Summer Collection, shot 109.

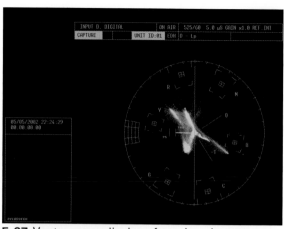

5.67 Vectorscope display of previous image.

5.68 Mask over blue blanket.

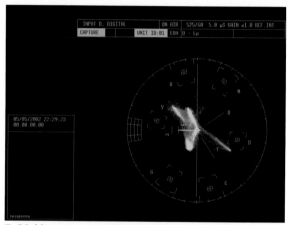

5.69 Vectorscope display of previous image.

5.70 Mask over blue dress.

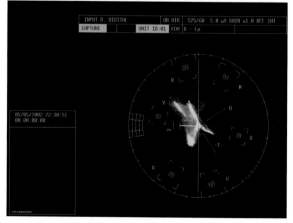

5.71 Vectorscope display of previous image.

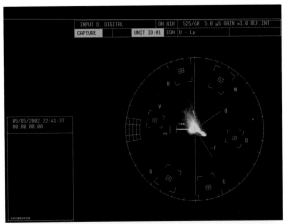

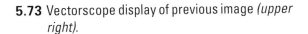

5.72 From Artbeats' Kids of Summer collection, shot 121 *(upper left)*.

5.73 Vectorscope display of previous image *(upper right)*.

5.74 Vectorscope display with sky matted out *(right)*. The vectorscope is displaying the image from Figure 5.46 on page 66.

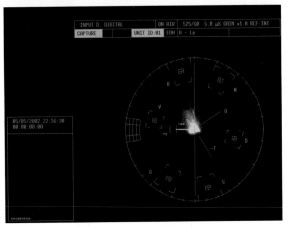

believes that West Coasters like more golden skin tones; the East Coasters like pinker skin tones; Midwest likes something in between.

Regardless of this, positioning skin tones is actually a fairly easy thing to do. The same instinctive understanding that allows everyone else to know a bad skin tone when they see it is the same instinct that helps you place it correctly in the first place. In addition to pure instinct, you are aided technically by the I-line on the vectorscope. This line, which runs from about the eleven o'clock position to about the five o'clock position, is widely accepted as the line where skin tones should fall. Obviously they need to be on the eleven o'clock side of the vectorscope instead of the five o'clock side.

The I-line is indicated on the vectorscope on the capture from a VideoTek VM330E, shown in Figure 5.75. Not all software scopes label this line. The I-line runs perpendicular to the Q-line. This vectorscope image is being generated from SMPTE bars, which have two large blocks of color that are meant to target the I- and Q-lines specifically. The I-block of color is a dull bluish/cyan color that sits in the lower left corner of the SMPTE color bar signal. You can consider this color the anti-skin tone since it sits on the I-line, directly opposite from where proper skin tones should be.

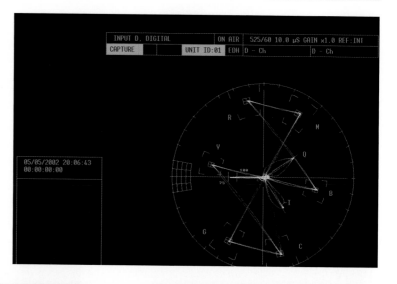

5.75 I-line on a VideoTek VM330E.

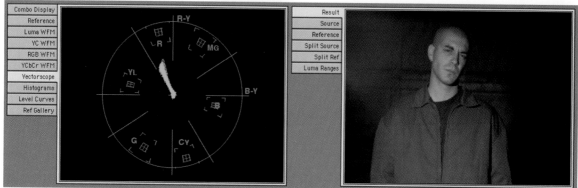

5.76 Screen capture from Synthetic Aperture's Color Finesse running in FCP2. The video image is from Artbeats' Mixed Cuts Collection, shot LM113.

Like any creative rule, this flesh-tone line is to be used as a guide, not an absolute dictate. Randy Starnes, the colorist for *NYPD Blue*, among other high-profile productions, explains:

> Generally people think that skin tones fall within 10° or 20° of the IQ vector, which lies somewhere between red and yellow. I've had engineers tell me that my job was not done correctly because it's obvious by looking at the scope that my skin tones were not on the IQ. So I lined up everybody and showed that everybody's skin tones were not the same, so they couldn't fall on the same vector. But it does generally fall within that vector.

The entire shot of Figure 5.76[4] is monochromatic except for the man's skin tones, which provide some warmth to the image. Human skin tones—regardless of race—all fall within a few degrees of the I-line. The color correction guide for FCP3 goes so far as to call this the flesh-tone line. While this is not tech-

---

4. Unattributed images in Chapters 5–7 and Appendix A are courtesy Steve Hullfish/Verascope Pictures.

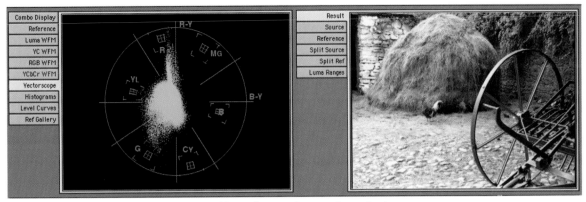

5.77 This one-sided trace gets most of its yellow-red tones from the hay.

nically accurate, it is certainly a good rule of thumb. Look at Figures 5.66 (page 74) to see how closely African-American skin tones line up with the Caucasian skin tones in Figure 5.76.

As a test, check some of your own flesh-tone video on a vectorscope to get a feel for where the pleasing skin tones land. Part of increasing your experience as a colorist is to develop an understanding of where certain colors should land. If you can, look at unusual, affected skin tones in spots or TV shows that you like and see where they land in comparison to the flesh-tone line. Try downloading spots or trailers and importing them. The colors that were intended for broadcast probably won't be quite the same as these imported files, but if you view them on a broadcast monitor, you can at least see where a professional colorist was able to take a certain skin tone to create a certain look.

Figure 5.77 shows a fairly one-sided vectorscope trace. There is virtually no magenta, blue, or cyan. The largest portion of the trace lands in the yellow/red vector. This is mostly from the pile of hay and the hay between the cobblestones. The spike that just misses the red target is the rooster's cowl and the red of the wheel. The green is coming from the trees, the grass in the cobblestone, and the green of the farm machine. The reds are a bit on the illegal side. It would be a good use of secondary color correction to define that particularly strong red component and draw it back into the legal zone without affecting the farm machine or the hay.

In Figure 5.78 (page 78) the black, gray, and white tones, which vary from the bluish cast of the paper towel to the subdued warmth of the rocks, create the bulk of the middle of the trace. There are spikes towards yellow, orange, and red from the colors in the watercolor palette. The intense spike to blue is coming from the fold of blue cloth in the upper left. The whites are running a little cool, which may be appropriate for this shot, or it could be easily warmed up for a different feel.

The vectorscope in Figure 5.79 (page 78) shows lots of blue, from the lifevests and the sky. The red life vest is almost hitting the red target perfectly. The trace extending between red and yellow is the yellow oars and gunwales of the boat. Yellow in real life is rarely the yellow of the yellow vectorscope target.

The specific hue of yellow that is indicated by the yellow target on the vectorscope is not the most pleasing yellow color. It is the yellow of color bars. Most people prefer their yellows to be a bit more golden. And a golden yellow is a yellow with more red in it.

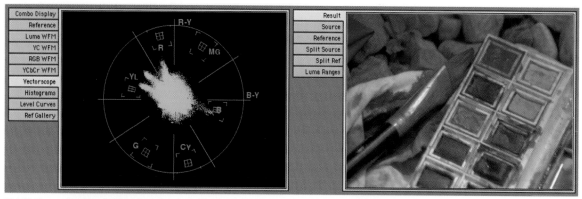

5.78 From Artbeats' Recreation and Leisure collection, shot RL123. The black, gray, and white tones create the bulk in the middle of the trace.

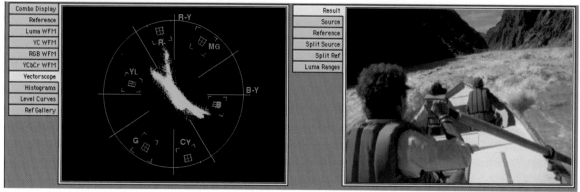

5.79 Heavily blue image from Artbeats' Recreation and Leisure collection, shot RL117.

Randy Starnes says the yellow of the vectorscope's yellow target is a color most colorists avoid:

> I think most colorists will turn the yellow vector a little bit away from green to compensate for what television does to yellow. The yellow of color bars is not the yellow of print art, so we turn that a little. Most people do. An example: in longform telecine, if you're doing an hour or two-hour story, quite often a lot of us will take the yellow secondary and move it two or three degrees away from green and then load the list, so the yellow is a little less green in your whole show.

The colorful shot in Figure 5.80 is like a good break in a game of pool. The yellows are going close to the yellow target, but are a few degrees toward red. The blue sky is heading towards cyan. And the red balloons are pretty close to hitting the red target exactly.

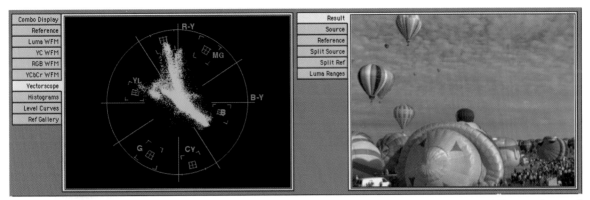

5.80 From Artbeats' Recreation and Leisure collection, shot RL101.

Info Palettes
and Other Numeric RGB Readouts

Another useful tool for color and tonal analysis is provided in the form of an eyedropper or **Info Palette** in many programs. Most imaging applications have them. The one in Figure 5.81 is from Synthetic Aperture's Color Finesse. The feature allows you to sample pixels and see what their specific RGB makeup is.

This feature allows you to click on various areas of the picture and see a readout of the RGB values of a specific pixel on the screen. Using this feature on pixels that you believe should be white, black, or neutral gives a great deal of information about color casts in those areas. Just as the vectorscope displays the absence of chroma by placing the signal in the middle of the monitor, it is possible to detect the absence of chroma with numerical RGB information. The absence of chroma with this means of analysis is indicated by the numerical similarity of the three channels to each other.

Pure white in RGB 8-bit color space is R255,G255,B255. Pure black: R0,G0,B0. 50% gray is indicated by R128,G128,B128. If the balance of red, green, and blue values are not identical or nearly identical, you have information that can help you eliminate the difference.

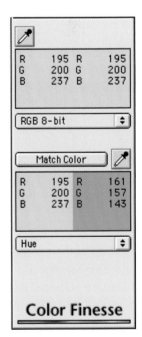

5.81 Info Palettes and eyedroppers in Color Finesse.

For example, use the eyedropper to sample an area of the screen that should be neutral gray. If the numerical RGB readout for this sample reads R60,G62,B94, then you know that your image is too blue. If the readout indicated R200,G200,B100, then the image would be too yellow. Yellow is the secondary color between red and green on a vectorscope or color wheel. Instead of saying the image is too yellow, we could also describe it as not being blue enough. Blue is the complementary color opposite yellow on a vectorscope or color wheel. Until you have memorized the relationships between the primary colors of red, green, and blue and the secondary colors of cyan, magenta, and yellow, refer to your vectorscope or a color wheel. If you are trying to use RGB controls to reduce magenta, then decreasing red and blue will solve the problem. To reduce yellow, decrease red and green, or increase the complementary color, which is blue.

The other important concept to remember is that adding a color that you need or subtracting a color that you don't want affects the picture in two different ways. Consider the previous example. If you decrease the amount of red and green to make a picture less yellow, then you are also decreasing the overall brightness or tone of the image. By increasing the amount of blue to make the picture less yellow, you are also increasing the overall brightness of the picture.

Let's see how this actually works. To simplify, we'll take a yellowish green color and attempt to make it more pure green. Analyzing the color as RGB numbers, it is R104,G194,B0. But let's also look at this color as hue, saturation, and brightness, which is H88,S100,B76. If we attempt to swing the hue more toward green, we could simply eliminate the red in the image. What does that do to our RGB numbers, though? For a pure green hue, this means that we get R0,G194,B0. The trick is, that even though the hue is now perfectly on green (120), the saturation and brightness have also remained the same in the HSB numbers, but if you look at the two colors, the first looks brighter than the second.

You could also try to increase the greenness by simply cranking up the green channel. Starting from our original example of R104,G194,B0, we would increase the green channel to its maximum, which manages to swing the hue around to 96. Dropping the amount of red gradually swings the hue closer to our green destination of 120, but it isn't until we get red back down to 0 that the hue gets all of the way to 120. Our final color here is much more saturated than our result in the first example, since we've cranked the green channel to its maximum number. The apparent brightness still does not match the original example.

Now let's try to swing the hue by looking at our color wheel and using complementary colors. If we want to reduce yellow, we add its complementary color, which is blue. If we are trying to compensate for the amount of red in the image, we could simply match the intensity of the red with the same intensity of blue. So, an image of R104,G194,B104 does actually swing the hue right where we want it: 120. However, now our green is a pretty pale shade of light green.

Our final attempt is to split the difference between red and blue instead of simply adding blue. Since our original example was R104,G194,B0, we'll cut the red amount in half and add that amount to the blue, giving us R52,G194,B52. This gives us a much more saturated image and maintains the hue at 120. If we were trying to maintain the look of a certain brightness or contrast of the image, we could now raise the amount of green either up to its maximum of 255 or lower it. But if we want to maintain the hue, we can only lower the amount of green down to one level above the red and blue numbers. In the current example, this would be R52,G53,B52. When the values of all of the channels match, remember, we have no hue at all because there is no chrominance. And if green drops below the red and blue numbers, we are left with the complementary color of green, which is magenta.

5.82 This window in Avid's Xpress DV color correction engine allows the selection of 3x3 averaged color sampling instead of single pixel color sampling.

Averaged color sampling

Rudimentary implementation of RGB sampling tools—or *eyedroppers*—sample a single pixel as a reference. However, selecting an individual pixel in an area may not actually be representative of the actual color in that area of the pixel. In most recent applications it is possible to define the size of the sample that is taken. That RGB sample is then averaged over a small area of pixels; for example, a 3×3 grid of pixels (see Figure 5.82) or a 5×5 grid of pixels. Depending on the area you are sampling, this averaging is much more useful than sampling individual pixels due to the possibility of noise in the image or subtle color variances from one adjacent pixel to the next.

Sampling RGB info with single pixel samples does have its uses. It can help you analyze areas that you think may be clipped. Areas of pure white or pure black can be a telltale sign that clipping has occurred. This test can be performed by watching the RGB numbers as you slowly drag the eyedropper inside an area of deep shadow or bright highlight. Minor fluctuations mean that the areas sampled have not been clipped. They can also mean that there may be some noise in the signal that can be addressed by the noise reduction tools that may exist in your arsenal of color correction or effects filter tools.

Not all random noise is a bad thing. With highly overexposed or underexposed portions of a film image, many colorists point to the fact that the film grain still creates "life" or "texture" in these portions of the image, while on video, an overexposed highlight merely results in lost detail, making it much less interesting.

Numeric RGB samples can also assist you in creating reference points for matching shots in a scene. You can compare skin tones, product colors, or even the depth and contrast of shadows. When using RGB sampling for this purpose, it is wise to use an averaged sampling to reduce the possible randomness.

One interesting use for these numerical readings could be in determining the strength of contrast between the shadows and highlights of shots that are in the same sequence and should match. You can quantitatively measure the ratio between the darkness of a shadow and the brightness of a highlight and compare that ratio with the same areas of another shot.

Even shots created with meticulous quality control and the highest level of professionalism are subject to these variances. Peter Mavromates, postproduction supervisor for David Fincher's *Panic Room*, explains the scope of issues that can cause these changes:

> When you think about the making of a movie, movies are at minimum, shot on really short schedules of 15 days and most long schedules of 80 or 90 days, and there are schedules that are even longer than that. Maintaining consistent lighting, quality control, etc., over that amount of time is impossible. If you're shooting on location outside during the day, the light changes minute by minute if it's a weather situation where there are clouds coming in. And if you're on a set and you actually manage to maintain consistent lighting over a number of weeks, you've got other issues that come in; you've got photochemical processes that drift, telecine scanners that drift. A number of different issues make it different: Actors, who despite their professional training, will go out and go to the beach over the weekend, and they come in on Monday in the middle of the same scene, and they've got a suntan. Stuff like that. You could make a list of a thousand things that affect how something looks.
>
> Now on *Panic Room*, what I just described was particularly difficult because it was one set for a large number of days. We're on one set day after day after day, and the inconsistencies creep in there. They creep in there a lot of times even though the lighting is all the same on the same set, what happens is that you move the camera and you're shooting an actor a certain way. Well, by shooting that way you suddenly find that the light kicks very strongly on the wall behind them. And what that means is that their side has become bright even though none of the lighting has changed, but just by the fact that the light is being bounced more directly into the lens, that angle is brighter. The wall in the background is brighter and so now no longer matches the reverse angle of the other actor.

Let's examine some sample images using RGB sampling.

The following are RGB samples taken from various portions of the image in Figure 5.83:

5.83 Frame grab from Artbeats' Kids of Summer Collection, shot KS109.

- Yellow hat: 222, 155, 43.
  This really nice hue of yellow has a lot of red in it.

- Blue dress: 14, 63, 237.

- Bluish/white blanket: 238, 244, 252.
  While the blanket looks fairly white, on video, this sample gives away its bluish cast.

- Flesh tones, girl in blue dress: 125, 69, 46.
  Flesh tones, girl in yellow: 121, 55, 30 and 151, 82, 49.
  Race does not change the basic hue of flesh tones.

- Grass: 43, 110, 30.
  A very nice grass color.

- White color on blue dress: 183, 197, 235.
  Fairly blue.

- Highlight on yellow flower: 252, 250, 237.
  If this was a straight highlight, the blue would be a little deficient. On a yellow flower, though, this is an appropriate highlight.

- Pigtails: 2, 2, 2 and 11, 4, 5.
  Pretty good numbers here. The 11, 4, 5 numbers are a little high on the red side, but sampling numerous points on the pigtails shows a wide spectrum of subtle colors in the blacks. Averaged out, these numbers are appropriate.

5.84 A nice day for a row in Ireland.

The following are RGB samples taken from various portions of the image in Figure 5.84:

- Shadows: 4, 10, 9.
  Many shadow samples came back with a similar red deficiency that we may want to correct.

- Skin tones: 197, 144, 157.
  He's Irish, so we may forgive the pink skin tones, but maybe we can pull down some of the blue. Notice the flesh tone numbers in the previous example. They all descend smoothly. But not our ruddy friend here. Pulling some blue out will reduce the magenta cast to his skin.

- Bright water reflections: 204, 235, 240 and 236, 246, 246.
  All's in order here.

- Sky: 253, 253, 253.
  Sampling of the sky showed there was still detail there, and the white is about as white as it gets.

- Boatman's coat: 133, 147, 163.
  Similar to the flesh tones, if we want this coat to be truly gray, we'll need to notch down the blue in the midtones. Our blacks and whites have the right amount of blue, so be careful to isolate the blue reduction to the midtones.

The image in Figure 5.85 is a little dark. We'll fix that in one of the tutorials. What else can the **Info Palette** reveal about where we should start? RGB samples are:

- Several fence readings: 30, 44, 34 and 32, 55, 38 and 22, 39, 28.
  All show this to be a little cyan. We are looking for a nice weathered gray. That means pulling down the green and a little notch down on blue.

- The blacks of the post: 8, 9, 10 and 5, 5, 4 and 9, 13, 12.
  This shows that blacks are in good shape. These good blacks are a warning that any color casts we attempt to fix will need to be limited to the midtones.

5.85 Dark fence.

The image in Figure 5.86 looks a little blue. What do the numbers tell us?

- Wood on front boat: 95, 41, 22.
  This doesn't tell us much.

- Red kayak paddle: 187, 47, 78.
  This seems a little blue if we want a red that's right on target.

- White from various outboard motors: 187, 221, 196 and 202, 237, 215.
  Now we're learning something. Reds are deficient and greens are a bit high.

5.86 Blue boats.

- Green from trees: 20, 54, 44.
  This seems blue as well.

- Sky blue: 146, 209, 223.
  Seems very green for a blue sky.

- Gray of second boat: 122, 180, 195.
  Another revealing number. Red is deficient. Since this is very close to that center number for 24-bit color images, we know that to balance this, we need to work on midtones.

Summary

We've seen the variety of information we can glean from the waveform and vectorscope. One more important analytical tool remains: the histogram, which we'll discuss in the next chapter.

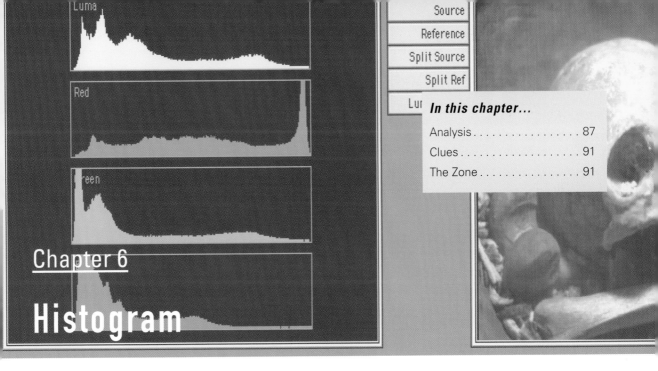

Chapter 6

Histogram

Another powerful tool for analyzing video images is the histogram. A histogram is a graph that breaks the video signal down into individual pixels and distributes them on a graph where the x defines the luminance of the pixels—with the darkest pixels to the left and the brightest pixels to the right—and the y displays the number of pixels at each luminance level.

In addition to showing the overall brightness levels of the pixels, the histogram can also display the individual red, green, and blue channels, graphed in the same way. This information can be very valuable in figuring out whether a given color channel has problems in the shadows, midtones, or highlights.

Analysis

Let's take a look at those sample images again to see how they appear when analyzed using a histogram.

The histograms in Figure 6.1 show pretty much what you'd expect from this image. Lots of shadows and some bright midtones. The only bright element is in the red channel. Nothing looks like it's clipped or crushed.

These are nice histograms in Figure 6.2. No clipping or crushing of the signal. The sky may be going a little green. We might want to pull those blacks down a bit to add some richness. The spike of

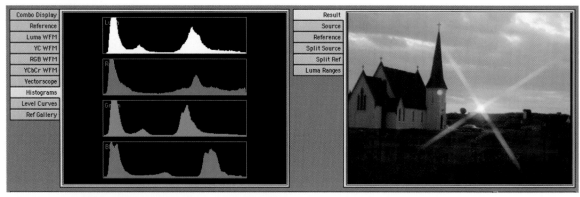

6.1   No surprises in this histogram.

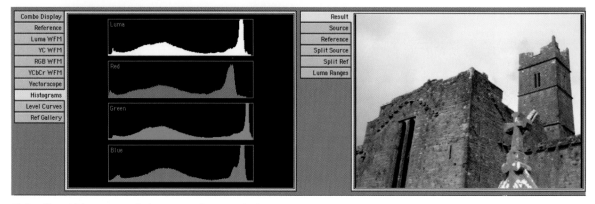

6.2   Good histogram, little correction needed.

luminance at the top is definitely sky. There might be enough detail there that we can make the sky more interesting.

Not a lot in the way of blacks in Figure 6.3. We can pull down the shadows to create some richness. It looks like the red channel clipped a bit on the high end. Rolling down the highlights a little will help this look less washed out.

In Figure 6.4 seems to be plenty of room to work with the shadow detail. Blacks could come down a little since there's some space at the low end of the luma histogram. The large spike of dark in the luma histogram can probably be spread out a little, improving detail in the blacks of the mine structure. It does seem like the sky has been clipped rather severely. Not much we can do to salvage that. You could pull the entire bright highlight level down. This wouldn't bring back the highlight detail, but it would make it easier to see the detail in the blacks because your eye wouldn't be so flooded with light. This is a careful balance, though, because you don't want the sky to look too dreary, unless that is the intent.

The blacks of Figure 6.5 seem very washed out. The low end of the histogram can definitely be pulled down to create some nice, solid blacks. Whites appear to be clipped, but there is still some highlight detail in the bright whites.

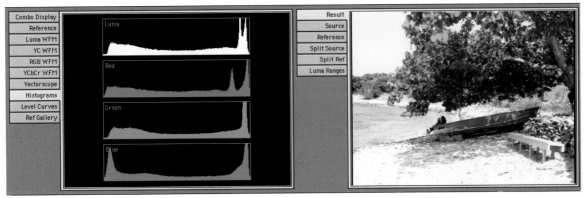

6.3 Not many blacks to work with.

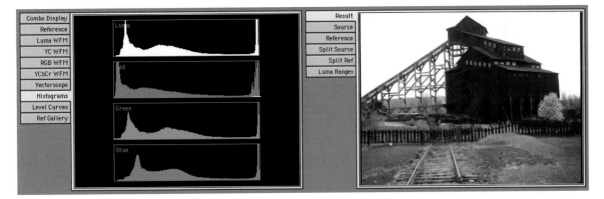

6.4 Plenty of shadows.

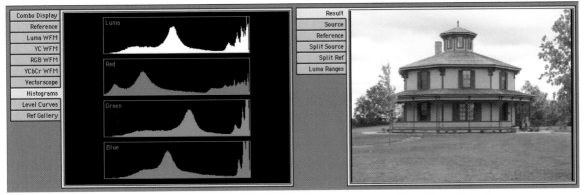

6.5 Faded blacks.

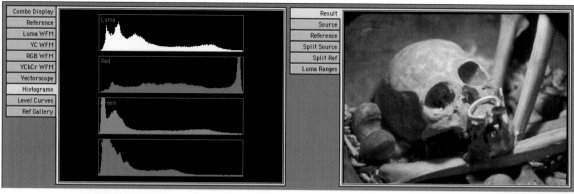

6.6   Green and blue surprise.

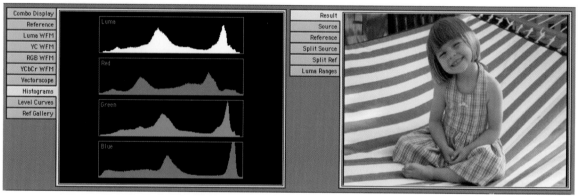

6.7   Excellent histogram, but note the midtone spikes.

Figure 6.6 shows some surprising histograms. The amount of blue and green in the low end of the histograms is unusual. There is the expected peak in the red channel histogram, but it is not clipped. Also, the luma histogram shows most of the picture sitting in the shadows, but the overall impression is of a fairly bright image. There is very little bright highlight, but that is as it should be. Other than the highlight of the ring sitting on the skull, very little else should be bright white. Correcting the red would be possible since nothing's clipped, but the red adds a lot to the image.

This is a beautiful histogram in Figure 6.7. The blacks could be pulled down to give some definition to the picture, but there's not much in this picture that should be pure black. Same with the whites. They could be pulled up some to add some punch and sparkle, but there's no definite bright white. The large spike of blue in the highlights gives reason to look at pulling down some blue in the highlights. The skin tones appear very nice, so any blue correction would need to either improve the skin tones or at least not make them worse. The green of the hammock and the warm colors of the girl's dress are evident in their respective histograms. The large spike of midtones in the luma histogram is a possible clue that midtones could be moved down to create a richer picture.

Clues

Like looking at a waveform monitor, there is no way to tell just by looking at a histogram that the image is good, but the histogram can give you some definite indications that something may be wrong. Some things to look for are:

- posterization, which can be seen as bands of pixels with similar levels

- clipping, with large, sharp peaks of pixels at either far end of the spectrum

- an overly large percentage of pixels in the middle of the spectrum, with none on the ends, indicating that your blacks and highlights are not well-defined

- missing levels of luminance—called *combing*—indicating data loss, probably due to some color space conversion (This is pretty rare to see in video color correction, but it can happen with imported images.)

The Zone

Although there is no "correct" histogram, the famous photographer Ansel Adams developed his Zone System for properly exposing and printing photographs. This system could give you an indication of what to shoot for. The goal of the Zone System was to match the exposure of the negative with the ability of the final print paper to reproduce that image. This created a series of zones that certain tones of the scene were supposed to fall into. The main point was to figure out which zone you wanted to place a certain element (like the skin tone of your subject, for example) and to properly expose and then develop so that that particular element ended up in the intended zone of the final print. The Zone System also helps photographers predict how the other elements will print in comparison to the main subject's zone. The other goal was not to lose important detail in the highlights and shadows. Adams didn't have histograms to analyze his photographs, so he broke each image into 10 zones based on their tonal range, and attempted to distribute the exposure of the film so that the darkest and brightest zones usually had some exposure, but that there were very few spots on any prints that went pure white or pure black to the point where detail was lost.[1]

Most critics consider Ansel Adams as a master of tonal range. He knew how to control it and what to do with it to provoke an emotional response. Yet, Adams' perspective on the importance of this skill was not that it was used to perfectly portray the *reality* of any given scene, but that it portray *the way the scene felt*. Another interesting note on the subject of Adams is that even in the 1960s, 70s, and 80s, he was still making prints of negatives he had taken back in the 1930s. As he aged, his prints changed to become much more bold and contrasty in comparison to his earlier prints of the same negative. This should make a clear statement that picking the "correct" tonal range for an image is very much a subjective undertaking and one that can and should be interpreted using more than just technical terms, but also emotion and feeling.

---

1. For more information on Ansel Adams's Zone System, see the Bibliography and Glossary page 194.

Many people who are unfamiliar with Adams' processes may place the entire weight of his artistic ability on his skill with a camera, but most photographic enthusiasts know that his skill in the darkroom—which is very analogous to the art of color correction for video—was as crucial to the success of his prints.

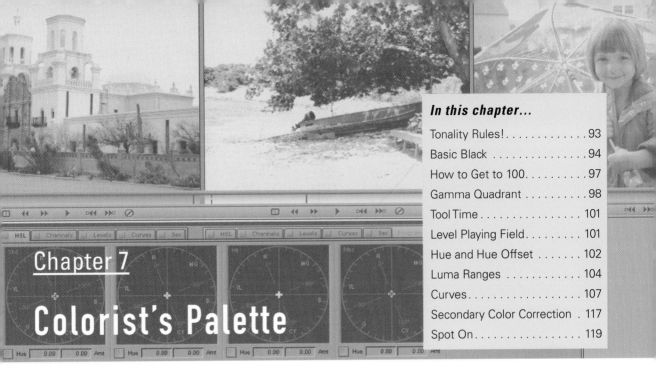

Chapter 7
Colorist's Palette

Now that we have an understanding of how to examine the images, we'll delve into the tools that are available to manipulate these images. The two main alterations performed by the colorist are color palette manipulations—balancing the color of the image—and tonal range manipulations. You'd think that since colorists are called colorists, the most important of these manipulations involves color. However, the thing that really transforms most images from mundane to marvelous resides in the tonal correction tools.

Tonality Rules!
(Or Colors Drool)

The tonality of an image is basically expressed in the range of luminance levels from black to white and where they fall in relationship to one another. The basic color correction tools have the ability to expand or compress the overall tonal range and to adjust the balance of how that range is weighted. To do this, the color correction engine basically remaps the levels of the incoming footage to new final output levels. The two main levels to remap are the highlights and the shadows. These define the limits of the tonal range of the image.

The other important element in manipulating the tone of the image is to decide on where the center tones of the image will be remapped. This is called the gamma. Some programs or tools will offer very basic controls over gamma, and others allow you to create complex gamma corrections, similar to parametric EQ in audio, instead of simple bass and treble controls. The advanced tools allow you to determine multiple gamma ranges and to determine the slopes of each gamma curve and how they blend into and out of each other.

Before delving too deeply into gamma, let's take a look at manipulating the extremes of the tonal range. These corrections are very standard. At their root, they are the basic controls that editors have almost always had with the basic TBC controls of brightness and setup. One of the first things that you will want to manipulate when doing a correction is to set the upper and lower limits of your image. To turn this into a highly generalized statement, you would want your blacks to be black and your whites to be white, without violating the legal limits. To simplify this discussion we will set these limits at 100IRE on a waveform monitor for the top end and 0IRE for the bottom. (Also see page 46 for a discussion of legal limits with various scopes, formats, and video standards.)

Hammer and saw of color correction

As you experiment with the following tonal corrections, use the basic **Master HSL** sliders for now. Each graphical user interface for each product will call this something a little different, and new versions of software will rename the old tools as they go. The tools we want to use now are the most basic color correction tools at your disposal: black level, gain, and gamma.

Basic Black

The first thing you should adjust in any correction is the black level, sometimes called *pedestal*, *lift*, or *setup*. The reason for this is that in most color engines, all of the other computations are based on this level. Normally if your picture looks a little washed out or there is not much detail in the blacks, you need to look at this level and get it to around 0IRE. The exception to this rule is if there is nothing in your image that *should* be black. If your image is:

- shot through a fog or smoke

- is mostly snow or

- is a long focal length shot of some distant skyscrapers

then there probably isn't anything that needs to be pure black. In cases like these, you should rely on your subjective judgment.

One of the primary indicators to set luminance or black levels is on the waveform monitor. The specific position the deepest black on the waveform monitor or the level of the brightest white is not as important as watching how compressed the waveform is at the top and bottom. If you lower the setup to get it down to 0IRE, but notice that the lower levels of the waveform are starting to compress into a single, thick line at the bottom, you know you're losing detail down in the shadows. Sometimes this means compromise. Usually you want that black point to be all the way to 0IRE, but if you start compressing the shadow details before you reach 0IRE, then you may need to use your eye to tell you when the blacks are rich enough.

The clue that you are clipping is not really the position of the waveform, but the overall shape of the waveform. Examine it carefully as you move the shadows toward 0IRE and the highlights toward

100IRE. When the shape—or excursion—starts to compress into a single, tight line, then you know you are killing detail in the highlights.

There was a good example of this in Chapter 5 on page 63. Reexamine Figures 5.37 and 5.38 and notice how Figure 5.37 has a certain shape to the brightest picture potions. When that level passes a certain point, the shape of the excursions change. That is the point where you start to really focus your adjustments. Just like scrubbing a piece of audio to find the very first bit of sound, you can increase and decrease the level while watching for that crucial point when the black level is low enough, but the shape of the wave is maintained.

Throw caution to the wind

Randy Starnes warns about allowing these adjustments to become too detailed:

> The more a person grades film, the more quickly they can recognize the perfect exposure of the film. That process can take five minutes; it can take fifteen minutes. If it starts to take longer than fifteen minutes, you'll start to lose your audience. Make the moves bold. Don't be constrained by technical limits. See what you can do. You can always come back. One of the most frustrating things for a client to participate in is a slow, deliberate manipulation of the image. You lose track of where you are and where you want to go.

> If you make big sweeping moves, you can do the same thing quicker. And you provoke more feedback from your client. They see it and you see it. One of the things that we have to watch out for is that our brain compensates for a lot of what we see. If you move too slowly—if you're too cautious—your brain may tell you that the image is right. But following a plan or a philosophy of making large changes keeps your brain from catching up or from convincing you that you've gone as far as you can. You make multiple changes. You go in three or four different directions, you save those and you compare them, and you quickly winnow out the ones that are not pleasing to you or your client. You narrow down your choices.

Back to black

Getting the blacks low without deforming the shape of the waveform near the bottom helps preserve shadow detail. There are certainly times when you may want to intentionally eliminate detail in your pictures, but this is rarely a good thing. Keep an eye on your waveform monitor when doing these first steps to insure that you are exploiting as much of the picture information as you can.

To better understand this, let's look at three waveform images in Figures 7.1–7.3 as we attempt to find the proper setup for an image. The image we're trying to correct here should have a full range of luma values, from black to bright white.

The waveform image in Figure 7.1 indicates that the picture probably looks a little washed out. No part of the waveform is sitting on the 0IRE line. The image in Figure 7.2 is properly set up. Notice the way the shadow area of the waveform looks. Now compare it to the third waveform image, Figure 7.3. In the third image, the shadows have started to compress into a tight line. The broad, open excursions of shadow detail are compressing. This indicates that shadow detail is being crushed. If we are trying for

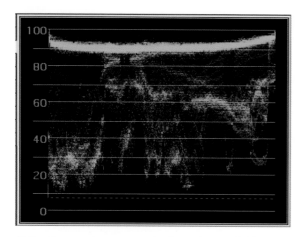

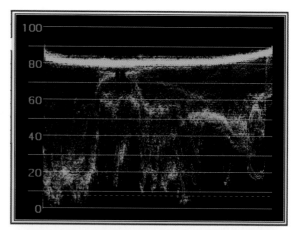

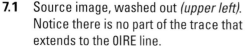

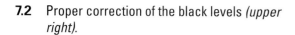

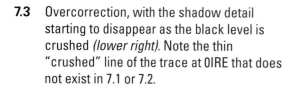

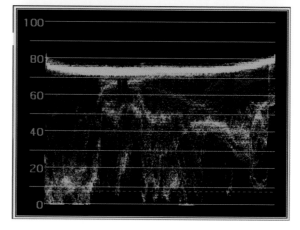

7.1 Source image, washed out *(upper left)*. Notice there is no part of the trace that extends to the 0IRE line.

7.2 Proper correction of the black levels *(upper right)*.

7.3 Overcorrection, with the shadow detail starting to disappear as the black level is crushed *(lower right)*. Note the thin "crushed" line of the trace at 0IRE that does not exist in 7.1 or 7.2.

an optimal image, there is a lot of detail being lost in this lower range in Figure 7.3.

Once setup has been properly tuned, we can look to adjust the bright end of the image. If your waveform shows that you don't have any parts of the image that extend all the way up to 100 IRE (the highest luminance), you may want to raise your luminance levels so that things that *should* be very bright hit that mark. If your image doesn't have anything that *should* be completely bright, then use your eye to determine the maximum luminance level.

Value of 100IRE

While all colorists agreed that not every image should be brought all the way to 100IRE, Randy Starnes pointed out that nearly every image should reach the extremes in terms of tonal range:

> Not every image should hit 100, but the majority of the time you will find in any image rich blacks and bright whites. We broke the rule along time ago that whites had to be 100%. They don't need to go there, but you'll have a better image if you have a full volt of video somewhere in your picture.

(One *volt* of video refers to the full 700mV of video signal that is equal to 100IRE, plus the 300mV of sync.)

Starnes continues,

> Since you're dealing with a television image that is transmitted, a low signal is going to give you more noise-to-signal and your goal is less noise-to-signal. Transmission introduces noise inherently. Our equipment has gotten better and better, so the post process—editing and color correction—is not introducing noise; transmission is introducing it. So in order to preserve that image with the lowest signal-to-noise ratio, you want to be able to build in a volt of video.

> If you have a night scene, you're not going to have bright whites, but if you have a night scene with a practical inside a window, you're going to have an opportunity to have a volt of video. That carries over well. You're not going to see a lot of commercial images that don't have the full range or at least a volt of video. And most of the time, you push it to 100% and past so it jumps out at you. So it carries across better. Obviously a white that is less than 100% is going to be a duller white.

Beyond the basic question of correcting images so that some point reaches 100IRE is another question of exceeding that range. Most broadcast specs actually allow temporary specular highlights to reach as high as 108IRE. Most professional camcorders do not clip images until around the 110IRE mark. Check with your dub house or broadcast client for specifics, but if you have an extra 8IRE of range to make chrome bumpers and sparkling water pop a little more, then use it.

How to Get to 100

When adjusting the upper range of your image, there are many tools that you can use. For now, let's discuss the **Brightness** and **Gain** controls. You may only have one of these controls. You may also be provided with *both* of these options. If you only have a single option, then you would follow a similar procedure to the one outlined for setup. You need to bring the brightest portion of the waveform up or down to create the brightest possible legal limit, assuming that your image has something that should actually be pure white.

You want to look out for the same kind of compression in the highlights that you were on the lookout for in the shadows. Don't take the brightness up so high that you lose detail in your highlights. Just as with the crushing of shadows, the loss of highlight detail is seen as a squeezing or compressing of the excursions in the upper portion of the waveform. On a monitor, an experienced colorist sees that the highlights begin to flatten out and lose texture. When your highlight levels have been set, revisit your black levels. Depending on how your **Brightness** or **Gain** control works, you may have slightly altered your set-up level, so you may need to make several small adjustments of the setup and brightness controls as they interact with each other. If you only have a **Brightness** control, instead of a **Gain** control, then you will have to perform an annoying little Texas two-step as you move back and forth between brightness and black until both levels are where they belong.

Math class

If your color correction controls provide for both gain and brightness, then you'll need to understand how they differ from each other. Inside the brain of your color correction engine, many of the controls work like a basic spreadsheet. You simply take every digitized pixel in the image, assign it a number and run it through the spreadsheet, which has a simple formula. The finished equation becomes the output image value.

For brightness control, the equation is additive. If you increase brightness by 2, you are simply adding 2 to the master RGB value of every pixel. The bad thing about this simple process is that it means that if you have already set your blacks at 0IRE and you add 2 to every value, your blacks are now at 2IRE. Brightness takes the entire waveform and moves it, lock, stock, and barrel, up by the same amount. Sometimes that may be just what you want, but usually you want more control than that.

That's where the **Gain** control comes in. Gain is usually done multiplicatively. That means that if you make an adjustment of 10 to **Gain,** your carefully set 0IRE black level is unaffected because 0 times 10 is still 0. If you increase a pixel with a value of 10 by 10%, it only goes up 1 value, while a pixel with a 90 value will go up 9 values.

Other color correction programs use different formulas to alter brightness. You don't need to know the specifics, but sometimes it does help to understand exactly what's happening under the hood.

The other complex equations that come into play involve luma ranges. When you do a gain adjustment to highlights, midtones, or shadows only, the multiplier that you choose with the slider also has to take into account an additional factor of where in the range each pixel resides. The multiplier is then modified by the percentage determined by its position in the specific luma range you are correcting. That's how you are able to control very specific tonal ranges of the image.

Enough math. Let's move on.

 Tip _____

A word of caution: When you create computer files—such as QuickTimes—you need to understand that PCs and Macs have significantly different gamma sensitivities. Macs generally displaying gamma much higher than PCs. It may be necessary to run some cross-platform tests and possibly specific platform adjustments of your output to ensure a quality image across the board.

Gamma Quadrant

With the top and bottom range of your image set, your image may still appear too dark or too light. The solution to this comes from the **Gamma** control. Gamma correction is one of the notable improvements over the basic TBC controls that editors are accustomed to. It is one of the secret weapons in many colorists's arsenals because it seems to solve a lot of difficult problems. Gamma correction allows you to maintain essentially fixed levels in your shadows and highlights while adjusting the midtones up or down independently. This allows you to keep your image legal while still altering the perceived overall brightness of the scene. Another change that gamma correction makes is that the image is perceived to increase in contrast as gamma is lowered and decrease with increased gamma level. Often when a picture is a little washed out despite having proper black levels, dropping the gamma will give it a nice, rich feeling.

In or out

If you just tried out the previous little gamma experiment using your color correction tools and got exactly opposite results, this may be time to explain a confusing aspect of altering gamma. Mainly this has to do with whether your color correction engine is making the gamma corrections on the incoming image or the outgoing image. After Effects' **Levels** control gives you gamma control of the incoming image, so this is one of the tools that may react the opposite of what you might expect. The reason this behavior seems backwards is that if you watch a waveform monitor while adjusting the gamma in a program that does the remapping based on the incoming gamma, then as you move the gamma down, the midrange values go *up*! Most video people will feel that the tools that control the outgoing gamma are more intuitive, since moving the gamma down will move the middle values on the waveform down as well.

The explanation of why incoming or outgoing gamma corrections behave in opposite ways means more math. We'll keep it brief, though. Let's assume that to the computer, gamma means 50. This number is the same whether it is incoming gamma or outgoing gamma. Remember, these corrections are usually just based on doing an equation to an incoming number to get an outgoing number. Well, if your color corrector affects the *incoming* signal that means that it sees 50 and, by default, wants to map it to 50 for the outgoing image. When you move the gamma down by 10, you're telling the computer, "Now I want the gamma of 40—which is darker than 50—to be mapped *up* to 50," so decreasing gamma in this situation means *raising* the level. This is fairly counterintuitive, but there are a lot of color correction engines that use this model.

For other engines, it sees a default of 50 for gamma on one side and a 50 on the outgoing side. Now, when you raise gamma, if you are raising the *outgoing* gamma by 10, you are saying, I want the digitized value of 50 to be remapped *up* to 60. This provides the behavior most people would expect.

The other thing to think about is that these gamma corrections are like a rubber band. As you compress the values on one side of gamma, you are stretching the values on the other. This can result in banding in gradients as a finite number of brightness values are spread out. Imagine if you were to draw vertical lines as tightly as possible on a rubber band that was stretched evenly between two points. Now, if you were to grab the center of that rubber band and pull it straight toward one of the end points, the lines on the side that is being pulled tight start to spread apart. The lines on the side you are pulling toward start to compress.

This can also be visualized by doing gamma corrections on a horizontally gradated image, as shown in Figures 7.4–7.6.

To further refine gamma adjustments, some programs provide controls for gamma knee adjustments. This parameter allows you to control the position of a secondary range within the gamma. You can think of it as upper gamma and/or lower gamma. The controls allow you to control the center position or the target luminance and the width of the secondary range which defines the spread of the luminance values. It then allows you to alter this second gamma range by increasing or decreasing the values in the specified area.

Most color correction plugins or built-in color correction engines have many ways to accomplish the same task. Sometimes it is because a certain tool offers an easier way to approach certain problems and sometimes it is because different editors prefer to think about their images in different ways and are

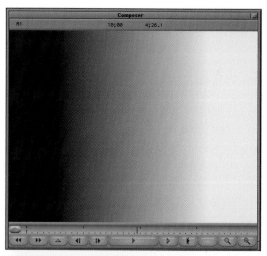

7.4 BWRamp test signal with no correction.

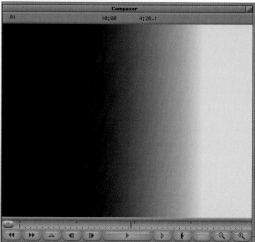

7.5 The same signal after lowering the gamma.

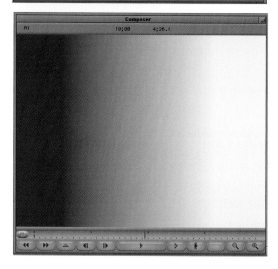

7.6 The same signal after raising the gamma.

more comfortable with certain tools. By adding many different ways to approach the same corrections, they make everybody happy.

Tool Time

Setup, gain, and gamma controls have the widest range of tools to do the same basic job. You can use the basic **TBC**-like sliders or you can use **Curves** or even **Histograms** (sometimes known as **Levels**).

So far, we've discussed using slider controls to alter **Setup**, **Gain**, and **Gamma** controls. But there are more intuitive tools available that provide more precise control. One of those is the **Histogram** or **Levels** control.

Level Playing Field

To use the Levels tool, you must understand the histogram display as described in the previous chapter on page 87. To review briefly, the histogram shows the brightness of pixels as plotted on a simple x-y graph. The brightness is plotted horizontally, along the x axis while the y axis shows the number of pixels at each luminance level. Additionally, most histograms have pull-down menus that give you access to the level controls of the individual color channels. This can be very useful for fixing color problems, but for now let's stick to the overall combined brightness levels of all of the color channels. This is known by several different names, including **RGB**, **Master**, **Composite** and **RGB Master** levels.

 Tip _____

Some programs offer the ability to lower the luminance of just the highlights, leaving the mid-tones and shadows alone. Care must be taken when making major adjustments to a single range of the picture because you can end up creating a solarized look. In an extreme example, you could lower the highlights to black. Be careful to check the new adjustments you've made against the uncorrected image. This can help spot areas that have become clipped.

Although it looks like the histograms we used to evaluate our images in the last chapter, Figure 7.7 is really a **Levels** control in disguise. A histogram doesn't give you control over your image, but the **Levels** control provides control, usually by way of two small triangles placed at either end of the histogram/level interface, and another in the middle to represent gamma.

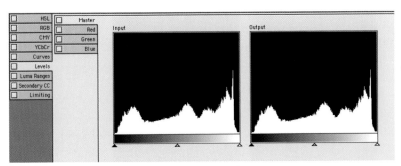

7.7   Level control. (Image from the Color Finesse Levels UI.)

Tip _____

Obvious Problem: Sometimes it's helpful to crank up the chroma quite a bit when adjusting hue or fixing color casts, so that the problems are actually accentuated. Or if you have an external vectorscope, you can take it out of its detente—also called the _unity_ or _neutral_—position and crank up the gain on the vectorscope to get the same clues to hue and color casts. Some vectorscopes also have a **Magnify** option that allows you to zoom in on the center of the vectorscope or on specific quadrants. Since the center position of the vectorscope is the absence of color and the outside edges are maximum chroma, increasing the gain makes it more apparent where subtle colors lie in relationship to each other. It also makes subtle adjustments in hue and RGB balance much more noticeable.

Some programs only provide you with a single **Histogram/Level** control. Others provide histograms for both the incoming levels (as digitized) and the outgoing levels (as corrected). Some provide a histogram for the incoming levels and just a slider for the outgoing corrections. Sometimes you can only adjust one side of the histogram, either incoming or outgoing. You have to do a little experimenting with these controls while keeping in mind the discussion on the difference between affecting the incoming or outgoing gamma and how the results of these two different adjustments affect the appearance of the image.

The main attraction of using this **Levels** tool is that you have graphic feedback as you make your level adjustments.

Hue and Hue Offset

Hue, as applied to the entire range of the picture, should really be set with color bars. It is rarely suitable for fixing color casts—like poor white balancing. All the hue control—sometimes called the _phase control_—does is rotate the hue of all of the colors the same amount.

Some color correction engines are capable of offsetting hue in specific luma ranges of the picture, and this is a great way to correct color casts. This is what was added to Final Cut Pro's interface with the transition to version 3. FCP users know this feature as the **3-way Color Corrector.**

Figure 7.8 is a screenshot from Final Cut Pro 3's **3-way Color Corrector.** This tool allows specific hues and saturations in specific tonal ranges to be balanced intuitively. Figure 7.9 is the **Hue Offset** control for the Avid Symphony. Both of these controls work similarly to the trackballs that Da Vinci colorists use to balance their colors.

To use the **3-way Color Corrector,** you analyze the picture—primarily with the vectorscope—and determine the specific color of the cast. One way to do this is to locate an area of the vectorscope that appears to indicate a white, black, or gray area of the picture. This area should be near the center of the vectorscope. If the vectorscope were displaying a portion of the image that was truly white, black, or gray, it would be perfectly centered on the crosshairs of the vectorscope. For an image with a color cast, that center position will be slightly offset. You can then use the **Hue Offset** controls to try to center that color cast. You can also use this feature while monitoring an **Info Palette**-type display that shows the RGB values numerically. By selecting a portion of the image that should have no chroma, the **Hue Offset** controls can be used to dial in the correct color balance. For example, if you use the **Info Palette** to analyze a piece of gray

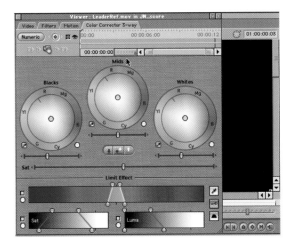

7.8 Final Cut Pro 3's 3-way Color Corrector.

7.9 Hue Offset control for the Avid Symphony.

asphalt in a road and see that the blue values are higher than the red and green values, you can use the shadow or midtone wheel to pull those tones toward yellow, which is the opposite direction—the complementary color—to blue.

Be careful to understand what luma range the color cast is affecting. If it is the whole image, then use the master **Hue Offset** wheel. If it is only in the highlights, then only adjust the **Highlights** wheel.

Hue Offset can also be used to great effect to create moods and special looks. Adding blue to the shadows, red to the midtones, or yellow to highlights, for example, may give emotional context that is not present in the "correct" white balance. Remember that color provides you with many important emotional clues that you can use to steer your audience.

Some plugins, like ViXen and FCP, have a kind of automated version of **Hue Offsets** built in to their plugin that works pretty much like using the white and black balance buttons on a video camera. You click on an area of the picture that should be black and "black balance" it; then you do the same with white. If there are no white or black areas of the image, you can select any neutral gray area of the image and click on the **Color Balance** button. This doesn't offer a whole lot of control, but it is very quick and intuitive. The problem with this approach is that in addition to centering the grayscale images in the center of the color wheel, they also adjust the luminance of the images, trying to take white to 100IRE and black to 0IRE.

There is also the old urban legend of a colorist who balanced his blacks on the black suit the talent was wearing and white balanced on his white shirt. Despite this, the colors did not look right. The problem was that the suit was really dark blue and the white shirt was really a light pink. So the shadows went yellow and the highlights went cyan.

It is possible for the **Hue Offset** wheels to introduce some fairly saturated chroma levels. High levels of chroma introduce bleed and noise pretty quickly. Use your eyes to tell you what's right, and keep an eye on your vectorscope to see what's legal and what's not. Dropping chroma below what's "normal" is often done for effect. It can also reduce noise or chroma bleed and can sometimes eliminate moiré in fine lines. Two schools of thought are available on making chroma adjustments. One is to make these at the beginning, using only color bars to set the levels. The other thought is to make them near the end to ensure that other adjustments that have been made have not seriously affected the chroma. For example, raising luminance will also raise chroma levels, and some RGB balancing could also raise or lower overall chroma levels significantly. Leaving chroma till the end lets you compensate for these adjustments, but you are essentially left doing this by eye. My rule of thumb for chroma adjustments is to err on the side of being desaturated.

Hue Offset can be very beneficial in maintaining the look of a nice picture that happens to have some illegal levels. Instead of pulling down the saturation of your entire image until the offending color hits a legal target, you can specifically hunt down the offending color and wrangle it into place without affecting any of the other colors.

Luma Ranges

As we touched upon earlier, when trying to adjust luminance and gamma controls or trying to eliminate color casts, one of the valuable features in a color correction package is to be able to isolate those adjustments so that they only affect certain luma ranges. For example, correcting a blue color cast across the entire picture so that skin tones appear correct may introduce a yellow cast that exists only in the highlights or blacks. With the ability to adjust the colors of highlights, midtones, and shadows individually, you can solve this issue easily.

But in addition to making these corrections on preset values for the descriptions of shadows, midtones, and highlights, many programs offer you the opportunity to carefully craft these descriptions using curves, as shown in Figures 7.10 and 7.11. Notice the correlation between the shadows curve and the histogram underneath in Figure 7.11.

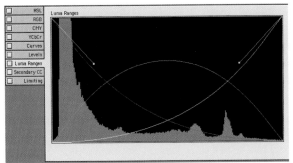

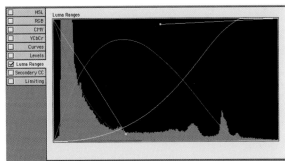

7.10 Default Luma ranges in Color Finesse.

7.11 A customized set of curves that exploits the specific tonal range of the image being corrected.

Using luma range corrections can also be a powerful and creative way to develop other-worldly effects with tremendous control. Look at what was accomplished by drastically altering the luma ranges of the image and then creating correction to those new ranges. Figure 7.12 shows how wild remapping of the luma ranges can affect even simple Hue Offset moves.

Figure 7.13 shows the drastic alterations to the luma ranges in Avid Symphony's **Luma Range** tab that created the image. The center image above the **Luma Ranges** is a special three-tone display that allows you to easily understand what you have assigned as shadows, midtones, and highlights. Shadows are displayed as black, midtones as gray, and highlights as white. You can see by this image

7.12 Remapping luma ranges.

that—after remapping the luma ranges—the new ranges have nothing to do with actual shadows, midtones, and highlights. Will you use this power for good or evil? Only the shadow knows.

The ability to radically change the luma ranges can also help when trying to isolate problem areas of a picture. If you're faced with mixed lighting, with a subject lit with tungsten or halogen and a bright blue window visible in the background, you can use luma ranges to isolate the bright window. Using **Luma Ranges** to isolate the window is a matter of describing the brightness of the window with a specific range, in this case the highlight range. Most programs provide a way to monitor what is being defined

7.13 Alterations to luma ranges in Avid Symphony.

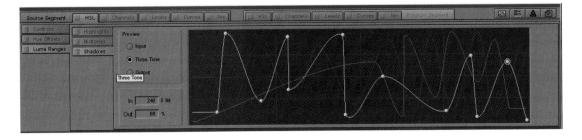

by a given range; for example, a three-toned representation of your image with black representing your shadows, grey representing midtones, and white representing highlights (see Figure 7.14).

Another important reason to dig into **Luma Ranges** is when a large portion of your picture sits in only one of the preset ranges. For example, you may have a very dark scene, where virtually the entire picture resides in the shadows. In order to effectively work on this image, you can alter the ranges so that the really deep shadows are represented by one range—shadows—while the middle shadows are represented by the next range—midtones—and the midtones and highlights are all represented by the highlight range. The object is to determine what you need to be able to change independently of the rest of the image. In the previous example, if you believed that the shadows were fine and there were really no midtones to worry about, you could isolate the highlight levels into midhighlights and bright highlights by adjusting the luma ranges.

The default shapes that define these ranges are gentle curves. However, on occasion you may want to affect a very specific portion of picture, and you can make the transition between shadows and midtones be a very sharp line. The danger in this is creating a posterized look at the transition. Creating a sharp delineation between ranges is often needed when rescuing detail in a sharply backlit scene where a window needs to be brought into control so that the rest of the image can be brought up enough to see shadow detail. If the luma range isn't sharply defined to specify just the luma range of the window, then bringing down the window will also bring down other levels that you may need to keep to provide definition in the shadows.

Despite the great benefits of controlling luma range, generally you will not have to manipulate luma ranges much unless you find you are not able to control the image as precisely as you want.

7.14 A three-toned representation of an image used while manipulating the highlight and midtone curves.

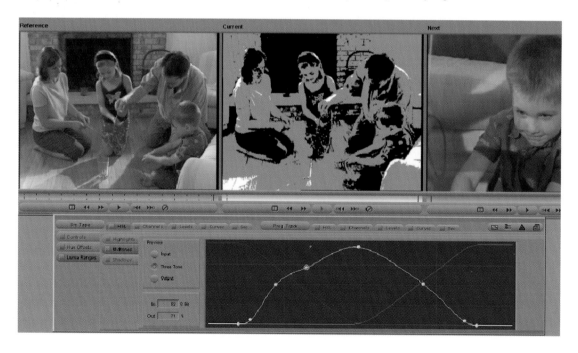

Curves

Figure 7.15 makes the name *Curves* seem like a bit of a misnomer. These are the default positions for the **Curves** controls, showing no change between input and output levels.

Figure 7.16 demonstrates the amount of control that is possible with **Curves**. Each color correction engine has limits to the number of points that you can put on a given line, but even with only four or five, the amount of control is much more specific than what is available with basic levels adjustments and luma ranges.

Curves are a powerful way to deal with color levels, although in some situations they are less intuitive than other methods. When adjusting levels in this type of graphical user interface, you are normally presented with four boxes with diagonal lines, one for each color channel (RGB) and another box representing overall composite level. Each box is merely a graph with the input (source) level charted on the *x* axis of the graph and the output along the *y* axis. The default of a 45° angle shows that the input and output are equal. So if you grab the diagonal line in the middle (the gamma) and drag it upwards, you are remapping the luminance of the middle pixels to be brighter. Similarly, dragging the same middle point backward will brighten the image as well, because you are asking to map a darker input value to the middle output value.

7.15 Curves controls defaults.

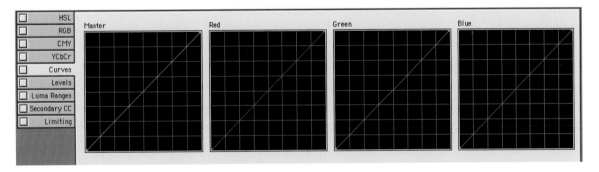

7.16 Control points in Curves.

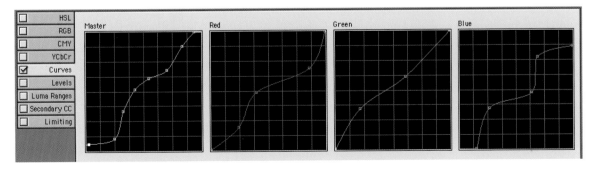

While these two adjustments seem to be having the same affect on the picture, they are actually doing two very different things. You can see the difference numerically in some programs by watching the starting point of the adjustment. If you select the true center point mathematically, it will be $128x$ and $128y$. Dragging this point straight up to, say, 168 means that all of the input values from 128 and below are being stretched up to a maximum level of 168 on output, and the levels above 128 input are being compressed between 168 and 255. By dragging the same point backward to, say, 100, you are mapping all of the input levels below 100 to spread out to a maximum value of 128, and all of the values from 100 and above are compressed into the range of 128–255.

Dragging the lower left corner to the right remaps the shadows so that the blacks are clipped. Dragging the same point upwards remaps the blacks so that the darkest input pixels now are much brighter.

The basics of curves

Let's take some basic examples and see what curves would provide the intended result.

In Figure 7.17[1] notice the look and levels of the waveform with the **Curves** in their unity, or default, position. Every input value matches every output value. This is taken from a screenshot of FCP running Color Finesse as a plugin. The other feature provided by Color Finesse from within the **Curves** tab is the ability to "eyedropper" blacks, whites, and grays. This provides an automatic white balance. It is an excellent tutorial in **Curves** to use these eyedroppers and see how it affects the curves.

The **Curves** in Avid's Xpress DV are really nicely designed to provide color-based clues as to what will happen by moving the curve in one direction or the other (see Figure 7.18). For example, pulling the blue curve up will add blue, while pulling it down will add yellow.

In Figure 7.19 we've dragged the lower left corner (representing black) and pulled it up, raising the black level so that what had been 0 on a scale of 0–255 is now 20. This moves the waveform monitor up from 0IRE to about 10IRE. Notice the numerical input and output values. What was digitized at 0 (input) is now raised to 20 (output).

The opposite move is made in Figure 7.20. We've taken the 0 point and moved it 20 levels to the right. This crushes all the pixels that had a luminance level of 20 and below down to 0.

In Figure 7.21 the highest point in the curve, 255 was moved backwards by 20. This moves all pixels with a value of 235 and above up to 255. The other tonal move that's happening with all these moves that is not as apparent is that when all of the values above 235 move up to 255, all of the values below 235 also move somewhat, spreading the 20 point move across all the values from 0 to 234.

In Figure 7.22 the highest point on the curve was moved down to 235. This remaps all of the pixels between 235 and 255 down to 235, effectively clipping whites at 235.

---

1. The image in Figures 7.17, 7.19–7.26, and 7.29 is courtesy of Artbeats' Mixed Cuts Collection, shot LM113.

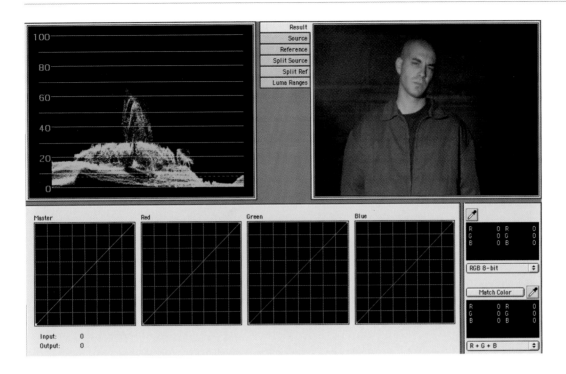

7.17 Curves in default (FCP running Color Finesse) *(above)*.

7.18 Curves from Avid's Xpress DV *(below)*.

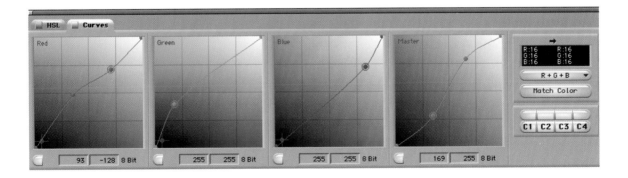

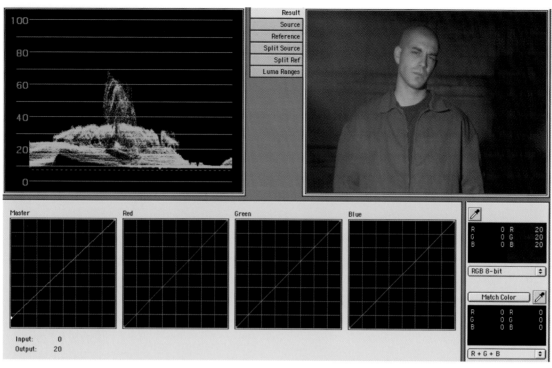

7.19 Raising the black level *(above)*.   **7.20** Blacks lowered *(below)*.

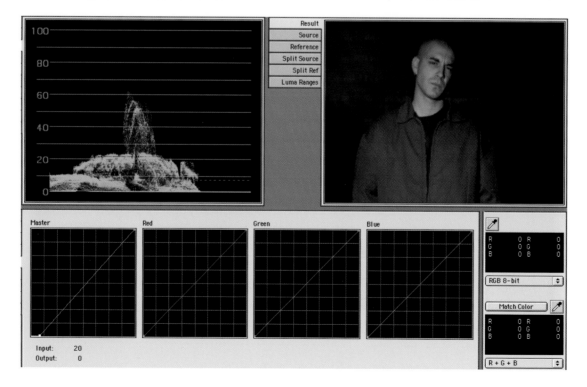

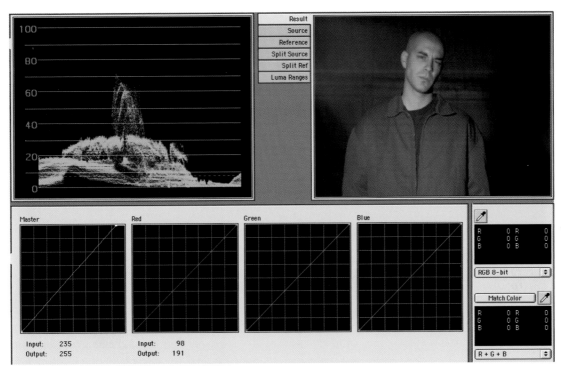

7.21 Highest point moved backwards 20 *(above).*   **7.22** Clipping whites to 235 *(below).*

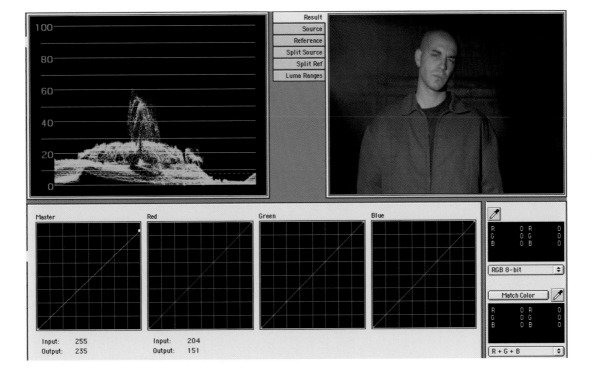

Figures 7.23 and 7.24 show two midrange moves with very similar end results. Figure 7.23 takes the input value of 128 and moves it down by 20, mapping pixels around the 128 level down to 108, darkening the midtones of the picture. Figure 7.24 shows the 128 midtone level pulled forward by 20, mapping the levels at 128 up to 148. Another variation of this move that would be even more similar would be pulling the point at 108 forward to 128. All of these moves would darken the midtones.

Again, two similar sets of moves with similar end results: Figure 7.25 shows the midrange point of 128 brought back 20 points to 108, brightening the midtones, by mapping 108 input values to 128 output values. Figure 7.26 shows the midpoint of 128 being brought up by 20. This also brightens the image, by remapping 128 input values to 148 output values. If the input and output numbers are not what you'd expect, remember that the original point on the graph is *not* the input value. The *direction* of the move indicates input or output changes. Any move that is vertical changes the *output* number while horizontal moves change the *input* value. Try some moves in **Curves** while viewing the input and output numbers.

If you have curves for each of the RGB channels, you can easily fix different color casts in the highlights, midtones, and shadows. If the midtones are too blue, but the highlights go green, pull the middle of the blue curve down and then adjust the top of the green curve down. You may need to make additional luminance and gamma changes after color fixes because the individual color adjustments will affect overall levels. Beyond fixing color casts related to the three primary colors, though, using curves to correct for color casts is much more difficult and less intuitive, because taking a magenta hue out means fiddling with pulling down both red and blue or understanding the complementary colors and adding green. Avid's new Color Correction tool for Xpress DV makes **Curves** much easier to understand when correcting individual color channels because of its unique color coding (see Figure 7.18, page 109). You should experiment with different ways to correct bad color casts before locking in to one. **Hue Offsets** is much easier for most casts than **Curves**, but many people prefer the control they have with **Curves**.

The benefit of **Curves** is to gain very precise control over specific luma ranges. If you only need general control inside a luma range—highlight, midtone, or shadow—then another tool may be faster and more intuitive. But of all the tools, the **Curves** tool gives you the most specific control when you really need it.

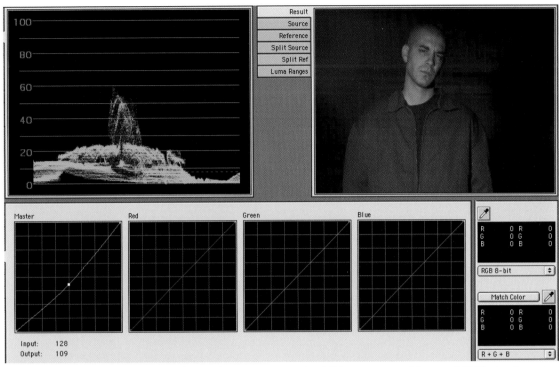

7.23 Midrange moved down 20 *(above).*   **7.24** Midrange moved forward 20 *(below).*

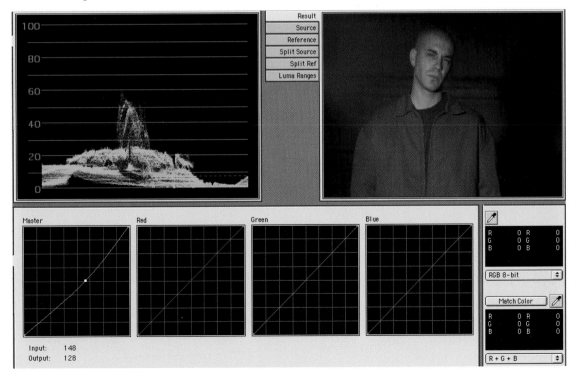

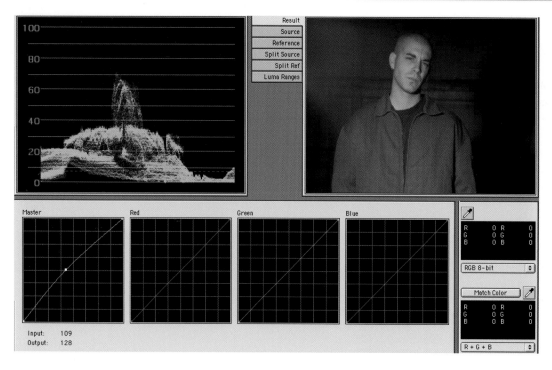

7.25 Midrange brought back 20 points *(above)*.   **7.26** Midrange brought up 20 points *(below)*.

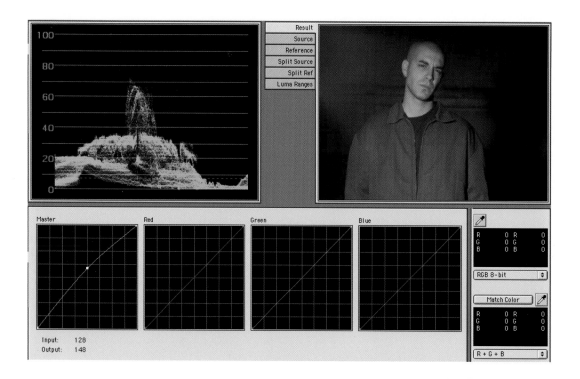

Precision control when you need it most

The **Master Curve** levels can solve very specific problems with difficult images. Figures 7.27 and 7.28 are from a tutorial that will be fully explored in a later chapter, but even a quick examination of the difficulties of correcting this image show where **Curves** really shine. It's all about control.

Figure 7.28 shows the amount of manipulation needed to control all of the fine levels of shadow to create a pleasing silhouette from a muddy, dark mess. To do this, it was necessary to hold some of the darkest shadows where they were, so there would be some definition in the blacks, but then add several points to the curve to begin spreading the shadow detail out. Also, curves were added in the blues, greens, and reds to manipulate the color of the sky, giving it a purplish twilight hue that would provide a color clue as to the time of day.

Tal, a veteran editor at Chainsaw in Santa Monica, California, color corrects on an Avid Symphony. For him, the **Curves** tab is one of the main staples of his color correction diet. He says,

> If you go to the **Curves** and you add a point about a quarter of the way down the luminance curve line and curve it up a little, and add another point a quarter of the way up from the bottom and push it down a little, you'll have a shallow S. That is the most effective, most immediate, helpful way to make a picture look better in 90% of the cases. Just that little curve makes things look a lot more like what you want them to look like (see Figure 7.29).

7.27 Dark original image and default Curves.

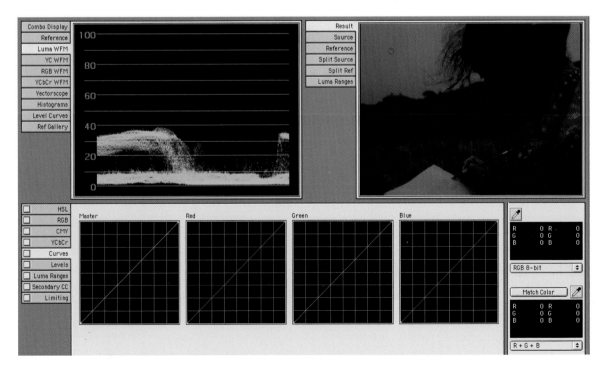

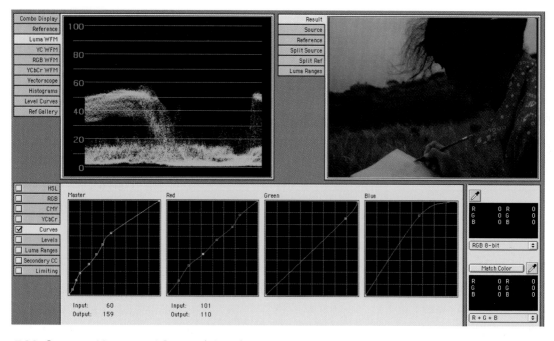

7.28 Corrected image and Curves *(above)*.

7.29 Example of using the curves to create a shallow S-curve in the luminance curve, which creates richer shadows and makes highlights pop *(below)*.

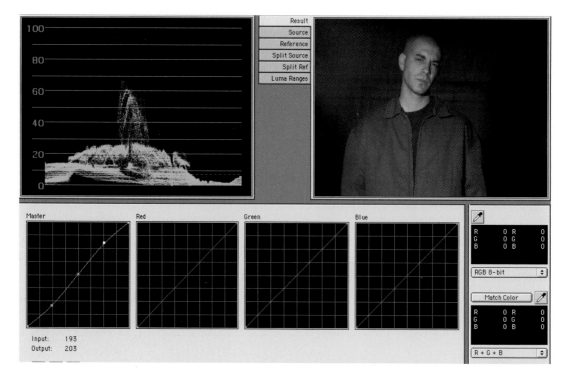

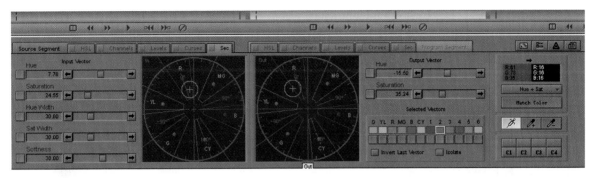

7.30 Secondary color correction UI for Avid's Symphony.

Secondary Color Correction

All of the corrections we've discussed so far in this article have been *primary* corrections, in other words, those that affect the overall balance of an image. Secondary corrections are those that affect just the parts of an image within a specified range of hue and saturation. The most obvious example of this is to take a shot of a car and select only the specific color of the car and change it to a totally different color while leaving all of the other colors in the picture—like skin tones, grass, and sky—untouched.

Each system works a little differently, but the basic operational method is to define the specific color that you wish to change. Usually this is done with some kind of eyedropper method. Then you select the new target color. Any pixels that are within a certain range of your specified color are then remapped to the new color. Figure 7.30 shows secondary color correction in Avid's Symphony.

One of the things that differentiates the high-end color correctors from the lower end tools is the ability to define the affected secondary range and to soften the effect of the color change between affected and unaffected colors. Otherwise, the secondary corrections look very electronic and noisy, because there are harsh cut-off points between the colors. Be aware of this difference if secondary color correction is important to your work.

Secondary color correction does not have to be limited to special effects. Sometimes it is an important tool in dealing with color gamut issues. Certain colors can not be very accurately captured on video. Kelly green is one of them. Many shades of yellow and red are also not reproducible on video. This can be a problem if one of those colors happens to be crucial to your client's brand identity. In this case, you can isolate the problem color and attempt to make it more closely resemble your client's vision, while not polluting the other colors with the correction.

Similarly, skin tones can be crucial to the look and feel of a project. Secondary corrections are often used to isolate skin tones, pulling the green out of black skin, or changing yellowish skin tones toward pink or pinkish skin tones toward golden while leaving the rest of the image's color palette intact.

The skin tones of the man rowing the boat in Figure 7.31 were sampled. This created a custom vector shape represented by the red circle to the left in Figure 7.30. This circle defines the range of hue and chroma of the sampled skin tones in the original image. The red circle to the right indicates the new position of that range which was moved away from the magenta skin tones in the original and more

7.31 Uncorrected image.

7.32 Corrected image.

toward a golden red. The resulting correction is seen in Figure 7.32.

Randy Starnes explained his use of secondary as he was correcting shots for an episode of MTV's *Making the Video*:

> I like my skin tone on this show not to be too red, and I like to have green grass and green screen shots to be cool green and a lot of green. So for green grass I take the green secondary. Of the six-vector color corrector, I take the green element only and turn it to cyan, away from yellow. I'll boost the saturation just of that green, and that always makes grass look better. If you take the green grass and move it away from yellow, it makes the difference between a springtime green and a fall green that's close to dead. Skies. Take a sky and keep it consistent by rolling the blue either down towards the cyan side or up toward a process blue or up farther towards magenta if I want it to be there for the time of day.

Mike Most is the visual effects supervisor for *Ally McBeal*. Before that, he was a sought-after colorist for primetime episodics and worked on such signature shows as *LA Law* and *NYPD Blue*. Most explains that this is a world where the primary skill is maintaining continuity:

> Secondary correction for me was a way of fixing what I couldn't get quite right with the basic primary controls, because secondary correction basically acts as a keyer. It keys whatever color you tell it you want to select or whatever range of colors you tell it you want to select and lets you change just those colors. That can be a great help when you're trying to make, say, a very green tree into a very fall, golden-leaf tree. And I used to have to do that quite often, especially on *NY[PD Blue]*. Short of that, it doesn't have a whole lot of use.

> If a cameraman has shot his film right—and let's face it, most professional cameramen shoot beautiful film. So given a decently shot piece of film, you should be able to get what the cameraman was seeing without having to do anything fancy with it: ripping the colors out of it and recoloring them to something else.

Now I used to use it sometimes to change my flesh tones a little bit because that tends to get a little out of hand with certain stocks, but generally I think that secondary color correction is way, way, way overused. Unless you're trying to achieve something totally unique, as in a commercial, there's very little need for it in most cases. And I think a lot of colorists go to it far too quickly. That's one of the things that I train people not to do.

Secondary color correction can be used to unusual effect. The following correction was done by sampling the blue sky values and swinging them very unnaturally to red (see Figure 7.33). The effect is striking (see Figure 7.34).

The large blue circle on the right in Figure 7.33 represents the sampled values of hue and chroma for the original sky. The circle on the left represents the output values of that secondary correction.

Secondary limits

There are several things that secondary color correction *cannot* do. These are important to note, especially if you have any kind of pre-pro contact with clients that are considering using secondary color correction.

Most secondary color correction tools can only alter hue and saturation, yet clients often request to alter the color in a way that requires a change in luminance. Also, the lower the saturation level of a color that needs to be altered, the more difficult it is to isolate that color shift from others around it. Think of it like a game of darts played on a vectorscope. The lower saturation images are in the middle and the higher ones are near the outside. If you toss a dart at a color near the outside, you'll either hit the one you were aiming for, or at least one that's adjacent to it. In the center of the dartboard, a near miss can still mean you've selected an image 180° from the one you aimed at.

In addition to the difficulty of isolating the color, lower saturation colors also offer less information to be able to increase the saturation, because increasing saturation means increasing noise.

Alex Scudiero, a colorist and principal at I³ in Chicago, was one of several colorists who cautioned against the use of secondary until later in the correction process:

Some inexperienced colorists will go right for the secondary to change something specific, but then they'll get further into the correction and realize they need that secondary for something else, so they've painted themselves into a box. Try to correct using the basics first.

Spot On

Another high-end feature is called spot color correction: the ability to select a specific geographic area in the picture and adjust levels within that area without affecting the other areas of the picture. Da Vinci colorists know this feature as Power Windows™.

One of the desktop systems to offer this feature is Avid's Symphony. Symphony's ability to make these spot corrections is very powerful since the regions of correction can be an infinite number of hand-drawn shapes. Most color correctors are limited to a handful of geometric shapes, like circles, ellipses, and squares. In skilled hands, though, this is more than enough control. Some of the more recent high-

7.33 Avid Symphony's secondary
color correction tab.

7.34 Image corrected by
swinging blue to red.

end color correction engines have evolved into a larger number of organic, hand-drawn shapes.

Although spot color correction is a fairly rare feature in name, it can be accomplished by almost all NLEs using simple wipes and mattes. Simply sync a corrected shot on one track with an uncorrected shot on lower track and use a wipe or matte to reveal the correction in only a specific geographic area. This obviously takes a bit more effort than a one-step solution, but the capability is certainly available to almost anyone.

Spot correction is useful in many applications. One of the most common is to *dodge* or *burn* the image, in much the same way that photographers do with prints in the darkroom. A specific area is selected—say, a blown-out sky—in an otherwise nicely exposed image, and the levels are brought down in just that portion of the image. This is one of the things that can assist colorists doing film transfers to translate the higher latitude of film to the lower contrast range of video. In an image where the sky might have held detail in the bright areas on the negative as well as in the shadows of the landscape, on video the only way to properly hold detail in both areas is to spot correct the sky and the landscape separately.

Another use of spot color correction can be to add the look of gradient filters to an image, for example, coloring a plain-looking sky to a rich sunset. In a film-to-tape transfer session, this is often done by actually using photographic filters in the filter gate. But spot color correction can also help you fix it in post without a full telecine session.

Randy Starnes, a colorist for many primetime TV shows, says Da Vinci's spot correction—Power Windows—allowed him to add just a little more glamour to your favorite stars and to subliminally focus the audience's attention to specific parts of the screen.

I use Power Windows quite often to give somebody a glow to their face. Separate them by putting an oval softedged window on their face. Bringing the luminance of their face up. And if you include their face and a little bit over the top of their head, behind them a little bit, it almost has the affect of a backlight or a halo. Make somebody look subtly a little special, kind, angelic.

I would use Power Windows quite a bit on *Dr. Quinn, Medicine Woman* to separate the star and make her look even more beautiful, more radiant.

A lot of people use them for vignettes. They can bring your attention to the center of the screen or wherever you want that attention. Place an oval window with a center where you want the eye to go and then softedge so you don't see it.

Another use is to add punch to lighting. To amplify the effect of a light—let's say a window and light that's streaming in—I'll often put in a Power Window, make it a long oval aspect, and rotate it from the direction that the sun would be falling in the window and soft-edge that. And inside that Power Window I'd increase the luminance, and probably outside I'd bring the blacks down, and that just makes the light more powerful.

Skies. I'm doing that right now. I've got a sky where I want the image at the bottom of the image to be bright. I want to keep the blue in the sky, so I'm going to make a circular Power Window, and I'm going to change the aspect ratio so it's horizontal lines, take the sky, separate

Before

After

7.35 Randy Starnes' special glow, using a spot correction.

that and then bring the luminance down inside the window. Add some blue to the sky and then soft-edge the window, and that keeps the lower end of the frame where all my talent is bright, and it doesn't blow out the sky.

Figure 7.35 shows a spot color correction similar to that described by Randy Starnes to give the stars of the show a special glow. A soft-edged oval was drawn around the face and the levels inside were increased and warmed up slightly. The levels outside the oval were brought down a little as well. The effect is that even in a fairly busy scene, your attention is drawn to the little girl's face.

Chapter 8
Common Corrections Tutorials

You've got the tools, so let's run them through their paces and make bad video look decent and give good video some real pop.

In the Dark
Improperly Exposed Video

One of the most common problems is video that has been improperly exposed. The basic TBC-type controls—hue, saturation, luminance, and black level—give just enough control to make the picture viewable. But with the addition of just a few color correction tools, we can really salvage a pretty decent picture.

1. Start by analyzing the image. Generally speaking we're looking for a full range of luminance values, from nice, rich shadows through a full range of midtones, all the way up to bright, sparkling highlights.

8.1 Starting point: a very dark image that appears to be unusable.

Our first example, Figure 8.1, is far too dark to be usable. We will bring it up to a nice fairly bright look, but examining the picture, there are clues that this image should not look really bright.

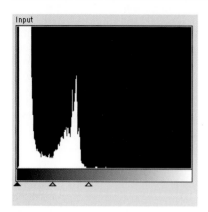

8.2   Levels correction.

Tip

Blur is another tool that "the big boys have" in their color correction arsenals. It is not included specifically in the color correction capabilities of most desktop systems, but it is usually available elsewhere on the system. The ability to blur a specific luminance range, especially highlights, is a powerful "color correction" capability because the sharpness of an image is a visual clue that our brains decipher as affecting contrast.

Before we can really analyze the picture, we're going to have to bring up the levels just to figure out what we want to do.

2. Use the **Levels** to do an initial adjustment, pulling the highlight triangle back all the way to the first semilarge bump in the histogram. Also move the gamma triangle up to see into some of the midrange shadows.

Now the image is viewable. Figure 8.2 shows the position of the **Levels** correction that was needed to bring up the detail out of the shadows. Blacks were left alone, and the highlight triangle was brought back to one of the first significant signs of luma in the image.

Instead of doing this with **Levels,** it's also possible to do similar tonal moves using the regular **HSL** controls or even using **Curves** if you're feeling adventurous. Basically, create a deep, rich black and as close to a nice, bright white as possible.

The black is pretty much as low as it can go in this instance. The highlights of this image are not going to reach 100. The main thing that will limit you—however you decide to set your main levels—is noise and grain. When you have an image this dark, bringing it up high enough will definitely begin to introduce a lot of noise in the image. Maybe this is acceptable to you or your client, but chances are that you will introduce unacceptable amounts of grain as you move your gain.

Some color correction plugins and all of the serious dedicated color correction boxes are equipped with noise reducers that could help in an instance like this. On the plugin side, ViXen is one of the plugins that provides noise reduction. Noise reduction may not seem like it belongs in a color correction tool, but it is instances like this—where you are limited in making a correction because of noise—that it becomes obvious why it is included in some color correction packages.

The main thing to look for in an image like this is shadows. Not luminance level shadows, but the type of shadows that are cast during daylight by the sun. With this image there really aren't any, and the ones that do exist are very soft. What does that tell us? It tells us the image was taken under either very overcast skies or it was taken at dusk, just after the sun went down, with only the evening sky as illumination. So when we try to settle on luminance values for this picture, we are not going to take the levels up too high, because they will conflict with the information provided by the shadows.

Note _____

David Fincher Tutorial: If you're interested in a detailed look at how a professional colorist approaches this, buy or rent the DVD collector's edition of the movie _Seven_, directed by David Fincher. Stephen Nakamura was the colorist for the home video release. One of the special features on the disk shows Mr. Nakamura color correcting the climactic last scene. As you watch the output of the Da Vinci 2K color corrector that he's using, he narrates what he's doing and—more importantly—why. It's a superb tutorial in itself.

What will bring this picture out of the mud more than anything else is not how much the highlights are raised, but where we put the shadows and gamma. Because so much of the picture is in deep shadows, using controls that only offer us control of shadow, midtone, and highlight will only take us so far. We can use the added control of the **Curves** tab to stretch out our deep shadows and provide some detail in the lower range.

3. Try several attempts at correcting each of these images starting from scratch. Use different tools.

This particular image in Figure 8.3 shows another approach to correcting this image that relied heavily on **Curves.**

4. Correcting midtones will also add some definition to the image. How much is too much? With the shadows, you definitely want to anchor some of the nice rich blacks so that there is a healthy

8.3   Image with Curves.

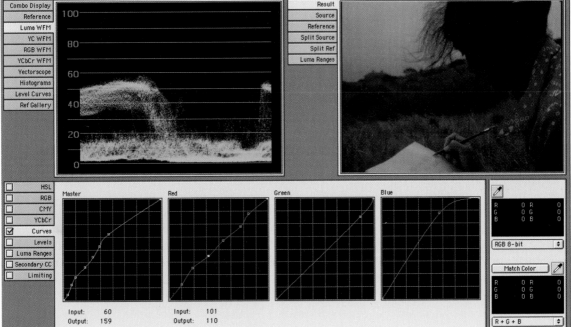

bottom to the image. Watch the image on the monitor and keep an eye on the waveform to make sure that blacks don't ride up too high. From then on, keep your eye on just your monitor to watch for encroaching noise as you bring up the shadows and midtones.

Since we have spread the luma values so much from their original position, we risk posterizing the image. This never looks natural, so when you start to see posterization—look at the sky around the wisps of hair and in the gradation in the piece of paper—you need to back off. It's better to leave the picture a little dark than to introduce noise and artifacts. Remember: First, do no harm.

Skin tones are a clue to latch on to for color balance. The face will remain dark, or the colors will become artificial and unnatural, but the skin tone in the hands should look right. After we address secondary color correction in the next chapter, you can use secondary color correction to attempt to turn the sky slightly magenta to hint at a late evening sky. That will help sell the luminance of the image.

5. Without resorting to secondary color correction, you can pull a lot of the green out of the sky and put in quite a bit of blue.

This is easy, because the sky is pretty much the only highlight in the image. I was able to go to the pure **RGB** controls, bring down green in the highlights, and bring up blue.

Most colorists will warn about the danger of focusing your attention on *just* the scopes or *just* the monitor. You must keep your eye on both. The scopes will keep you honest. They will warn you that something's not right with the monitor. Sometimes a monitor will drift or be accidentally set up wrong, and you'll find yourself fighting against the information that the scopes are telling you if you're really watching your monitor. They provide a check and balance to each other. If you feel there is a discrepancy between what your scopes says and what the monitor says, then check them both. Is the monitor set up correctly? Is everything terminated properly? Are the scopes properly calibrated?

If the scopes and monitor are in agreement, then you need to keep shifting your attention back and forth between them. However, with an image like this, we aren't going to need the scopes quite as much because nothing is going to get even close to the legal limit. Also, when correcting an image that needs this much work, you are going to be seeing more important clues in the monitor than on the scopes, because the artifacts that this severe correction will create are only going to show up on the monitor.

6. Watch for:

    -   banding or posterizing in the piece of yellow paper
    -   strange shades of gray blocking up the fine detail of the wisps of hair
    -   banding and clipping in the sky
    -   grain in the face
    -   hands becoming contrasty and noisy
    -   too much level or chroma turning the grass or the red shirt "electric"

7. Because this is a tutorial, you should take the image too far. Make big moves so that you can see the errors on the monitor. Crank the levels up until you start to see banding in the paper or grain in the

face or until you lose detail in the wisps of hair, then slowly notch it down until you can no longer see the artifacts. As with so many things, the best way to learn is to make mistakes. So try for the mistakes.

8. Save various corrections and then compare them to each other. Also, compare a few of your favorites in the context of the shots around them.

Saving is another important learning tool. On a Da Vinci, this would be done by saving stills or scratchpad memories. These are *reference frames*. They can help by providing you with a base correction that you can return to keep things consistent. They can also just be various corrections on the same frame, so that you can quickly toggle back and forth to determine which correction is best.

Figure 8.4 is the before and after of this image. You can see that even though the picture is still relatively dark, the image is now viewable and pleasing.

Tip

As simple as black and white. When setting tonal ranges, Chicago colorist Alex Scudiero likes to double check his corrections in black and white. He turns the chroma completely off on his monitor and looks at the image in its purely tonal form. He showed instances with high saturated colors where the vividness of the chroma was tricking the eye about the actual levels of the image. Some colorists also do this occasionally to "wash the eye" for a moment. Sort of like cleansing your palette before tasting a fine wine.

8.4 Before and after.

8.5 Bill, the original.

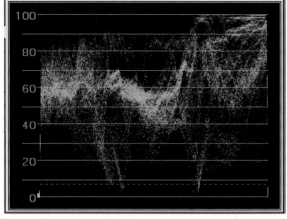

8.6 Waveform of previous image.

Bright and Flat

Let's take a look at an example that kind of comes from the opposite end of the spectrum: slightly over-exposed and fairly flat. The entire picture just lies there, lifeless on the screen with very little detail.

Figure 8.5 shows a still from an interview that was shot on video with no lights but quite a bit of bounce. The image lacks punch and contrast. The waveform in Figure 8.6 shows that there is very little bottom to this image. And the portions that *do* get close to black are not in areas that are helping to separate the central image from the background or to define the features of the subject. The only areas that drop much below 20IRE are in the man's collar and the canoe in the background.

You can see some of the problem by looking at the histogram of the image (see Figure 8.7). A statistician would love this beautiful bell curve, but for us, it means that almost the entire image rests squarely in the midtones with little to define the highlights or blacks. This histogram is actually a **Level** control, as you can tell by the small triangles along the bottom that allow for adjustments. This **Level** has been altered slightly to bring down the blacks a little lower than the midtones (by increasing the gamma level of the incoming image).

1. Bring the luminance values down to eliminate the glaring highlights from the sky and reflections on the water.

2. Pull down the black levels and adjust the gamma so that flesh tones are correct.

We're starting to rescue some detail from the overexposure. Now the face is starting to look nicely modeled, or shaped, by the light instead of being so flat. These adjustments also made the contrast in the canoe stronger.

The corrected image in Figure 8.8 pops much more, and its richer tones are much more pleasing and easier on the eyes.

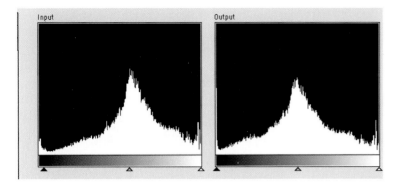

8.7 A great-looking histogram with no clipping at either end, but the large amount peak in the center of the graph indicates a lot of midtone, little definition to the top or bottom of the image.

The last final tweaks to this image use some advanced tools.

8.8 Bill, corrected.

3. Bring down the overall level of the scene and the highlight corner of the sky down even a bit more, warming it up just a bit to match the feeling of the afternoon sun coming through the trees.

4. Add some secondary color correction if you have the tools, creating a custom vector to match the leaves, pulling just those yellowish green tones more towards a full, rich green.

5. With that done, add a spot color correction to pull the subject's face back up, and add a bit of contrast and a bit of red in the flesh tones.

Film and Tape's Bob Sliga also offered additional comments on correcting this image:

> We need to isolate the subject from the background as much as possible to create the illusion of depth and make him stand out a little more. Try to find a more pleasing color in the trees, possibly by dropping the gamma, create a late afternoon feel by adding some warmth to the trees. Then maybe kick a little blue reflection into the highlights of the water. Drop the gamma. Pull some blue gamma out, and raise some red gamma slightly. Add some video gain until the white highlight on the cheek starts to blow out. Add more black to increase the contrast. You have to be careful of his eyes and eyebrows going away as you drop the blacks and gammas, so that will be a bit of balancing act. Possibly add some secondary correction to adjust the skin tones some more.

Casting for Colors

The image in Figure 8.9 has a range of problems. We'll try to correct them all. The biggest of them are the color cast and lack of detail on either end of the luminance range.

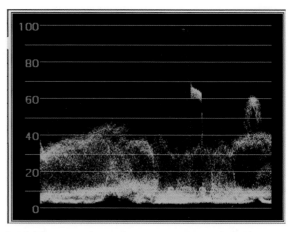

8.9 This image is dark and has strong color casts.

8.10 The waveform shows compressed shadows and a very low overall luminance.

1.   Start by analyzing the waveform (see Figure 8.10).

The image didn't have much contrast and it was very dark. Also, even though the blacks didn't look black enough, the shadows all looked compressed and lacking detail. Using **Curves** will be necessary for some serious manipulation of specific luminance areas. For example, the blacks needed to be pulled down, but other deep shadows needed to be stretched out to create some detail. Also, the columns on the house look blown out, but other areas of midhighlights needed to be raised so the picture doesn't look so dark.

Going to **Curves** will also be necessary because of the color issue. By examining some areas—like the blacks on the base of the hurdy-gurdy, the grays of the wooden sidewalk, and the whites of the columns—using the eyedropper or **Info Palette,** you can see the need to increase certain colors in some luminance ranges of the picture while decreasing the same color in other ranges. You can do that with a series of correction to each of the **R, G,** and **B Curves.**

Let's look at the clues we can get with the **Info Palette.**

- The black of the base of the hurdy-gurdy is around Red at 6, Green at 14, and Blue at 16 (or 6, 14, 16).

- The black of the man's hair is at (8, 15, 19).

- The black of the two small trees to the left of the man is at (4, 10, 12).

All of these numbers reveal a pretty clear pattern of reds that are about half the value of greens, while the blues are slightly elevated above the greens.

Gray tones show a little more variety, but are still similar to the findings in the black tones.

- There are obviously numerous values of gray in the sidewalk, but some random values include (77, 102, 102), (104, 121, 122), (47, 81, 89), and (86, 104, 108).

- The gray on the nose of the plush toy monkey is (91, 104, 100).

- The gray on the wheel of the hurdy-gurdy is a variation on the pattern (108, 135, 129.)
- The blue-gray of the "white" picket fence is (57, 115, 125) and (39, 99, 113).

The white values reveal patterns as well. The brightest part of the picture, which was located by looking at the waveform monitor, is the sky in the small patch, high in the center of the picture.

- A representative sample for the sky was (249, 250, 250).
- The white area at the front of the hurdy-gurdy looks brighter than the sky, but the brightest pixel in the entire area is (212, 229, 211).

This optical illusion could be due to the presence of surrounding colors. The area around the front of the hurdy-gurdy is all very dark, while the sky has lighter shades around it, plus it is close to the white pillar.

- The pillar to the right has quite a bit more detail than the pillar to the left. A representative sample of that column reveals (128, 165, 168).

So the blacks are not red enough by half, the grays are not red enough by maybe 25%, and the whites are about right, but the high midrange (right column) definitely needs more red too.

2. Without the benefit of an **Info Palette** or eyedropper, hue and saturation information would need to come from the vector-scope and from your eye.

The picture looks blue, though the lack of red in the blacks is very difficult to see with your eyes. Moving the red, green, and blue values in specific tonal ranges of the picture while monitoring the vectorscope will reveal the approximate place to put these values.

The vectorscope (see Figure 8.11) shows a lot of red (obviously the colors of the hurdy-gurdy); a little yellowish red, which could be the flesh tones and the little bits of yellow under the hurdy-gurdy; and plenty of cyan. There's also a small blip of low-chroma green, which is probably the grass. The cyan color is probably the same thing we're seeing in the numbers of the **Info Palette**, since green and blue make cyan.

3. The waveform (see Figure 8.10) and **Histogram** (see Figure 8.12) are the places to go for luminance information.

On the waveform monitor, the bright band of trace along the bottom is the dark shadow detail. But the blacks should be at zero, so they are slightly murky despite being dark. There is a very bright white on the waveform monitor, but other elements of the picture should also probably be reaching closer to 100IRE as well.

8.11 The vectorscope is the other key to chroma and hue information.

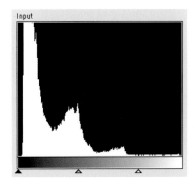

8.12 Histogram of the image as it was digitized.

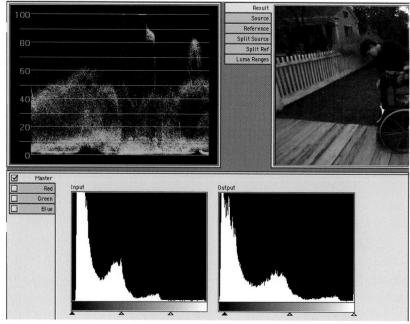

8.13 Waveforms and Levels after Level corrections.

Like the first tutorial, you can see that there are no harsh shadows, so this is another example where the entire image should probably not be too bright or too contrasty.

So now there is a game plan:

1. Bring down the darkest blacks.

2. Spread the lower blacks out to get some detail in the image.

3. Place the gammas where they'll look good.

4. Add red to the blacks and to the grays and maybe a little red to the highlights.

As with any correction, we'll start by setting our blacks. You could do this with a black level slider, but let's use the **Level** tab to set this while getting some visual feedback. Despite having a histogram, the real monitoring as you set these critical black levels is with the waveform monitor.

1. Bring the black level triangle on the **Levels** control up as you watch the lowest portion of the excursion in the blacks on the waveform monitor. Take them to black, but don't crush them.

In Figure 8.13 note the effect that the moves on the incoming **Levels** histogram have on the outgoing histogram (They always start out identical, so the outgoing histogram used to look like the incoming histogram, but now it is spread out.) Also, note the levels spread out in the waveform monitor.

2. Now walk the white (highlight) triangle down towards the midtones while watching the waveform monitor. Look at the shape of the excursion for the left pillar. As you move the white triangle to the left, the pillar brightens, and the trace begins to move from its old level, between 60 and 70IRE up to a new level between 80 and 90IRE. When the excursion compresses, notch it back a bit.

When the top of the excursion hits 90, it starts to change shape and compress as the highlight detail begins to clip. Depending on your look and the need to match surrounding shots, this is a good indication to leave the level where it is.

Gamma is done more or less to taste. Where do you want certain tonal ranges to fall?

3. To see detail, bring the midtones up. This may raise the blacks as well, so readjust those. Continue this little dance with the levels until:

    - The blacks are at zero, but not crushed.

    - The whites are bright but not clipping.

    - The midtones provide the overall look that you're trying to achieve.

All of this gets you an image with much better detail and overall levels. Looking at the waveform shows you that you've opened up the shadow detail quite a bit.

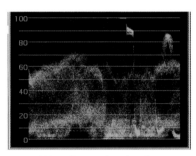

Figure 8.14 is the waveform after all of these corrections. Notice that the luminance range is much fuller and the shadows, which were very compressed to begin with, are now nicely opened up.

Now let's correct the colors. You can attempt this in a couple of ways. The goal is to isolate the color changes within luma ranges. So you need to be able to bring up a specific color in a specific range, because not all of the color casts are happening the same way in each range. One way to go would be **Curves**. The **Curves** in Figure 8.15 show the adjustments to the master curve as well as the curves for each individual color channel.

8.14 Waveform after luminance corrections.

You could also attempt to use **Luma Ranges** to effectively isolate just three ranges. With **Curves** you could have over a dozen individual ranges. This depends on the limitations of your software, though. Some only allow as few as three points to be placed on a curve. If you do not have access to individual RGB levels in **Curves**, you can adjust individual RGB levels in each of the tonal ranges with sliders or with **Hue Offsets**.

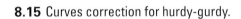

8.15 Curves correction for hurdy-gurdy.

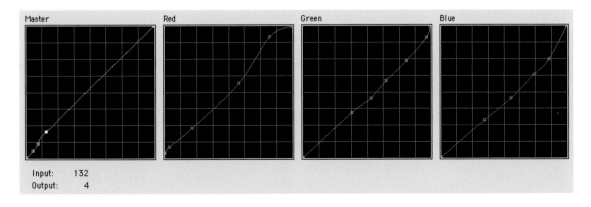

Input: 132
Output: 4

4. If you have all of these tools, use each of them to adjust the color balance, and save the result.

5. Clear and reset the color, and then try to balance with another tool.

This will help you understand what tools are best for you and what tools are best for specific jobs and problems.

For the software that provides control or customization of the luma ranges, the key is to set the luma ranges based on your need to isolate specific problems. So if your problem is only in one particular highlight area, then you can assign just that little area as the only thing the rest of the controls see as being highlights. Remember, **Luma Ranges** don't actually alter the image directly. They just define what the ranges are, so that as the other tools are adjusting things in terms of shadows, midtones, and blacks, *you* are the one who defined exactly what is meant by shadows, midtones, and blacks.

Figure 8.16 shows how the **Luma Ranges** were set for this image. Because there was so little highlight area, the highlights region was greatly expanded to include some high midtones. Most of the picture sits heavily in the shadows, so that was broken up with a very limited definition of shadow. The midtone definition was then centered to split the difference between these two ranges.

6. Check the final result in the waveform monitor (see Figure 8.14).

The blacks are sitting right at the legal limit, and the rest of the shadows have been stretched out a lot, providing much more detail in the shadows. By bringing the shadow detail up and correcting the red deficiencies, we can now see the case of the hurdy-gurdy is not black, but a dark red wood. Some of the highlights in the sky have been clipped, but the highlight detail is preserved in one of the two columns of the house.

7. Also, check the neutral colors with the **Info Palette** or eyedropper.

The whites of the columns, the grays of the sidewalk, and the blacks in the doorway—all have equal R, G, and B levels. The middle highlights—like the man's face, the sidewalk, and fence—have all been brought up enough to pull the entire image out of the shadows and give it some definition.

8. As a final fix to the image, do a secondary correction on the man's face to create a more pleasing skin tone.

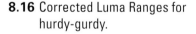

8.16 Corrected Luma Ranges for hurdy-gurdy.

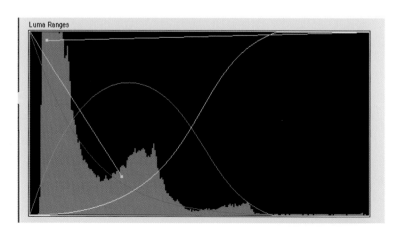

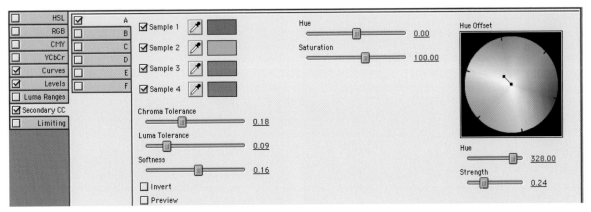

8.17 Secondary color correction UI from Color Finesse.

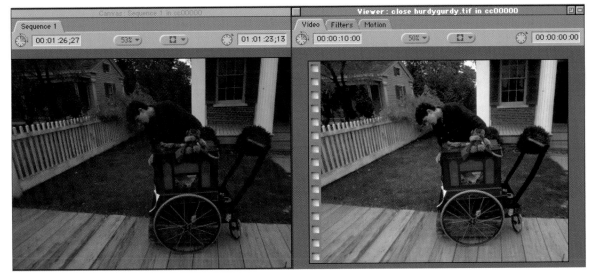

8.18 Final side-by-side comparison.

Four samples were taken from the man's face which created a custom color vector (see Figure 8.17). This vector was then spun to create a more pleasing, golden skin tone. Compare the original and the final result in Figure 8.18.

On the Fence

This weathered fence image in Figure 8.19 has several problems: low luminance levels, color casts, and low contrast. Take a look at the waveform image in Figure 8.20, and you can see how blocked up the shadow detail is. The thick, bright line at the bottom shows how crushed all of the shadow detail is. This image has black levels down at 0IRE. Remember, you need to know whether your blacks are

8.19 Fence image with problems of low luminance, color casts, and low contrast.

8.20 The waveform shows the crushed shadows.

supposed to be at 0IRE or at 7.5 IRE (see page 47 for a full explanation). The highest video levels barely reach 50IRE.

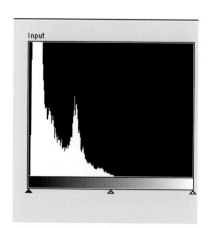

8.21 Histogram with clipped blacks.

Confirming these results on the histogram in Figure 8.21 shows that the blacks have been clipped drastically. The sharp, steep cliff wall at the lower end of the histogram is the clue that describes the clipped black level. It also shows that there are no pixels in the highlights range at all.

1. The first step is to get those black tones in line. As usual there are a number of ways to do this, depending on your tools. The **Level** tool is an option, or you can work with **HSL** sliders. A few quick level changes should open the tonal range up a lot, as is indicated on the waveform monitor in Figure 8.22.

That same tonal range is expressed on the histogram as a more even disbursement on pixels across the entire histogram. Notice the difference between the incoming and outgoing histograms in Figure 8.22. This **Level** change opened up the image nicely, especially spreading out the shadows, providing good detail in the blacks.

2. Finish placing this image in the proper tonal range by making gamma adjustments.

This is a good image to work with to begin the color balancing. Using the eyedropper method, or even using your eyes and a monitor, will show that the image is very bluish green. Any number of tools are available for this image. There is no need to resort to **Curves**, because precise control of specific tonal ranges is not required.

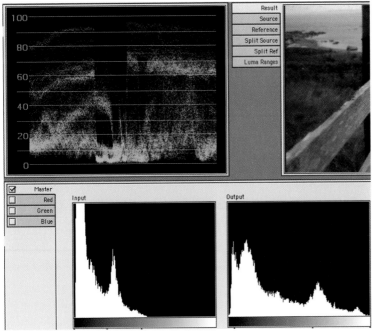

8.22 Waveform and histograms after Level corrections. Notice how the image has opened up.

3. **Hue Offset** is the most intuitive tool to use here (see Figure 8.23), though you could use RGB level controls or simple **Curves** adjustments.

This image cleans up fairly quickly. Things to watch for:

*   Try to keep the nice contrasty detail of the sea waves in the highlights.

*   By pulling out as much blue and green as you will need to, there are portions of the image—like the brightest highlights on the sea at the top of the image—that could start to go very red.

8.23 Final Hue Offsets used to balance the colors in the fence image.

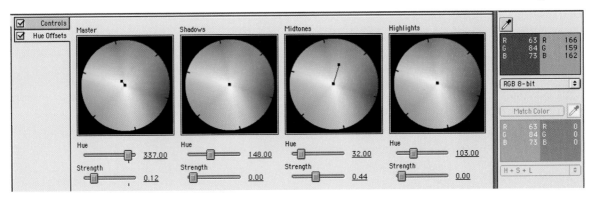

8.24 Before and after the corrections on the fence image.

Skull and Crosshairs

The skull image in Figure 8.25 is improperly white balanced. This is a common correction to make with tungsten fixtures in low-light situations. The tonality on this image is not too bad (see Figure 8.26). The main thing to discover here is whether the red cast is in all of the luma ranges, or is it primarily the mid-tones?

We can actually pass on the normal workflow of setting levels with this image. Not because we want to, but because they are already where we want them. Blacks are a little elevated, so those could be brought down just a little bit, but the rest of the tonality is basically where we want it. The other factor is that

8.25 Skull image, poorly white balanced.

8.26 Waveform of skull image.

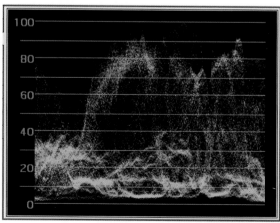

the majority of the picture is so heavily dominated by a single color that when we start making drastic color balance fixes, they will probably also alter the tonal ranges, which we'll have to fix after the color balance.

One step at a time

Mike Most, a former colorist on many primetime episodic TV shows and now visual effects supervisor for *Ally McBeal*, warns about changing the order in which you do corrections:

> I did things in a very specific order. I would balance blacks; then I would balance whites; then I would balance midrange. And I set it for both overall balance and [RGB] levels. And then I would start playing with it. But I would set a basic balance first. The only way to keep yourself from walking into no-man's land is to do it in a very, very disciplined straight-ahead way, and the best way I was ever taught was to do the blacks, then the whites, then the midranges. That served me well, and I think most good colorists tend to do things that way. You tend to overlap some of those steps if you're fast, but basically underneath it all, a good colorist is going about it in a very, very specific way.

> You have to set the overall levels to a close range before you start playing with the individual RGB levels, because otherwise, as soon as you start changing the overall level, you'll have to rebalance it. Be very methodical. Don't do things out of order; it's only going to get you into trouble. Be very methodical and stick to the method. Do things in a specific order because that's what works. Be very, very disciplined and pay attention.

> The nuances of color are something that comes with time. It comes with time and experience, and I think you need to do a number of projects and experience a lot of different kinds of film and video before you really have a feel for that. There's no advice that's going to get somebody there quicker. Part of it's talent; part of it's just a need to learn; part of it's being willing to spend more time doing it. But the basic advice is just be really, really disciplined.

8.27 Vectorscope of skull image.   **8.28** Histograms for the skull image.

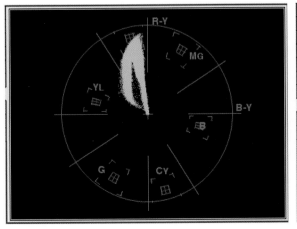
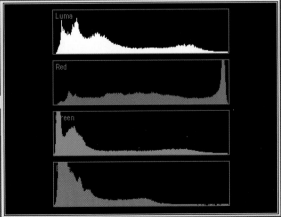

You have to learn how far those basic tools can get you, and they can get you awful damn far. I was a telecine operator, before we were called colorists, with just three sticks in front of me [RGB joysticks], and I think we turned out some pretty darned good pictures.

Back to the head

With that advice tucked away, we'll continue. Our levels are set, but our balance is not. The red cast is not an overall cast, but it is very strong in the midtones. So strong, in fact, that there is no way to reduce the red enough with the midtone **Hue Offset** wheel.

1.   However, with a combination of the **Master** and the **Midtone** wheels, you can bring the reds under control.

This throws off the color of the shadows and the highlights, which go a little cyan and green, respectively.

2.   So use the **Hue Offset** wheels to compensate for that (see Figure 8.29).

This gives a nice sepia image. There is still some reddish-yellow to the image, which is appropriate. The blacks are black, and the highlights go slightly yellow, which is nice. Without these two slight color casts, there would be no chroma at all.

Several other colorists suggested an approach for this image that involved pulling virtually all of the color out of the image and then working a specific color back onto the desaturated image. This is actually a quick approach, with results that are similar in the end.

Now let's turn our attention to our monitor and waveform in Figure 8.30.

3.   Blacks are starting to look a little milky, so bring down the setup a little bit. It's appropriate with an image like this to crush the blacks a little so that you can't see into the shadows. It makes it a little more mysterious and threatening.

8.29 Adjusted Hue Offsets for skull.

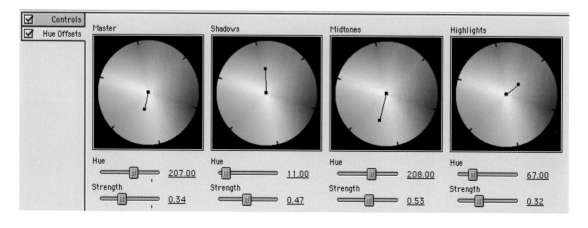

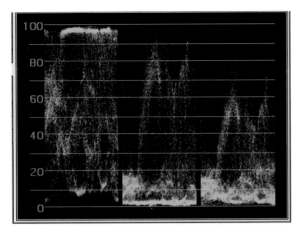

8.30 RGB Parade waveform of skull image.

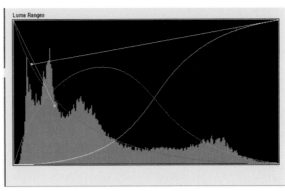

8.31 Luma Ranges of skull image.

4.   Crushing the blacks also kills some of the midrange shadow detail as well, though, so if you have separate **HSL** controls for each tonal range, then raise the gamma of the shadows.

This is different than raising the overall gamma. On the waveform monitor, you'll see the thick, dark band of the trace near the bottom start to spread out a bit. The dark shadows will start to open up.

Looking at the monitor, the highlights seem a little bright. They almost make you squint a bit. But looking at the waveform, they are not even at 100IRE yet. How do you set these brightness values? Watch the shapes of the trace. Because we're adjusting highlights, look at the shapes in the top of the waveform, especially the shape of the highest portion of the trace.

5.   There is a faint, tent-shaped area that peaks between 90IRE and 100IRE, depending on how you've adjusted your other levels. Watch this as you take your highlights up and down over the full range.

For a majority of the movement, the area has a specific shape. When you get too low, the shape tends to flatten out, and when you get too high, the same thing happens. With highlights, my rule of thumb is to take this area up until the shape starts to compress. With shadows, take them down until the shapes

8.32 Final waveform.

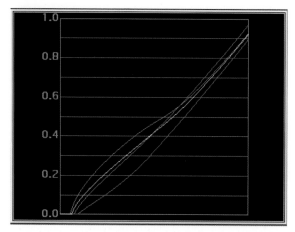

8.33 Corrected curves for the final skull image.

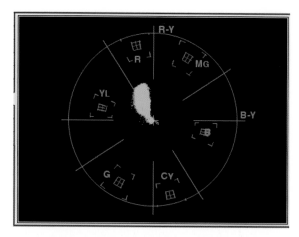

8.34 Vectorscope of the final skull image. Compare this to the original vectorscope in Figure 8.27 (page 139).

8.35 Side-by-side comparison of original and corrected skull image.

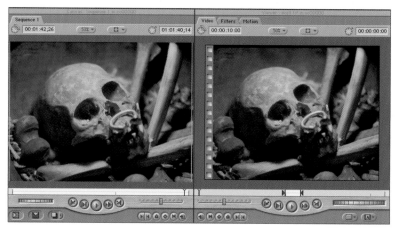

start to compress. But this image is one of the places where I would ignore the rule of thumb a little. Because I wanted that hint of mystery in the shadows, I brought the shadows down past the point where the shadow area started to compress.

Another possible area to work with in this image is the **Luma Range** control (see Figure 8.31). If your color correction engine allows you to set the definitions for highlights, midtones, and shadows, this image would be a good candidate for an adjustment.

6. Usually you can leave these levels at their presets, but this image doesn't have a lot of highlight detail, so reassign some of the bright midrange to be controlled by highlights.

7. We can also assign some of the lower midrange to control the brighter shadows and compress the amount of the image considered shadow so that we have more control of each portion of the image that is actually there (see Figure 8.31).

If we don't reassign these ranges, then any parameters affecting shadows will control most of the image, and parameters affecting highlights will do virtually nothing. Compare the final results with the original in Figure 8.35.

That's Blue
And I'm not Lion

Figure 8.36 was shot with the wrong filter set on the camera. Figure 8.37 has the proper white balance. Although these are both wide shots, it is common for a client to ask for two shots with mismatched white balance to be matched so that they can be intercut seamlessly. Matching shots like this is a large part of a colorist's responsibility.

This final tutorial image will address the classic daylight blue color cast. As an added twist, we'll try to match another shot at the same location that is correctly balanced. This is an everyday request made of many colorists, especially those working in video. Peter Mavromates, postproduction supervisor for the movie *Panic Room*, explains the importance of matching shots:

> You could make a list of a thousand things that affect how something looks, so that when it's cut together and Joe is talking to Mary, Joe's side looks bright and green, and Mary's side looks dark and red. You've got to bring them closer together so that every cut doesn't "hurt." Another way I put it is that each cut doesn't have an "eyeblink" factor.

> It's not that the average audience member will say, "Her side is redder than his," it's that there will be a discomfort level. Their eyes will blink. It works on a subliminal level as far as I'm concerned. If there's a discomfort level with the audience, they're distracted and they don't know why. And so color correction is part of that process of wrapping it in a nice package so that you're there watching the story.

8.36 Shot with the wrong filter.

8.37 To be matched with previous shot.

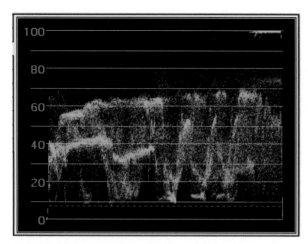

8.38 Original waveform for lion with the blue colorcast (Figure 8.36).

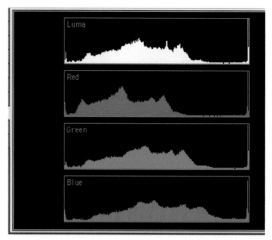

8.39 Original histogram for lion with the blue colorcast (Figure 8.36).

Balancing act

The basic levels for both of these lion shots match pretty closely, and they're both pretty much correct. Because the levels are set, we'll move on to color balance.

1. The main course of action with the color balance will be to attempt the fix in **Hue Offsets** (Figure 8.40).

This is a very quick and intuitive way to fix the color shift. This helps pull a lot of the blue out, but there are still some specific needs that have to be addressed as we try to match the shots.

2. For this fine tuning we're going to go to the pure **RGB** controls of the specific tonal ranges of the picture.

What happens with this image is that even when the particular shade of the Art Institute in Chicago is matched, other tonal ranges and hues do not match. A global correction is not enough. To effectively figure out what to do, think back to the experiments that were done earlier in the book with the gray chart.

At Chicago's Opt1mus, Craig Leffel explains how he uses one of the tricks of professional photographers to assist his clients in finding the perfect look for their images:

> One thing that I will do very quickly now is what photographers call a "Ring-around test." You set exposure, you get contrast, lights and darks, and details where you like them, and then you rotate through the color wheel. You go a little warm, a little neutral, a little blue, a little green, and then back to yellow and warm again. I don't always do it, but if there is confusion about where an image can go or wants to go, then that's a trick I use. Obviously we're not just swinging hue or phase, but pushing whites and blacks and midtones through those colors. If you're starting with a warm image or a cool image, it'll react differently to these hue swings. Each image has a number of different sweet spots. There might be a really warm, bright, sunny look we could get to. There also could be a nice, cool, completely workable ice-blue kind of

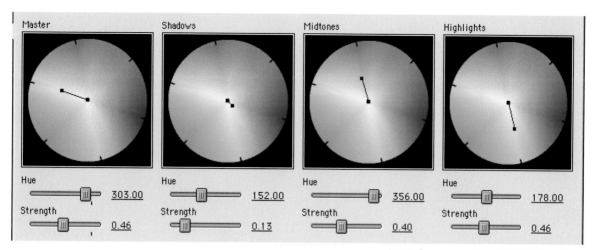

8.40 Corrected Hue Offsets for lion.

area. There aren't any rules. I know the technical limitations, but I try not to limit them creatively at all.

Lions and parades

3. Watching the **RGB Waveform Parade** and your monitor, the object is to try to make the various shapes in the trace match in level between the source you're correcting and the reference shot you're trying the match. One good way to attempt this delicate match is to use a split screen.

Now in the RGB controls, you have controls of nine different tonal ranges. Basically it's the high, mid, and low value for shadows, midtones, and highlights. It seems strange to be able to adjust the black level for a highlight or a highlight level for a shadow, but these specific ranges really do isolate portions of the picture that make a difference.

The adjustments that I had to make in this area were:

- In the **RGB Master** level, the green came down from 1.0 to 0.92.
- The green **Pedestal** went up to 0.01 from 0.
- The green **Gamma** went from 1.0 to 1.01.
  These adjustments helped get the sandstone color to match.
- In the highlights, I reduced the green **Gain** to 0.89.

In all of these instances, gamma is measured from a default of 1.0, **Pedestal** or black is measured from a default of 0, and **Gain** is measured from 1.0.),

- I added blue gain up to 1.05.

These corrections helped make the sky in the upper right corner match. The midtones—where most of the picture sits—were critical.

8.41 The lion's RGB Parade waveform before correction.

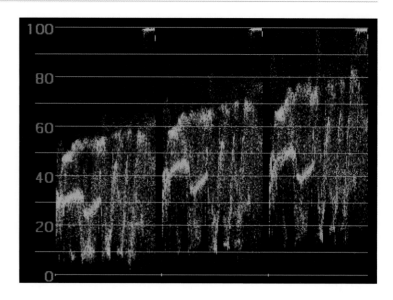

- The red **Gain** was moved to 1.21, green **Gain** and blue **Gain** to 0.98.
- The green **Gamma** went to 0.98, and the blue **Gamma** went to 0.96.
- The pedestal levels in gamma were set to –0.01 for green, –0.02 for blue.
- The shadow values included bringing green **Gamma** up to 1.15, the green **Pedestal** to –0.05 and the green **gain** to 0.98.

The green **Gain** in the shadows helped match the color of the pedestal that the lion is on.

4. Make a few general **Master HSL** level changes to compensate for some of the color balance changes.

- In the **HSL Highlights**, we brought **Gain** down a little (0.92) and **Gamma** up a little (1.04).

Once again, gamma ranges were critical because that's where so much of the image sits.

- **Gamma** in the midtones was brought up to 1.37.
- **Saturation** was brought down to 59.54 (nearly half).
- The **Pedestal** was adjusted slightly downward (–0.05).
- Then the shadows were adjusted with **Saturation** raised significantly to 235.11.

This move was done to add color and definition to the lion. After the **Hue Offset** moves, the lion was looking washed out and a little reddish.

- **Gamma** of the shadows went to 1.07.
- The shadow **Pedestal** went to –0.11.

Basically all of these moves involved watching the parade of RGB and figuring out which slider moved which part of the trace on the waveform. Once that was established, it was a matter of trying to replicate the look of the correct image. The other analytical tool that is invaluable is using a wipe between the reference image and the blue image. Be careful not to leave the wipe in one spot. A color change may not be noticeable in the spot where your wipe is positioned, but it may have a large effect elsewhere. That was the case with making corrections to the sandstone color of the building. You may get that color in balance rather quickly, but the lion may not match at all.

Summary
It wasn't broke, but now we have to fix it

In the end the two images are slightly different, but I think the image that had been blue is actually nicer. There is a little more definition in the shadows. To really match these shots at this point would mean correcting the "correct" image, too, possibly taking the bright sky in the right corner and moving it all the way up until it clips.

8.42 The left image is the reference image of the lion shot with correct filtration. The right image shows a split screen between the "blue" lion and the color corrected image.

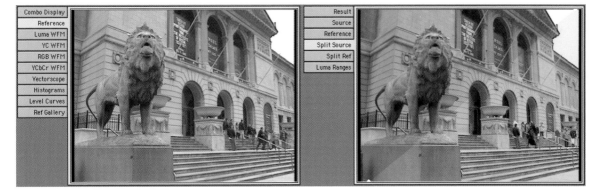

8.43 The left image is the reference image of the lion shot with correct filtration. The right image shows a split screen between the color corrected image and the reference image with normal filtration.

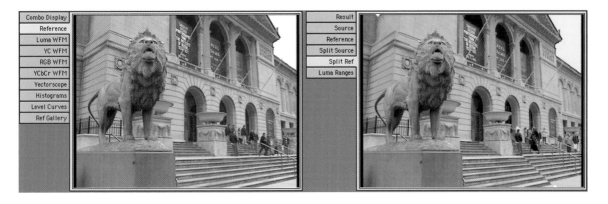

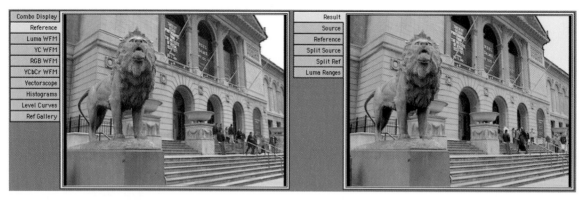

8.44 The left image is the reference image of the lion shot with correct filtration. The right image is the corrected image of the "blue" lion.

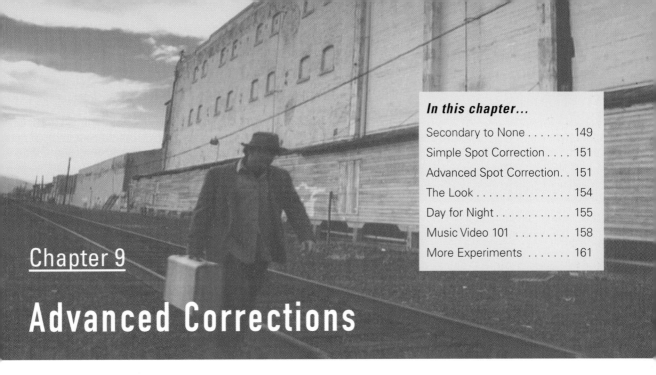

Chapter 9

Advanced Corrections

While the previous chapter was devoted to fixing bad images with the basic color correction tools, this chapter is devoted to more elaborate corrections and embellishments of images that are already pretty good looking.

The first image will involve secondary corrections on two vectors in the image. A *vector* is just a term for a specific area defined by hue and chrominance.

Secondary to None

The image in Figure 9.1[1] is very nice, and the exposure is just about perfect, but the skin tones run a little blue.

1. To solve that, we will use the basic controls, and pull blue out of the entire image. Once that is done, the watermelon doesn't look quite as nice.

2. We can isolate that vector (a very high chroma red) and rotate the hue until we are pleased with the color.

9.1   Image for vector correction.

9.2   Blue pulled out.

---

1. Figures 9.1, 9.2, and 9.4 are courtesy of Artbeats' Kids of Summer Collection, KS114.

9.3 Secondary corrections for the watermelon.

3. You can also crank up the chroma of this vector, but you need to keep an eye on the scopes, since this is already a very saturated red.

The other trick here is that the hue of the watermelon comes close at times to flesh tones, so finding the hue and saturation spread that best defines the watermelon alone will be a delicate dance. Figure 9.3 shows final settings for the watermelon correction, and Figure 9.4 shows the final image.[2]

9.4 Watermelon after correction.

The other thing that we're going to use secondary color correction for is—let's pretend—that the art director spent a lot of money painting the house that particular shade of yellow, and he wants to see it better. He remembers a more vivid, orangish yellow than what is on the monitor. Remember, people's color memory is toward a higher chroma image.

4. We can select the vector for the wall very easily.

5. By swinging it towards red, the prominence of the wall kicks up a bit, with no change in the foreground (see Figure 9.5).

9.5 Secondary corrections for the yellow wall.

---

2. Figure 9.4 courtesy of Artbeats' Kids of Summer Collection, KS114.

9.6 Girl in a busy background.

9.7 Girl after correction.

Simple Spot Correction
See Spot Walk

The next two exercises are spot corrections. The first one is rather simple. We have a fairly nice image of a little girl with an umbrella, but the image is so busy that she gets lost in the clutter a little (see Figure 9.6).

1. To pull her out a bit more, we're going to bring down the levels across the board, trying *not* to look at what we're doing to the face.

2. We can also add some yellow to the highlights and high midtones to suck out some of the blue. Watch the jacket color to find something that is pleasing.

3. With spot correction, create a soft-edged oval around the girl's face.

4. Raise the brightness, contrast, and saturation.

5. Add a bit of red to warm her up.

Now she punches through the clutter a bit more, as you can see in Figure 9.7.

Advanced Spot Correction
See Spot Run

With that as a warm up, let's see what can really be done with some serious spot correction. The original image is beautiful (see Figure 9.8), but the art director doesn't want the little boy in the center to have quite so much prominence. The only way to accomplish this will be with spot color correction.

9.8 The center boy is too much the star of this picture. (Image courtesy Artbeats' Kids of Summer Collection, KS108.)

9.9 A screenshot from Avid Symphony, which is capable of an infinite number of keyframable, organic-shaped spot corrections on a single image.

1. Take a look at the image[3] and identify the things that stand out too prominently and the things that are too hidden.

These are the areas we will isolate with spot corrections. The boy is too prominently lit. But there are three different areas of the boy that all have different characteristics.

2. We will isolate his head, the shoulder, and his pants.

3. The yellow flowers at the front of the picture are too hot, so we will put a window on that.

4. Then we will create two different windows for the girls in the background.

 Tip _____

When to Stop. When you're working with spot corrections, one rule is that your correction has to stop when you can see the shape of the spot start to appear on the image.

One would be easier, but the girl on one side needs different processing than the one on the other.

5. Let's bring down the boy's face first. Everything's going to come down: brightness, contrast, saturation, and gamma.

6. In the shoulder window, brightness, saturation, and contrast all come down, as well as a bit of blue.

7. Now, the pants window. The brightness and saturation need to come down, and we're going to pull a lot of blue out as well.

The reason we needed a window here is because the blue of the pants is almost glowing.

8. The flowers are too hot, so the window over them will get the brightness pulled down, and the saturation will come down a little.

_____

3. Figures 9.8–9.10 are courtesy of Artbeats' Kids of Summer Collection, KS108.

9.10 A more egalitarian view.

9. Then we'll pump up the individual channels for red and green to add yellow back into the blown-out highlights.

10. Finally, in the right window, we'll bring the brightness up and the contrast down.

11. Saturation will also come down. We need to bring the saturation down because bringing the gain up in this area also adds too much saturation. This is a common problem with increasing gain to dark areas and it is something to always be looking out for.

12. And in the left window, contrast and saturation will come down while bringing the brightness up.

13. We'll also pull some red and blue channel down.

The finished image is much more evenly balanced, sharing the spotlight with all of the kids (see Figure 9.10[4]).

Bob Sliga from Film and Tape provided some addition suggestions for this image:

> I'd draw a matte around the boy in front, then open up the right side of the picture with a soft-edged window and raise the gamma levels in this area. As you lift that up, you'll create a nice separation, but eventually you'll run into a wall. Stretch the black level and the grays as much as possible to see our separation in the shadows. Then I would pull some blue out of the gamma and roll a little bit of red in. There's nothing really clipping back in the shadows, so we could really open this up to look into the shadows.

> On the other side, I'd create another soft-edged window on the other side of the screen. You don't want to bring up a lot on this side, so we'll stretch gammas and pull the highlights up. That way you see into her eyes.

---

4. Figure 9.10 is courtesy of Artbeats' Kids of Summer Collection, KS108.

Once I had all of that taken care of, I would come back to the boy's face with a window and bring his gamma level down slightly, back the luma level down slightly, and pull some of the blue reflection out of his skin. You can't pull the whites down too much, or it'll start looking fake because the shadow is giving you a clue that he's in a very bright light. So what you want to do is feather that light. Possibly take a little secondary red and feather the black level down a little. That will give us a richer feel in his hair and that will take some of that stark whiteness, the blue whiteness out of his hair and bright skin.

Alex Scudiero, a veteran colorist and principal at I³ in Chicago, points out that before executing any correction—especially a tricky one like this—you need to watch the shot through from beginning to end. You may need to track windows with movement, or the light may change after a while.

The Look

This correction involves creating a specific look for the image. We're going to revisit the skull image from the earlier tutorial chapter (see Figure 9.11), but this time Craig Leffel from Opt1mus in Chicago will take the controls and provide a more distinct look than the basic correction that we did in the last chapter. Craig did these manipulations on a Da Vinci 2K.

Analyzing the image, Leffel noted the obvious red color cast and pointed out that detail was missing in the whites that could not be recovered.

1. To take care of the color cast, Leffel simply desaturated the image, which removed the red and magenta tones (see Figure 9.12).

2. With a desaturated image to use as a base, he spun the phase or hue around to more of a yellow tone and walked in a bit more blue.

3. Using the Da Vinci's ability to generate mattes on luma or chroma, Leffel isolated the reds in the shadows and brought in a colder, more detached look by adding back some blue.

9.11 Red-cast skull original.

9.12 Desaturated skull.

9.13 Final correction, with added blue and green. The specific look created here is quite eerie and disturbing compared with the other two images of the skull.

4.   As a final touch, Leffel vignetted the edges and turned the corners of the image slightly green.

You can see his final product in Figure 9.13.

Day for Night

Colorist Alex Scudiero, of I³ in Chicago walked through a beautiful day-for-night example with me on his state-of-the-art Da Vinci 2K. The tools he had to perfect the image were so numerous and powerful that we felt we needed to approximate his look in a lower-end tool, so we chose Avid's Xpress DV.

1.   To start, Scudiero suggested pulling a lot of the chroma out of the image. Then he pushed a lot of blue up into the darks.

9.14 Night will shortly fall on this castle.

To approximate the range of the Da Vinci's ability to add color, we needed to do this in several ways on the Xpress DV.

2.   First, we added blue to the shadows and the midtones in **Hue Offsets**.

3.   We also pulled down luminance more than in half and pulled down the gamma as well.

The colors still weren't quite right, so we did some additional corrections using the **Curves** control. These included additional tonal range corrections as well as some subtle and not so subtle color casts.

4.   Using the blue curve, we crushed the blacks and then lifted more blue in the deep shadows.

5.   Then we clipped the whites.

This didn't actually raise the level because the luma has already been pulled down so drastically. It just served to flatten out the sky. Actually, the more I pulled the highlights down in the master curve, the brighter the sky appeared.

9.15 These are the corrections made in Avid Xpress DV's Hue Offset control.

6. Then I pulled down some of the midtone levels, which pulled back some of the highlights of white that are part of the castle wall.

7. Finally, the color looked too magenta, so we crushed the red curve black levels, pulled down the reds in the highlights a lot and a little less in the midrange.

8. One of the final elements that Scudiero added to his correction recreated the eye's loss of detail in low light by softening the highlights fairly significantly and adding a small amount of softness to the entire image.

We did not approximate that look for this example, but it is certainly possible on the Xpress DV platform with any number of AVX plugins or on Final Cut Pro with After Effects plugins.

Film and Tape's Bob Sliga also provided some suggestions for this correction, too. His additional suggestion was to pull a matte using the luminance of the sky that could be used to separate the corrections done to the sky from the corrections done to the castle. This key could actually be used to insert a whole different sky into the image. The separation of these elements allows you to create a specific feel for the kind of a night that it is, since the tonal differences between the building and the sky give you your best clues as to how dark the night really is.

9.16 These are the adjustments made to the Curves controls to achieve the day-for-night look.

9.17 Night falls, with our help.

9.18 From Artbeats' Lifestyles Mixed Cuts collection, LM112.

Music Video 101

Finally, let's take a shot at the kind of stylized look that you might see in a music video or TV spot. We started out with an image that has a cool look on its own (see Figure 9.18).

This correction would have been a little easier on a Da Vinci, but we're going to try it on an Avid Symphony. We're going to build a multilayered correction with a mask to cut through from one correction and reveal parts of the other correction.

1. On the first layer of video, pull out *all* of the saturation.

2. Then using **Hue Offsets** or the method of your choice, add a bunch of red to the shadows, blue to the midtones, and yellow to the highlights.

3. We'll also add a bit more yellow using the **Master Hue Offset.**

4. Now let's bring the pedestal, gamma, and gain down.

This will make the background not as distracting later because we've darkened it and pulled out contrast.

5. Now pull out even more level in the highlights to cut down on the glare factor.

6. In the midtones, lower contrast more by lowering the gain and raising the pedestal and gamma.

Be careful about lowering gamma too much, or the image turns dark and moody—which may be what you want! Figure 9.19 shows our corrections so far on the bottom layer.

7. With that correction in place, copy the same clip and paste it to the track directly above it.

9.19 The bottom layer, corrected.

8. This track is going to be basically unchanged, but we will add a little chroma and some reddish yellow warmth to the whole image.

9. If you have the tools, you can also add a small amount of blur.

The blur and warmth will help humanize the subject as he walks through a cold, steely palette (see Figure 9.20).

10. Now, on a third track, add the same footage again, synced in time to the footage below.

9.20 Chroma, blur, and warmth added.

9.21 Third track, contrast up, chroma out.

11. Crank the contrast all the way up and pull out the chroma (see Figure 9.21).

12. We will use this as a matte to cut a hole through the one image, down into the other.

13. Adding some blur to the matte will help blend the two distinct corrections better (see Figure 9.22).

14. Now if you drop a matte key on the top of this signal, it will cut a hole through the human correction down into the contrasty, blue/yellow world. Our final version appears in Figure 9.23.

9.22 Blurring the corrections together.

9.23 Final version of a new story.

Film and Tape's Bob Sliga also gave his take on providing this image with a look:

> The first thing I'd have to think about is the storyline involved. As nice as this image is, we can go a multitude of different ways. This scene could take on a nice, magic-hour look. It could go stylized, cooler, skipped-bleach kind of look, which makes the whites superwhite and the blacks fairly black, but then we really pull the gamma detail so that it takes on a scariness. That bluer, eerie look would set the story up for danger and something bad about to happen.

> How we would do that is to isolate the sky area. We're going to really play up the height of the brightness and the contrast. And we're gonna have hot, hot whites in the skin tones. The gamma is buried with a blue feel in it. The blue gamma is up around 20IRE, and everything else is well below that.

> With another look, we could set it up so he's blown out with a neutral to a cool feel. Isolate the suitcase and keep that warmer. The story could be that he's leaving home, but he's got the picture of his baby girl in his suitcase. It's a country and western song I'm writing right now! The beauty of this is that you don't have to do it in camera, and we can start telling the story with colors to let the audience know where we're headed without any dialog or plot at all.

More Experiments

There's no reason to stop here. Find some images that you've come across recently that needed some work. Take a few minutes to analyze what the image's deficiencies are. Figure out how to fix them. Use several different approaches. Learn which ones yield the best results for you or which ones are the best ones for certain problems.

Color correction is like any other skill. It must be practiced. Challenge yourself. Try to experiment when you don't have a client or when there is no deadline. If there's a tough image in a production that you don't have time to perfect in the course of your deadline, save it and experiment with it after the job is done. You need to have the freedom to experiment and make mistakes.

Develop your eye by analyzing the images you see on TV and in the movies. How are they using color to affect your perception of a product, character, or moment in a story? Fashion magazines are always visually striking. How can you incorporate those looks into your next project? Save various images that appeal to you so that if you are having trouble communicating a look to your client, you can show them a range of possibilities. Often, the look they want will not be in your folder of clippings, but it can start the discussion about how to approach the look.

Good luck exploring this brave new world of color correction.

Appendix A

Software and Plugin Capabilities

As the popularity and importance of color correction functionality grows, more and more vendors are getting color correction products into the market or beefing up the capabilities of the products that are already there.

Despite the rapidly changing and expanding marketplace, this appendix will provide an explanation of color correction capabilities for some of the most popular products and platforms.

Avid

Historically, color correction has been included as part of the effects capabilities of most Avid products and was performed by dropping a **Color Effect** on any clip in **Effect** mode. The Avid Symphony introduced a powerful, full-function color corrector in late 1999 with release 2.1 and added secondary color correction in version 3.0. Some of those features are beginning to make their way into other Avid products, such as the Xpress DV in version 3.5, released in the summer of 2002, and other Avid products in subsequent releases (after release 11/5 of the Media Composer/Xpress family). First we'll address the capabilities of the widely available Avid Color Effect.

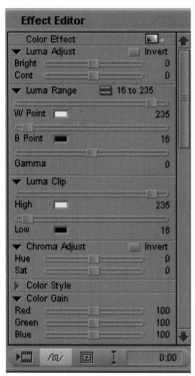

A.1 Avid Color Effect.

Avid Color Effect

Color Effect (see Figure A.1) offers control of **Brightness** and **Contrast**. The **Luma Ranges** sliders provide the ability to set white point and black point levels and to adjust overall gamma levels. **Luma Clip** allows for clipping of the top or bottom of the luminance range. **Chroma Adjust** offers controls of **Hue** and **Saturation** levels, and **Color Gain** provides access to the individual R, G, and B levels. There are no controls for individual color control over shadows, highlights, and gamma. This means that if you're looking for real control over the color and tonal values with most Avid products, you'll need to turn to third-party expertise.

The exceptions to this are Avid Symphony and Xpress DV 3.5. Avid will also be moving some of Avid Symphony's color correction capabilities to its other products after version 11 of the Media Composer and version 5 of the Xpress.

Xpress DV Color Tools

The Xpress DV3.5 (see Figure A.2) has a very nice set of tools brought over from Symphony. These are accessed from the **Toolset** menu. By clicking on **Color Correction**, the entire UI reconfigures to a new set of tools specifically designed to put all of the color correction tools you need in one place. The two main tabs are **HSL** and **Curves**. In the **HSL** tab are two more tabs. One

A.2 Xpress DV Color Tools.

is called **Controls**, and one is called **Hue Offsets**. **Controls** offers the basic TBC controls, similar to the Avid Color Effect: **Hue, Saturation, Brightness, Contrast**, and **Clipping** controls. There are also color matching controls that allow you to sample colors from reference frames to match colors from scene to scene.

The **Hue Offsets** tab includes three **Hue Offset** wheels, one for each luminance range, but none for overall **Hue Offset**. Additionally it includes controls for gain, gamma, and setup. Also on this tab is another set of color matching controls. For quick fixes, this is the tab where you can get the most done with the least work.

In the **Curves** tab, there are four different curves, one for each primary color plus a master curve. Each curve can have four points, which is enough for many corrections. There is also another set of color matching controls. The color matching controls on each tab offer a slightly different capability, especially the one in the **Curves** tab, which provides a function called **Natural Match**. All of these tabs have buttons called **Color Buckets** that allow the user to save various setups for quick recall and reuse from shot to shot.

In addition to the easily accessible **Buckets**, each correction can be saved in a bin. These corrections can then be named and used from the bin like any Avid effect, by dragging and dropping. The naming convention for color corrections is usually to name it after the clip that it corrected, but it can also be a simple description of what the correction does, such as "crushed blacks, cool gamma" or "Kurtis blue fix."

To assist in color correction analysis, Xpress DV3.5 includes a much improved waveform and vectorscope display than the older software.

Avid Symphony

Avid Symphony (see Figure A.3) features such a broad tool set that we'll only skim the surface here. The Symphony color correction mode is enabled by entering a user interface completely separate from the three standard modes of editing, trimming, and effects. Color correction can be accomplished on both the source and on the entire sequence.

A.3 Avid Symphony.

Tabs provide the editor with access to a number of ways to correct color. Each tab is an additive correction that is applied in addition to any correction that occurs in any other tab. The tabs include: **HSL, Hue Offsets, Channels, Levels, Curves,** and **Secondary Color Correction.** Spot color correction is not performed in the **Color Correction** mode, but as an effect, so it is accessed through the **Effects** palette.

The **HSL** tab is mainly for making the basic TBC-type adjustments to hue, saturation, and brightness. It also includes controls for **Contrast, Gain, Gamma, Setup,** and **Clipping.** The important thing with all of these controls is that the tab allows each of these adjustments to be made on either highlights, midtones, shadows, or the master. This tab also allows viewing and altering the definitions for each individual tonal range.

The **Hue Offset** tab is presented as one of the subtabs of the **HSL** tab. The **Hue Offset** UI can be configured to display either as wheels of color or as vectorscope-like images. As with all of the other tabs in **Color Correction** mode, it allows controls for color matching with an eyedropper. Avid suggests that **Hue Offsets** are "especially well-suited for correcting color casts."

The **Channels** tab allows you to blend color channels by changing the percentages of each color channel or color component. You don't have to do this blending in RGB alone. You can also change the proportions of the YCbCr color space. Another great tool in this tab is the ability to view the individual color channels as black-and-white images. This feature is provided in this tab because one of the main reasons for color correcting using **Channels** is to correct a problem with a specific color channel, such as an image where the red and green channels may look fine when viewed separately, but the blue channel is too noisy or dark due to a poor white balance or camera problem. **Channel Blending** allows you to use the two good channels to compensate for the deficiencies of the bad channel. For those that have the time to really investigate the deficiencies of an image, this is great because you can actually see a bad color channel. The clipping or low levels or lack of contrast becomes obvious when you view an individual channel.

The **Levels** tab is the Symphony's histogram control, although there is a **Curve** graph and color matching functionality as well. You can access histograms for input *and* output levels of the red, green, blue, master, composite, and luma levels. The difference between **Master, Luma,** and **Composite** is that **Master** adjusts the levels for all three color channels, **Composite** is for ensuring that the Composite video level is legal, and **Luma** only adjusts the luminance values, for maintaining legal luma values. Using the **Composite** and **Luma** tabs works well when the **Safe Color** feature of Symphony's color corrector is set to warn you of illegal levels. There is a **Safe Color** feature that can automatically *limit* levels, but setting it to *warn* you of improper levels allows you to make specific determinations about how to maintain legal levels while affecting your image in a specific and appropriate way. Using the **Warn** feature of **Safe Color** while monitoring the **Levels** tab is a great way to make creative decisions about maintaining legal levels.

The **Curves** tab is pretty straight forward, providing you with **Curves** for each color channel and a **Master Curve.** The curves in this tab allow for a great deal of control: they provide up to 16 individual points on each curve to be adjusted (compared to Xpress DV's limit of only four or some other software which allows only three points—one for black point, one for white point, and a floating gamma point).

The **Secondary** tab allows for control of adjustments to regions of the image that are specifically defined by a range of hue and chrominance—called a *vector*. Ranges can be set by customizing preset color vectors, each basically matching a color on the vectorscope, or can be created by color sampling in a custom vector.

One of Symphony's strong points in color correction management is the ability to quickly assign a correction made on a single shot in an image to other shots based on clip name, tape source, or other options. This is ideal for an entire tape shot with the same incorrect color balance, an entire scene shot with the wrong filter or a stock footage reel with the same age-related color errors.

Symphony also provides the ability to affect the overall color of an entire sequence in addition to the individual shot corrections. An overall look can be designed and executed for an entire show or spot or a specific segment of a show or spot. This could allow for specific emotional beats in a show to be color corrected at the same time. For example, all of the first act could be warmed up. Then all of the second act could be slightly desaturated, while the third act had cool tones with deepened blacks.

Avid|DS

Avid|DS (see Figure A.4) provides its color correction capabilities as an effect that can be applied to a clip. The DS color correction is arranged in tabs, similar to Avid Symphony, for **Basic** (HSL corrections), **Hue Offset** (called **Balance**), **Adjust**, **Curves**, and matte generation or **Masking**. The **Basic** page has **Hue**, **Saturation**, **Brightness**, and **Gain** controls for the overall image. The **Balance** page allows for **Hue Offsets** in **Shadows**, **Midtones**, or **Highlights**. **Adjust** allows for selecting specific tonal ranges for color channel adjustments. And the **Curves** page allows for moving points on curves for each color channel or a master curve. The **Masking** function allows for color correction adjustments to be limited to an area assigned by an alpha channel mask or any other externally generated mask source.

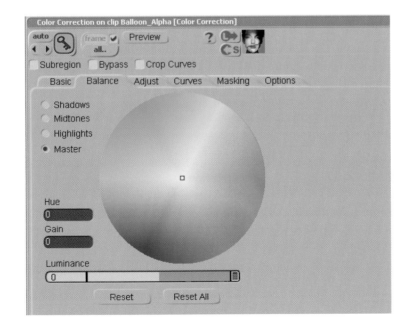

A.4 Avid|DS.

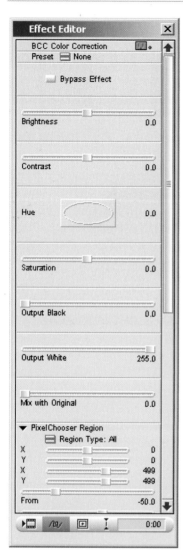

A.5 Boris FX 6.

Boris

Boris FX 6 (see Figure A.5) offers a number of color correction options in addition to the 3D effects for which Boris is best known. It allows brightness and contrast control and master RGB color controls. It also offers basic TBC control through the **Color Correction** filter and **Gamma Control** filters. The only filter that distinguishes Boris FX 6's controls from Avid's **Color Effect** is the **Color Selected** filter, which allows you to isolate a selected range of colors in the image to be corrected.

Boris also has a set of plugins called Boris Continuum Complete, which includes a color correction plugin for Avid that provides brightness, contrast, hue, saturation, output black, and output white controls. Also the **Pixelchooser** gives many options for applying these controls to very specific portions of the picture based on a list of matte-generating features, as well as the ability to selectively mix the correction back with the original image.

Digital Film Tools

Digital Film Tools' Composite Suite (see Figure A.6) offers basic HSL (hue/saturation/luminance) control plus sliders for gamma and overall RGB sliders. Additionally, there are RGB sliders for shadows, midtones, and highlights as well as a feature called **Flash Amount**. This is terminology borrowed from cinematography and describes the optical process of brightening and lowering the contrast of an image by flashing it with light. Basically, **Flash Amount** just adds a simple tint to the image and is done by choosing a color with an eyedropper or RGB sliders. Digital Film Tools' full Composite Suite package provides these color correction capabilities. They also have a color correction only package called Composite Suite Color Correct.

GenArts

GenArt's Sapphire package (see Figure A.7) also has some color correction capabilities. As an Avid AVX effect, Sapphire does not put all of its color-related controls together in one effect, so you must drag several individual effects onto the clip to have full control, but Sapphire is available on several other high-end NLEs and compositors that group the color effects together into a single effect on those machines, including Discreet Systems, Quantel systems, Nothing Real, and Alias|Wavefront Maya Composer. Control from this product includes the basic TBC controls, gamma, and various specialized color effects.

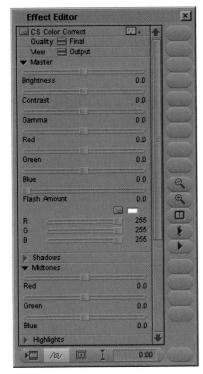

A.6 Digital Film Tools' Composite Suite *(above)*.

A.7 GenArt's Sapphire *(middle)*.

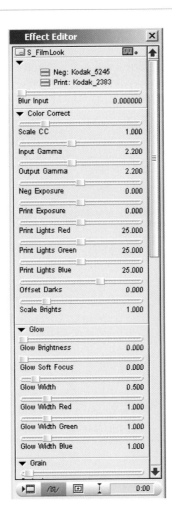

A.8 3Prong's ColorFiX.

3Prong

3Prong's color correction offering for Avid AVX, ColorFiX (see Figure A.8), provides lots of control for isolating colors and luminance ranges. It also allows the image to be re-white balanced and re-black balanced using eyedroppers. ColorFiX has two sets of controls that it calls *paths*. The **Main** path provides overall color correction and the **Select** path is more closely related to secondary color correction, allowing for the replacement of specific colors with different colors without affecting the rest of the image. The controls in this plugin are very advanced and provide very detailed control, allowing corrections to one part of a picture, such as shadow, to be done without affecting other areas. Also, the **Color Difference** controls allow for unusual color vector movement that is not available in any other plugin. Of all of the AVX color correction plugins, this would be at the top of the list. Most of the other plugins provide color correction tools secondarily, as support for the more important effects tools. ColorFiX offers nothing beyond color correction, but it does it very well.

Final Cut Pro

Internally, Final Cut Pro 3 provides most of its color correction effects through the **Effects Menu>Video Filters>Color Correction** path. The main tools that you'll access from here are the **Color Corrector** and **3-Way Color Corrector** (see Figure A.9). FCP3 also offers a set of scopes, including a histogram and parade waveform which are accessed through the **Windows>ThreeUp** path or simply **Windows>Toolbench**. These scopes can be arranged in various configurations and, best of all, can be expanded to full-screen size. There are also color correction options in the **Effects Menu>Video Filters>Image Control** path, which was the main path for color correction before version 3.

Under **Image Control**, **Brightness** and **Contrast** offers simple sliders for general control across the entire image. **Color Balance** provides sliders for R, G, and B levels for highlights, mid-

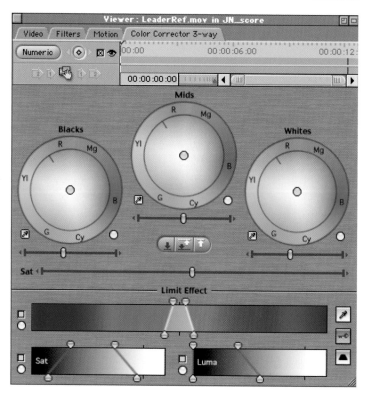

A.9 Final Cut Pro 3's Color Corrector and 3-Way Color Corrector.

tones, and shadows. **Gamma/Pedestal/Gain** provides sliders for gamma, pedestal, and gain in each of the color channels. Also, **Levels** provides sliders for master RGB and individual R, G, and B color channels with control similar to that of an editable histogram. Finally, the **Proc Amp** controls give the basic TBC-like controls that many editors are used to: **Setup**, **Video**, **Chroma**, and **Phase**.

Premiere and Wintel Plugins

Adobe Premiere (see Figure A.10) offers a pretty decent array of color correction tools built in to the basic software. Before the advent of FCP 3 and Avid Xpress DV 3.5, Premiere had the best built-in color correction capabilities, but it has been surpassed by both of these programs. Also, the color correction plugins available for programs such as Xpress DV and FCP3 are also better than the plugins available to Premiere.

In Premiere 6, under the **Video** tab, you will find the **Adjust** folder, which includes **Brightness** and **Contrast**, a **Channel Mixer** allowing you to blend color channels, and **Color Balance** with **Red**, **Green**, and **Blue** sliders, allowing you to modify the amount of each color in the overall picture. It also includes the powerful **Levels** option, which provides you with a histogram that allows you to individually adjust the shadows, highlights, and gamma on the composite RGB signal as well as individual **Red, Green,** and **Blue** channels. **Levels** is where much of the color correction on Premiere should probably be done.

In the **Image Control** folder, you will find controls for **Color Balance,** which is different from the control in the **Adjust** folder: it provides **Hue, Lightness,** and **Saturation** sliders. A **Color Pass** control, which allows you to isolate a single color and turn the rest of the image to grayscale. **Color Replace** allows you to replace one color in your image for another. This is kind of a poor-man's secondary color correction. However, this control allows no softening or blurring of the replaced color with the ones surrounding it, making it much less useful. A **Gamma Correction** slider and a **Tint** control allow separate mapping of whites and blacks to different tints. This could be used effectively to provide a certain look, but there are better controls to use if you are trying to correct for mistakes in the footage. In the **Video** folder are controls for **Broadcast Colors,** which essentially acts as a video limiter, allowing you to ensure that your levels are legal.

Available plugins for Premiere include Xentrik's ViXen (see Figure A.11) and Synthetic Aperture's Video Finesse (see Figure A.12). ViXen is available for Premiere and several other PC/NT-based NLEs. It includes a built-in waveform monitor and vectorscope that update very smoothly, even on a low-powered laptop. In addition to the normal TBC or proc amp controls, ViXen gives sliders for **Gamma, Knee,** and **Slope** (**Knee** and **Slope** provide additional control over the upper range of the gamma portion of the image.) It also provides three buttons to automatically correct white and black balancing in post. For those who like to get their fingers dirty, slider control is also given for the **R, G,** and **B** channels for the highlights, midtones, and shadows. Beyond all of this, ViXen offers several other options for

A.10 Adobe Premiere.

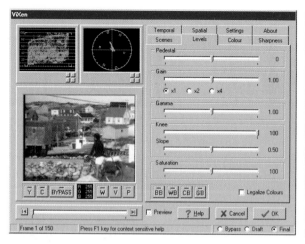

A.11 Xentrik's ViXen.

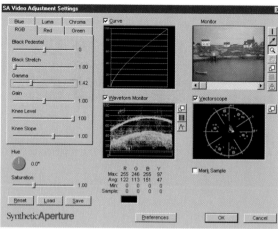

A.12 Synthetic Aperture's Video Finesse.

improving the look of video, including both temporal and spatial noise reduction and sharpening or softening of the image.

Also available for Premiere is Synthetic Aperture's Video Finesse. A waveform and vectorscope are included. It also includes a curve-monitoring tool. It would be really nice if you could alter levels with this curve, but it is not interactive. Video Finesse has much of its power in its **Channel** controls. These allow you to control either the master RGB levels or specific color channels. Each of these can be confined to a specific luminance range. Like ViXen, Video Finesse also has a nice range of features beyond color correction, including a **Blurring** filter, **Skin Detail** filter, **Gamut Limiting** filter (for getting colors to legal broadcast levels), and a **Video Bandwidth** limiting filter, to help with moiré patterns. There are also filters for **Sharpening** and **Softening**.

Both of these filters can be applied to the master image or individual color channels or just luminance or chroma. There is a **Defect Removal** filter for dirt, drop out, and other small picture defects and a **Noise Reduction** filter. One of the nice features about Video Finesse is the ability to get the picture, waveform, or vectorscope blown up to full screen for detailed analysis. And for those who may have more of a leaning toward camera work than post, Video Finesse can add zebra stripe highlights, just like many cameras.

After Effects

After Effects 5 has quite a bit of control in the area of color correction. In the **Effect** menu, under **Image Control**, there are a few offerings, including **Change Color** (a decent secondary color correction tool), **Color Balance, Colorama, Equalize, Gamma/Pedestal/Gain, PS Arbitrary Map,** and **Tint**. However, under **Adjust** there is an even greater wealth of control, including: **Brightness and Contrast, Channel Mixer, Color Balance, Curves, Hue/Saturation, Levels, Posterize,** and **Threshold**. Not surprisingly, these are very similar to the offerings provided in Adobe's editing product, Premiere. In After Effects,

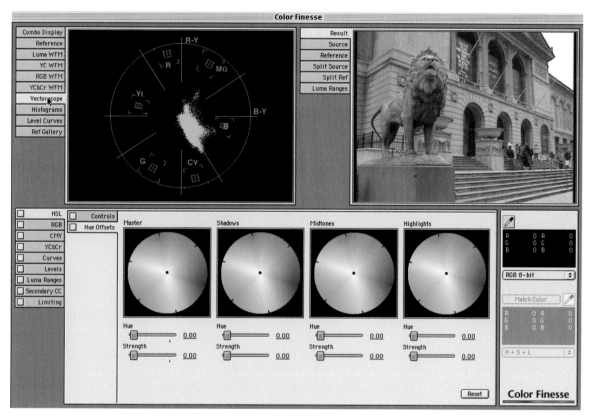

A.13 Synthetic Aperture's Color Finesse.

the **Hue/Saturation** filter is very effective at isolating color ranges and providing controls to alter those specified ranges without altering other ranges. It is this kind of control that really helps in doing effective color correction. The **Curves** filter also provides great control of the overall signal as well as individual color channels using **Curves** that provide hands-on graphical control of very specific areas of highlights, gamma, and shadows. Additionally, the **Levels** control provides intuitive graphic control over individual color channels and their highlights, gammas, and shadows by providing an interactive histogram display. **Levels** would be my home base for doing most color correction in AE.

Color Finesse Plugin

Synthetic Aperture has an After Effects–compatible plugin for color correction called Color Finesse (see Figure A.13). This plugin also works very well in all versions of Final Cut Pro. It has many useful features that make it an excellent tool, even when used in Final Cut Pro3, which already has substantial color correction horsepower. One reason for using Color Finesse within FCP3 is that you can execute all your corrections with a single filter.

Color Finesse has a very complete range of tools with which to inspect and analyze the footage. There are software waveform and vectorscopes built into Color Finesse. Sampling colors with an eyedropper is an excellent way to analyze your footage. Color Finesse provides this common feature, and adds the ability to choose a single pixel or an averaged sample from a 3×3 pixel area, a 5×5 pixel area or a 9×9 pixel area.

Another nice feature is the **Reference Gallery.** which allows you to have access to a list of images that can be used as references for matching colors from one shot to the next. They are available across all projects, which is very convenient. You can use this feature for a client who has approved a certain color for their product or a certain skin tone for talent. (This stuff happens, believe me!) Once it has been approved for one project, you can then match that color for any other projects.

Matching skin tones from one scene to the next is as easy as clicking with an eyedropper using Color Finesse's **Color Matching** feature. This is a great thing for people looking for more automated corrections. You can also use the eyedropper in the **Curves** tab to set white balance, black balance, and gray balance. This is a quick and intuitive way to get rid of color casts and to set basic levels.

For more hands-on specific, manual control of your image, there are a wide range of choices that closely match the capability of Avid Symphony. There are **Hue Offset** wheels, **Levels**, and **Curves** in addition to the standard **HSL** controls. All of these controls can be applied to specific luminance ranges of the picture, providing excellent control.

Synthetic Aperture also manufacturers a product called EchoFire that delivers imagery from your computer to a video monitor, and its integration with Color Finesse is a real bonus. EchoFire can also be used with other products, like PhotoShop, so artists can accurately judge what their work will look like on television.

Discreet Logic

Discreet has numerous products ranging from the desktop software product, Combustion (see Figure A.14), all the way up to Inferno. Most of these products are generally acknowledged as effects products, with the exception of Smoke, which is Discreet's NLE product. The excellent thing about this entire product range is that the color correction capabilities and UI are standard throughout. Obviously there are features and speed that the higher-end products deliver that aren't available in products below it, but if you can use Combustion, you will understand how to do color correction throughout the product range.

Discreet has really made color correction an important part of their products, and they have developed some fascinating color management technology, including their Color Warper. There are also sophisticated color correction plugins for Discreet, including the Anvil plugin from The Foundry in the U.K.

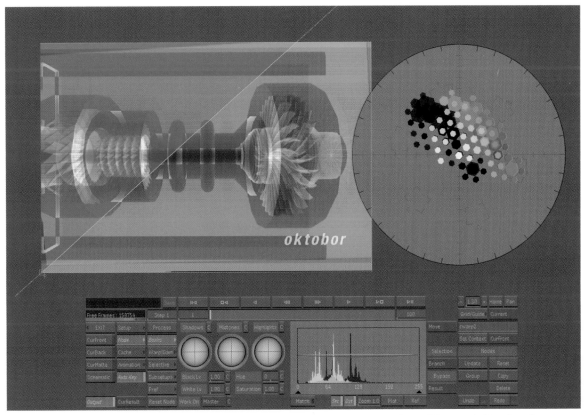

A.14 Discreet's Combustion.

Glossary

2:3 pulldown The process in telecine created when a film, shot at 24 fps, is transferred to video at 30 fps. Every other frame of film is held for an extra field of video; thus the fields run in a 2:3 order. Used in NTSC telecine only.

2-pop A 1,000-Hz tone emitted for one frame 47 frames before a reel begins. Used to establish sync with a SMPTE leader 2-frame. Also called a *sync pop*.

4:2:2 Also 4:4:4, 4:1:1, 8:8:8, and others. Subsampling rates used in digitizing video images. The higher the number, the better the sample. Higher numbers also create more cumbersome file sizes and complex pictures. The first number refers to the luminance of the picture. Second and third numbers refer to color. Sometimes a fourth number is also included, which refers to a key or alpha channel. See *subsampling*.

A neg Exposed negative that is telecined and used for cutting. A neg comprises the circled takes on a production.

A-roll Also referred to as *single-strand conforming*. A method of conforming a single strand of negative, used primarily for 35mm film.

A/B strand conforming Also referred to as *dual-strand conforming*. A method of conforming two strands of negative, used primarily for 16mm film.

Aaton code A type of timecode used in Aaton cameras. Aaton code is accurate to within a 10th of a second, but readable only through Aaton Keylink telecine database systems.

Aaton file A telecine log format whose suffix ends with .flx. Also known as a *flex file*.

absolute frames A method of measuring film, as opposed to footage + frames. Absolute frames do not count feet. Thus a 35mm footage count of 1+00 would be 16 in absolute frames. Used commonly by animators and CGI.

absorption The retention of light without reflecting or transmitting.

academy leader Leader placed at head of release prints, counting from 11 to 3. As opposed to SMPTE leader.

achromatic Having no color; gray, white, or black.

Acmade A company that manufactures ink number printers used for reference along the edges of film and mag stock. Used when conforming workprint and mag stock. Not commonly used with NLEs, Acmade numbers can be entered into Avid Film Composer databases. Acmade numbering systems have two leading characters for 16mm film and three leading characters for 35mm, followed by four or five footage count numbers, as in AA-10256. These were developed originally for the English method of shot counting vs. scene numbering.

adaptation The process of the human visual system's adjustment to the conditions under which the eyes are exposed to light.

adaptive white Color stimulus that an observer—adapted to a set of viewing conditions—would judge to be perfectly achromatic and white.

additive color Color formed by adding a mixture of primary light sources: red, green, and blue.

ADO Ampex Digital Optics. A video digital effects system manufactured and sold by Ampex.

AgX Silver halide used in motion picture film.

ALE Avid Log Exchange Format used for converting telecine files. Also an application for converting telecine files created by Avid Technology. ALE is used as a log import format for Avid and other NLEs.

ambience Also referred to as room tone or presence, production sound used where there is no dialog to establish a setting. More traditionally, *ambience* refers to outdoor locations; *room tone* refers to interiors.

analog Continuously variable electrical signal.

answer print The first film print combining sound and picture that is submitted for filmmaker approval.

ASA Exposure index defined by the American National Standards Institution. Originally defined for black-and-white films, it is also used for color films.

aspect ratio Ratio of picture width to picture height. 1.85:1 is the most common film aspect ratio in the United States, 1.66:1 is more common in Europe. Standard definition television is 4:3. Most HDTV pictures are 16:9.

assemble list Also known as the cut list. A cut list that includes all the edits in a sequence in the order in which they occur chronologically. Used for conforming negative or work print.

ATSC Advanced Television Standards Committee. The group that is developing standards for high definition and digital television as well as compression schemes for broadcasting them. Currently there are 18 different types of HDTV.

autosync Feature that allows for synching and combining of audio and picture clips on an Avid NLE.

B neg Exposed negative that is usually not telecined. Noncircled takes.

balancing The process of creating and maintaining a footage balance between cut reels. Reels used for screenings normally are

1,000 feet long. Balancing the reels maintains consistency in length without interrupting the flow of the film.

batch digitize   The automated process of digitizing previously logged clips in a batch on NLEs.

batch list   Import log format for Final Cut Pro. A telecine log must be converted into a batch list before it can be digitized into a Final Cut Pro NLE. The equivalent of an ALE file for Avid or Power Log file for Media 100.

best light transfer   A method of telecine transfer where each scene is corrected to look its best, without consideration of continuity of color between scenes, as in a scene-by-scene transfer.

bin   A container where workprint is stored hanging from pins. The editor's completed scenes are normally stored in a separate bin. A bin normally consists of a series of hooks that overhang into a nonfibrous bag. The clips are attached to cardboard trim tags that visually identify the scene, take, edge numbers, and a short description. The tags and clips are hung on pins and cascade into the bag. Should one of the clips fall off of a hook, you are immediately introduced to the film editor's sport of bin diving. NLEs have virtual or electronic bins, where pointers to media files are located. NLE bins are used in much the same way as film bins, with the added feature of the ability to copy clips into several different type bins.

bin diving   The act of having to fish out or find a clip that has fallen into the bin.

bi-phase   Electrical impulses from the telecine tachometer, used to update the footage encoder for each frame of film transferred.

bit   Contraction of binary digit, normally having a value of 0 or 1. The smallest unit of information that a computer can store.

bleach bypass   Popular lab technique used to reduce contrast and desaturate color in a film.

blow-up   The process of optically enlarging the scale of an original frame, a method of increasing the scale of the frame to show only a part of the original. Also can refer to the process of enlarging a film from one gauge to another, i.e., blowing up a 16mm film to 35mm film. Could also refer to an editor when too many changes are made.

brightness   Attribute of visual sensation to which an area appears to exhibit more or less light.

burn-in   Refers to character-generated numbers superimposed on video telecine transfers. Typical burn-ins would include video timecode, audio timecode, and key numbers.

calibration   Process of correcting any deviation from a standard set of specifications.

camera roll   A roll of motion picture film used in production, usually 400 feet or 800 feet long. Each roll is assigned a unique number for reference. Also called cam roll.

camera report   A report issued for each camera roll by the camera department of a motion picture production. Includes scene numbers, takes, circled takes, footage, and other information. A copy of this multicarbon form should be sent to the editorial department.

capture   To input video and/or audio into an NLE format. Also known as *digitizing*.

CCD   See *charged coupling device*.

CCIR An abbreviation of the International Radio Consultive Committee, an international body that sets television standards. Now referred to as *ITU-R*.

CCIR 601 A document issued by the CCIR which recommends specifications for digital component video. Now referred to as ITU-R BT.601.

CCIR-709 A document issued by the CCIR which recommends specifications high definition television signals. Now referred to as ITU-R BT.709.

CES Abbreviation for color encoding specification.

change list A list of instructions comparing an updated cut of a sequence to its previous version. Simplifies changes for the person conforming by only listing updated revisions and new edits.

changeover The point where the projectionist switches between reels during display of a motion picture. Changeover cue marks must be made 24 frames before the last frame of action (LFOA).

characterization Process of defining color characteristics for a model of an input or output device, used with color management modules.

charged coupling device A sensor used in digital video cameras and other photoelectric devices to convert light into electricity.

chroma Color component of a video signal.

chroma subsampling Technique for sampling image information, usually for storage on videotape, in which luma is stored at full resolution but chroma components are reduced. Often referred to by ratio, where 4:2:2 would refer to four pixels of full luminance, two pixels of horizontal chroma for each channel of chroma information, and two pixels of vertical information for each channel of chroma information.

chromadynamics Human response to color, be it psychological, physiological, or cultural.

chromatic adaptation Process of the human visual system's adjustment to the average chromaticity of the light to which the eyes are exposed.

chromaticity Property of a color stimulus, apart from its luminance, described by its chromaticity coordinates. For example, CIE *x, y* values.

chrominance Referring to the properties of color.

CIE The International Commission on Illumination. The organization responsible for international recommendations for colorimetry, such as the CIE LAB and CIE XYZ color spaces.

circled takes Refers to method of circling takes that the director wishes to print during production. Takes are circled on camera and sound reports as well as on facing pages in the script supervisor's notes. When referring to the film, circled takes are also known as the *A neg*. Noncircled takes, not normally telecined, are called *B neg*. These terms are not to be confused with *A-roll* and *A/B roll* methods of conforming film.

CIS See *color interchange standard*.

clapper The two striped sticks used on a slate that aid in establishing sync on a shot. By clapping the two sticks together, visual and aural reference for sync is established on film.

clip name A name given to a shot used in an NLE to identify it. Clips are usually named after a scene and take number, e.g., "16/1" for scene 16, take 1.

clipping Also called *white clip*. A condition where the variation of input luminance signals can produce no further variation of an output signal. This usually occurs when brightness is overdriven, causing little or no variation at the highest point of luminance in the signal and an irrecoverable loss of image detail in the clipped areas.

CMX The most common format for EDLs, CMX was one of the first computer controlled editing machines and a pioneer in nonlinear editing machine development. CMX 3400 EDLs have two audio tracks; CMX 3600 have four. Originally a co-venture of CBS and Memorex.

CMYK Abbreviation for cyan, magenta, yellow, and black (K) inks used in the subtractive color process.

codec Compressor/decompressor, based upon a specific compression scheme, such as motion JPEG, MPEG, and so on. Codecs come in both hardware and software form.

color cast *1)* A bias towards a single color in an image. This color cast is usually due to improper filtration or white balance—such as using a tungsten white balance outdoors—causing the entire image to appear bluish. They can also be used intentionally for a creative effect such as a sepia color cast to give the impression of age. Color casts can affect an entire image or only exist in certain luminance ranges of an image. For example, the shadows can have a blue cast while the highlights have a yellow cast. *2)* Situations where sources or modifiers cast colored light on other objects in an image; for example, a setting sun casting orange light on the ocean.

color correction The process of adjusting film colors using a color correction system. A component of telecine and, more recently, of nonlinear editing systems.

color encoding Numerical specification of color information.

color encoding specification Fully specified method of color encoding used for encoding color on an individual system.

color gamut Referring to the limits of the array of colors that can be captured or reproduced by a device, or represented by a color-encoding metric.

color interchange standard Fully specified color interchange scheme that includes colorimetry specifications and a set of reference viewing conditions. It can also include specifications for data compression and file format information.

color management Appropriate use of color hardware and software to control color in an imaging system.

color management module (CMM) Digital signal-processing engine for processing image data through profiles.

color primaries (additive) Independent light sources—usually red, green, and blue—that can be combined to form various colors.

color primaries (subtractive) Colorants—usually cyan, magenta, and yellow—which absorb light of one of the additive primaries.

color stimulus The energy from that portion of the electromagnetic spectrum between approximately 380–780 nm which is perceived as light and color by the human visual system.

color timer Also *negative timer*. The person, usually employed by a film lab, who is in charge of timing an answer print for film. The timer makes recommended adjustments to the film's brightness, contrast, and color.

color timing   Also called *timing* or *grading*. The process of adjusting color balance for each scene from a conformed negative.

color wheel   Similar to a vectorscope but without I&Q or any reference, a color wheel is used in color correction to examine the amount of color in each color vector—usually red, green, blue, cyan, yellow, and magenta.

colorant   Dye, ink, or other agent used to impart color to a material.

colorimeter   Instrument that measures color stimuli in terms of standard observer responsivities.

colorimetry   The science of color measure.

colorist   A person who adjusts electronic signal processing equipment in the transfer of motion pictures to video or data. In the industry, one who has distinguished themselves as a color artist and craftsperson with an extensive background in image manipulation with a high degree of understanding of color management.

component video   Video signal that separates the various components (i.e., chrominance, luminance, or other variables) rather than combining all elements, as in composite video.

composite print   A positive print that has both picture and sound. Also called *married print*.

composite video   Video signal in which chrominance and luminance are combined.

compositing   Process of combining two or more images to form a single image.

compression   Process of reducing data file sizes for storing images.

cones   Photoreceptors in the eye, located in the retina, which receive the information that initiates color perception.

conform   To assemble workprint or negative according to a list, usually a cut list. The term has been expanded to refer to assembly of a videotape sequence from an EDL or an audio sequence from an EDL. Can also refer to assembling an online high-quality video finish from an offline video edit, as in "online conforming."

continuity reports   Could refer to notes made by a script supervisor regarding script continuity. Also refers to reel continuity, where an editor reports durations of reels, last frame of action and last frame of film.

contrast   Degree of dissimilarity of luminance in two or more different areas of an image.

crushing   The artifact that occurs when the pedestal (also called the *black level*) is adjusted too low during the shooting or reproduction of an image. Crushing tends to reduce contrast in dark elements of an image.

CRT   Cathode Ray Tube.

cut list   An EDL for film. Instead of timecode numbers, edge numbers are used.

cyan   Subtractive primary color which absorbs red light and reflects or transmits blue and green light.

DAC   Digital-to-analog converter.

dailies   The results of a single day of shooting. Usually refers to workprint made from a single day of shooting, but can also refer to a videotape transfer of the footage. Referred to as *dailies* because of the traditional method of shooting, developing, and printing overnight. Same as *rushes*.

dark surround Area surrounding an image being viewed having a lower luminance than the image itself. Images viewed with dark surrounds are perceived to have lower luminance contrast.

DAT Digital Audio Tape. Audio tape recording format used by many sound recordists and audio engineers. SMPTE DAT is most commonly used.

datacine A telecine capable of scanning and creating large image files that go beyond the constraints of SDTV video. Datacines can be used for storing color corrected frames of film and the files they create can be scanned back onto film, avoiding the need for color timing.

Da Vinci One of the first companies to develop a color correction system for film. Da Vinci systems can now be used to color correct practically any type of media. Considered by many as the standard bearer for color correction.

daylight Combination of skylight and direct sunlight.

daylight illuminant An illuminant having the same spectral characteristics as daylight.

device-dependent color space A color space in which the gamut of color reproduction is defined by characteristics of the device itself.

diffuse Referring to scattered light.

digital A signal that contains information in a binary form. Digital signals are often perceived incorrectly as being lossless. However, some are compressed; others are not.

digital color timer Another term for a *datacine colorist*. Some consider the term less flattering.

digital cut A video output of your project direct from an NLE.

digital encoding Referring to the transformation of color stimulus into digital values.

digital intermediate See *digital interpositive* and *interpositive*.

digital interpositive Also called a *digital intermediate* or *interpositive*. The files scanned from film during the datacine process, which are stored digitally on large drive arrays. These files are color corrected, then scanned back to negative film, using a film recorder.

digitize Also known as *digitalize* in some European circles. To input video and/or audio into a digital NLE format. Also known as *capturing*. The process of converting analog signals to digital values. In some cases, a process of transferring digital values from one storage medium to another.

display Device that presents images to an observer. Could be a monitor, television, etc.

DNR Digital Noise Reduction. An option used in telecine that can virtually eliminate all sources of noise on the film. Potentially hazardous to use, as it can also remove grain, which might be desirable.

double strand See *A/B roll*.

drop frame Timecode-counting method that reflects real time. In order to compensate for the base 30 timecode count and the actual frame rate of NTSC video (29.97 fps), drop frame timecode skips ahead two frames in the count at the top of every minute, except the 10th minute of time.

DTV Digital television. DTV is a standard for broadcast that incorporates transmission of a digital signal vs. traditional analog. Often confused with HDTV, which is a format.

dual strand See *A/B roll*.

dupe A duplicate. When one or more frames are used twice in an edited sequence. Short for "duplicate," as in duplicate frames. Dupe lists are generated to determine which frames will need to be duplicated before a list is conformed. The neg is copied onto an interpositive, which is then duplicated (see *IP*).

dupe list A list of frames that need to be duplicated before conforming a cut list. Dupe lists are checked frequently during editing to prevent the high cost of duplicating negative.

edge code A broad classification of film frame numeration which could be either key numbers or ink numbers. Printed numbers on the edge of film that identify frames; a method of keeping track of edits through a simple numbering process. There are two types of edge numbers. Acmade or ink numbers can be printed on the edge of synced workprint and mag track by an ink-jet printers. Key numbers (also called *latent edge numbers*) appear on the edge of the film when it is developed. Key numbers are more commonly used with NLEs.

edit bench The place where much of the non-digital work takes place. Synching and conforming are done here. Also known as the bench or work bench. Typically contains rewinds, a gang sync, and a splicer.

EDL Edit Decision List. A list of edits in a sequence showing timecode numbers for both source and record tapes. Used for online video editing, sound conforming, spotting, mixing, and in some cases, for comparison with telecine logs for match-back. Can be used with some computerized video editing equipment for automatic conforming.

EOP End Of Picture. The very last frame of projectable film on a reel. Usually occurs a second or more after the LFOA to accommodate for human error when switching between reels. Also known as *LFOP*, Last Frame Of Picture.

Evertz Manufacturer of motion picture equipment. Also refers to a telecine log format whose files end with an .ftl suffix.

excursion The thickness of the trace signal of luminance on a waveform monitor that determines chromatic values of an image. Normally observed and adjusted by a colorist when neutralizing color cast of what should be an achromatic chart or image.

exposure The quantity of light that is captured by a receptor.

facing pages Pages printed on the back of three-hole punch paper used in conjunction with a script so that the editor can see both script pages and script supervisor notes. Contain scene, take, camera, and other details recorded while on location.

field In interlaced video formats, a single scan of the raster that includes every other line of resolution; comprising one-half of an interlaced video frame.

flare Stray light which is usually reflected from a medium but is not part of an image.

flat transfer A telecine transfer where color and luminance are kept in the middle ranges. Flat transfers are used for footage that will be color corrected later in the postproduction process.

flatbed   A film editing system for playing back conformed workprint. Flatbeds are flat tables with viewing screens attached. Most common are KEMs and Steenbecks.

flesh-tone line   A line which is used in some color wheels and software vectorscopes to give colorists a reference point for the natural color of human skin. Interestingly, there is very little variance between this reference and the variety of human skin coloring.

flex   Also known as *flex files* or *Aaton files*, a telecine log format whose files end with an .flx suffix.

fps   Frames per second. Used to measure video or film playback rates.

frame handles   See *handles*.

gamma   *1)* The slope of the straight-line portion of a CRT that relates log luminance to log voltage. *2)* The portion of an image which normally defines the midtones. Adjustable by a colorist to create more contrast in lower luminance areas or higher luminance areas.

gamut   The limits for a set of colors within a given color space.

gamut boundary   The outermost boundary of a color space.

gamut mapping   Process of replacing color values which are not physically realizable by an output medium with appropriate values for that medium. Depending on the method of mapping, even some attainable colors may be replaced.

gang sync   A gang synchronizer. Used to synchronize picture with one or more sound tracks on an edit bench. Measures footage and frames.

gate   The aperture assembly in which film is exposed in a camera or projector.

grading   Also called timing or color timing. The process of adjusting color balance for each scene from a conformed negative.

grayscale   Usually indicated on a chart, a progression of achromatic values from black to gray to white.

GVG   Grass Valley Group. A manufacturer of video and television production equipment. Also an EDL file format. GVG EDLs usually refer to their software versions. Most commonly used are 4.0–7.0.

hamburger   Slang for the **Fast Menu** used to access preview mattes in an Avid.

handles   The number of extra frames required for splicing, usually when conforming the OCN. With some splicers, adjacent frames are destroyed during conforming. By adding a number of frames as a handle in your cut list, you can determine whether or not adjacent frames need to be used in other edits, which would require a dupe.

hard   Can refer to a film emulsion or a set; having high contrast or harsh contrast.

hard matte   Term used when shooting OCN with a matte in place. As opposed to a soft matte, where no physical matting is done during the production phase.

HDTV   High Definition Television. A system having greater spatial resolution than that of standard television signals (SDTV) whose standards are recommended by the Advanced Television Systems Committee (ATSC). Currently there are 18 different formats for HDTV.

histogram A graph representing the amount of pixels in an image between a set number of luminances—usually between 1 and 255.

hue An attribute of a visual sensation that defines a specific shade of color. Hue is mapped on a vectorscope, which indicates degrees of red, green, blue, yellow, cyan, and magenta.

I & Q Points on a vectorscope which indicate a 123 degree deviation from U and V channels, respectively. See *YIQ*.

ICC The International Color Consortium, formed in 1993. The ICC promotes interoperability of color imaging systems.

illuminant A light which may or may not be physically realizable as a source defined in terms of its spectral power distribution.

ink numbers Also called *Acmade Numbers*. Inkjet numbers that are added to a work-print and mag stock for reference. Can be used in some NLEs. Also used for preview code. Key numbers are more commonly used for digital editing.

interlock projector The projector used for screening workprint and dailies. It consists of a film projector and mag track player that can be interlocked and thus remain in sync.

interpositive Also referred to as a *digital interpositive* or *digital intermediate*. Digitally, this is the files scanned from film during the datacine process, which are stored digitally on large drive arrays. These files are color corrected, then scanned back to negative film using a film recorder. Non-digitally, this refers to an intermediate form of a film which can be used for opticals, effects, and other outside work before going back to a negative format.

IP Interpositive print. Created from the OCN, this positive print is used to duplicate a negative. IPs are created for items on a dupe list.

ISO International Standards Organization.

ITU International Telecommunications Union, a United Nations organization that regulates all form of communication.

ITU-R BT 601 A document issued by the ITU which recommends specifications for digital component video. Formerly referred to as CCIR-601.

ITU-R BT-709 A document issued by the ITU which recommends specifications high definition television signals. Formerly referred to as CCIR-709.

jutter Also called judder. A stopping and stuttering motion of video caused by pulldown in the telecine process. 2:3 produces the most telecine jutter. PAL B pulldown produces very little.

Kelvin Also referred to as *kelvins* or *K*. The degree of color temperature variance based upon a scale of light emanating when a black body of mass is heated. For example, lava has a color temperature of around 1,200 degrees Kelvin, while ordinary tungsten light creates a yellowish-toned color temperature between 2,800 and 3,200 degrees Kelvin.

key numbers Latent edge numbers that appear along the edge of the film near the sprocket holes. The numbers are adjacent to Keykode, a bar code system used in telecines to identify the frames. Not to be confused with Ink or Acmade numbers, which are printed on the edge of film after the film is processed. Key numbers are generally used for digital editing more often than ink numbers.

keycode   Refers to the barcode reference which is machine readable and is placed adjacent to key numbers on a film. Keycode can be read by a telecine to generate a database of numbers during a telecine transfer. Commonly confused with *key numbers*.

keycode reader   A machine used in telecine that reads the latent bar code on film. Keycode readers are located on the telecine scanner, usually connected to a character generator which can put key number burn-in windows onto a transferred videotape.

keyscope   A telecine log format using files that end with .ksl.

lab roll   A roll of negative stored in a lab configuration. Most lab rolls are 2,000 feet and consist of combined camera rolls.

lab standard durations   The standard durations for opticals of A/B conform films that can be created by the lab, thus bypassing more expensive optical print. The lab standard durations are 16, 24, 32, 48, 64, and 96 film frames.

lateral brightness adaptation   A perceptual phenomenon where a stimulus appears more or less bright depending on the relative brightness of its surround.

leader   Film-like materials that are attached to head and tail of a reel of film. Clear leader is used as a protecting agent and threading guide for a reel and is attached at the head and tail. Picture leader contains writing that identifies the reel and its contents. Picture leader is usually placed at head and tail. SMPTE or Academy leader provides a countdown before the picture content of a film begins. SMPTE or Academy leader is placed at the head of a reel adjacent to picture content.

LFOA   Last Frame of Action. The last frame of action intended for projection on a given reel. The LFOA is preceded by motor start and changeover cues.

LFOP   Last Frame Of Picture. The very last frame of projectable film on a reel. Usually occurs a second or more after the LFOA to accommodate for human error when switching between reels. Also known as *EOP*, End Of Picture.

light   That portion of the electromagnetic spectrum between 380–780 nm that is visually detectable by a normal human observer.

light source   A physical emitter of electromagnetic energy between 380–780 nm.

lined script   A script prepared by the script supervisor, marked with vertical lines to determine coverage of a shot, indicating which characters are on camera for a given take at a given time. Used by editors for easy reference.

liquid gate   Also *wet gate*. A process where film is immersed in a suitable liquid at the moment of exposure to reduce scratches and abrasions.

log   The entering of information about clips which could include timecode, key numbers, and so forth. Can also refer to a medium on which the logging data is placed, such as a file or paper. See *telecine log*.

lok box   Also known as a *lock box*. A videotape player connected to a gang sync, used for conforming a negative. Can also refer to the output of an NLE to videotape which is used for conforming.

lookup table Also called *LUT* (pronounced "luht"). A reference file that converts images from one color space to another. For example: a lookup table to convert RGB pixels to YCbCr pixels for video. A LUT can also transform raw information from a device (like a video camera) and compensate for differences in the way the device behaves by using a cross-reference table designed specifically to correct for the compensations. LUTs are often used in monitor profiles, Color Management Modules (CMMs), and digital transfers to film.

luma The achromatic part of a video signal that refers to a quantity of light.

luminance The measure of an object that correlates with the perception of brightness.

luminance contrast The apparent rate of change from lighter to darker areas of an image.

mag stock Sometimes, but not always, used with dailies, mag stock (a.k.a. *mag track*) is magnetic audio tape attached to a plastic backing which resembles film and consists of sound portions of the film. It is normally synced on an editing bench with the dailies, which are projected for the director to look at and make notes. Mag stock is cut with workprint on flatbed and upright film editing machines. For digital purposes, mag stock and workprint are used to conform a film.

magenta A subtractive primary which absorbs green light and reflects red and blue light.

married print A positive film print with both picture and sound.

matchback A process which allows generation of a film cut list from a 30 fps video based project. Matchback lists can be ±1 frame accuracy per edit. A method of converting from one frame rate to another, i.e., from 30 fps video to 24 fps film. Matchback provides ease of use with the ability to generate both EDLs for video and cut lists for a telecined film. Commonly used process for television where a conformed print will be required for distribution in other formats. Could also refer to the application which generates a matchback list.

meta speed An option used on Cintel telecines that allows for an extraordinary variety of frame rates during telecine transfers. Meta speed transfers can range from –30 fps to +96.

monochromatic Having a single hue. Electromagnetic energy of a single wavelength. Frequently confused with achromatic, which is without color.

MOS From German: "mit out sound." A scene that is without sound.

motor start A cue given to the projectionist as to when to begin running the motor, but not the projection lamp and sound head, on a second projector before a changeover occurs. Motor start cues must be given 200 frames (8 seconds) before the last frame of action (LFOA).

mute print A print with no sound. Picture-only print.

negative timer A person who sets the exposure and color of motion picture film by adjusting the timing lights as the original camera negative is printed—usually as an answer print or interpositive. See also *color timer* and *digital color timer*.

neutral Achromatic; without hue.

NLE The term for a nonlinear editor. A digital computer system application that features editing in a nonlinear method. Also known as DNLE or digital nonlinear editor. Manufactured by Avid Technology, Media 100, Lightworks, Apple (Final Cut Pro), and others.

nondrop frame   A timecode-counting method that reflects 30 fps instead of the more accurate 29.97 fps of NTSC video. As a result, this method of counting frames is not duration accurate, but each number correctly accounts for each frame without skipping ahead, as drop frame does. See also *drop frame*.

normal surround   An area surrounding an image that has a luminance factor of around 20% and chromaticity equal to the observer adaptive white. Also referred to as *average surround*.

NTSC   National Television Standards Committee. The group that developed the standard for color television in the U.S. NTSC signals have 525 lines of vertical resolution at a rate of 29.97 fps.

OMFI   Open Media Framework Interchange. A file format that is used primarily for transferring audio files and sequences from one work station to another. Platform independent.

one light   A nontimed exposure of the OCN to a positive copy of the film. It is not the prettiest copy of the film, but presentable.

one-light telecine   Also called a *lab transfer*. A telecine transfer done with color correction on the fly, used for editing purposes. Much less expensive than a best light transfer or a scene-by-scene telecine.

opticals   The separate creation of dissolves, fades, and superimpositions by an optical house. A-roll conformed films must create opticals of all such effects. A/B roll conformed films must create opticals of any effects that are not lab standard durations.

original camera negative (OCN)   The original film shot on location. Most films are shot with negative (not reversal) film.

PAL   Phase Alternating Line. Standard (as opposed to NTSC) used in many different countries. Features 625 vertical lines of resolution and 25 fps.

PAL telecine A   The method of transferring film shot at 24 or 25 fps to PAL videotape via telecine running at 25 fps to achieve a 1:1 frame ratio with the OCN. PAL A telecine shot at 24 fps will have a speed increase of 4.166% when played back on videotape. Some NLEs have speed correction capabilities to adjust it back to original shooting speed.

PAL telecine B   The method of transferring film shot at 24 fps to 25 fps PAL video, using a pulldown field every 12th frame to adjust the timebase so that the two match in duration, but not frame for frame accuracy. PAL B has all of the trappings of NTSC 2:3 pulldown, but with less frequency. Also known as *25@24*.

pan and scan   A method of transferring wide screen images to SDTV, where the telecine operator can zoom into a part of the widescreen image and pan across it, filling the SDTV screen, but eliminating some elements of the wider original picture. Pan and scan is a time-consuming and expensive method of transfer.

parade display   A three-part, waveform-like graph which displays individual channels of red, green, and blue separately. Parade displays give colorists an idea of the volume and levels of each individual primary channel.

phantom telecine   A system that plays back previously telecined films from a drive storage array. Used for color correction on motion pictures.

phosphors   Materials on the screen of a cathode ray tube that, when irradiated by an electron beam, emit light.

picture leader   Placed adjacent to SMPTE or Academy leader, a picture leader has information written on it that consists of project name, reel number, and running time.

pixel   A single point of an image. Contraction of picture element.

power log   Import log format for Media 100. A telecine log must be converted into a batch list before it can be digitized into a Media 100 NLE. The equivalent of an ALE file for Avid or Batch List for Final Cut Pro.

Power Windows   Da Vinci tool used to select portions of an image using geometric patterns. Used for spot correction and secondary color correction.

preview code   Ink code reference that applies to changes on a conformed work print.

primaries   The base colors used to make other colors additively or subtractively.

pull list   A type of list sorted usually be source, i.e., camera roll, so that the person conforming neg or workprint can pull each shot from that roll at one time prior to assembling the cut.

reddy-eddy   A circular gauge used in film cutting rooms that calculates film footage to running time and vice versa.

reference spot   Sometimes used in telecine suites, a reference spot is a 6,500 degrees Kelvin light source that a colorist will use for matching physical elements with colors in a film. Also used for visual system adjustment to the proper color temperature.

retina   Layer on the back of the eye interior containing photoreceptors called rods and cones. The retina is attached to the optic nerve, which in turn sends signals to the brain, where they are interpreted.

reversal   Film stock that produces a positive image and requires no printing, as opposed to negative.

reverse telecine   The process of removing pulldown fields in an NLE so that the digital picture matches the OCN at a 1:1 frame for frame ratio. Process can occur either during or after digitization, depending upon configuration.

rewinds   Devices used for winding rolls of film backward and forward on an edit bench.

RGB   An abbreviation for Red, Green, and Blue. The primary additive colors, also can refer to a specific color space.

rivas   A butt splicer commonly used in film editing rooms.

rods   Photoreceptors in the eye located in the retina which detect light and initiate the process of scotopic vision.

roller splicer   Film splicer manufactured by CineTrim. Uses a round blade to cut film in an unobtrusive manner which is safer for careless or left-handed editors.

room tone   Production sound used where there is no dialog to establish a setting. Also referred to as *ambience* or *presence*. More traditionally, *ambience* refers to outdoor locations while *room tone* refers to interiors.

rushes   The results of a single day of shooting. Usually refers to workprint made from a single day of shooting, but can also refer to a videotape transfer of the footage. Referred to as *rushes* because of the traditional method of shooting, developing, and printing quickly for editorial use. Same as *dailies*.

saturation The colorfulness of an area judged in proportion to its brightness.

scanner Also known as a *film scanner*, *flying spot scanner*, or *telecine scanner*. The physical machine where the film passes through a scanner and is converted to video.

scene-by-scene telecine A method of telecine transfer where color is carefully corrected for best exposure of a film and continuity between scenes is also carefully calibrated. Unnecessarily expensive for editing, a scene-by-scene is sometimes used after a cut has been made of a film for video distribution or promotion.

script supervisor The person responsible for maintaining script notes and circled takes. Produces facing pages and notes for editing.

SDTV Standard Definition Television. Refers to current television standards, such as PAL, NTSC, PAL-M, and SECAM. As opposed to HDTV, High Definition Television.

sequence Another term for an edited master, cut or program created in an NLE.

short end Term for a short roll of film, typically cut off for use on another shoot. Commonly used on low-budget projects.

signal-to-noise ratio The ratio of signal strength to the strength of undesirable "noise" in the signal. Usually measured in decibels (dB), high signal-to-noise ratios are desired. Low signal-to-noise ratios are undesireable.

single strand Also referred to as *A-roll* conforming. A method of conforming a single strand of negative, used primarily for 35mm film.

SMPTE Society of Motion Picture and Television Engineers. A society that develops standards used for television and film.

SMPTE DAT A digital audio tape (DAT) machine that uses SMPTE timecode. SMPTE DATs are far more expensive than a conventional non–timecode DAT.

SMPTE leader Countdown leader placed at the head of each built film reel. SMPTE leader counts from 8 to 2 seconds. When the first 2 frame appears, a 1,000 Hz tone pops with it (called the *2-pop* or *sync pop*), and an additional 47 frames of black are shown before the reel starts. As opposed to Academy leader, which counts from 11 to 3.

SMPTE timecode The timecode standard approved by SMPTE, as opposed to other standards, such as VISCA timecode. The most commonly used format of timecode.

soft matte Term used when shooting without a matte, with the intention of inserting one during negative printing. Soft matting allows for adjustments to be made to the frame optically if necessary. Also allows for a 1.33:1 aspect frame to be displayed on videotape or DVD.

sound report A report issued for each sound roll by the sound department of a motion picture production. Includes scene numbers, takes, circled takes, SMPTE timecode, and other information. A copy should be sent to the editorial department.

specular highlight An intense highlight created by the reflection of a bright light on a shiny surface, such as glass or polished metal.

spot correction A method of secondary color correction to change aspects of one color or one element of a picture. Spot correction on a Da Vinci system, for example, can be achieved with Power Windows.

subsampling (chroma) A method of reducing data within image files for transmission, usually to videotape. Subsampling is represented by a ratio of three or four digits, where the leading digit, usually 4, is representative only as a luminance sample relative to the amount of horizontal and vertical color samples. A fourth digit may be added to this notation to indicate alpha channel. Alpha channel sampling, when used, will always match luminance sampling.

subtractive color Color formed by the subtraction of light by absorption. CMYK primaries work as subtractive colorants.

surround The area within a viewer's range of sight that surrounds an image to be viewed.

surround effect An effect which is caused by lateral brightness adaptation where an image is perceived as having lower or higher luminance contrast depending on the average luminance of the surround relative to that of the image.

sync pop A 1,000 Hz tone emitted for one frame 47 frames before a reel begins. Used to establish sync with a SMPTE leader at the 2 frame. Also called a *2-pop*.

take The filming of a single shot.

TBC Time Base Corrector. A device which aligns the timing of the various portions of the video signal. In most uses of the term, however, it is used to describe the TBC's function as a signal processor, allowing adjustments to hue, saturation, brightness, and black level.

telecine The process of transferring film to videotape. A telecine maintains a consistent relationship between film and video frames. Not to be confused with a *film chain*, which is not as accurate.

telecine log converter An application within Trakker's Slingshot™ matchback suite. Converts telecine files to NLE usable import files. Could generically refer to all telecine log converters as well, including Avid Log Exchange.

telecine logger A computer system used to database the relationship between keycode from an original camera negative to video timecode recorded on a telecine transfer videotape.

three perf A 35mm system that records a single frame using only three perfs instead of the traditional four. Used mostly for television production, three perf requires a specially equipped camera and a telecine with metaspeed or other speed alteration device.

time logic control A method of transferring film to videotape where the pulldown remains consistent between stop points or edits. If a telecine stop occurs on an A frame, the next recorded frame will be a B frame. Commonly referred to as TLC, not to be confused with Slingshot's TLC or Telecine Log Converter files.

timecode A numbering system used to measure frames of video. Nondrop frame is most commonly used on film, has a direct number to frame correspondence but is not completely time accurate due to the actual video rate of 29.97 fps (NTSC). Drop frame does not have a direct frame-to-frame numbering correspondence but is time accurate.

timecode reader A machine used in telecine that reads timecode, usually connected to a timecode character generator which can put timecode burn-in windows onto a transferred videotape.

timing   Also called *grading* or *color timing*. The process of adjusting color balance for each scene from a conformed negative.

trichromatic   Three colors, such as RGB.

trim tab   A small white tab that indicates the content of a clip in the trim bin. West coast trim tabs are usually rectangular. On the East coast, they prefer cross-shaped tables.

tristimulus values   The amounts of three color stimuli required to match a particular color stimulus.

upright   A vertical viewing system for film. Also used for cutting. Moviolas are the most common uprights used. Vaguely resembles a sewing machine with two pedals attached, one for sound, the other for picture.

viewing conditions   Description of the characteristics of an area where images are viewed.

wet gate   Also *liquid gate*. A process where film is immersed in a suitable liquid at the moment of exposure to reduce scratches and abrasions.

white point   A point of viewer reference which is perceived as being white. Even under extreme lighting conditions, the brain detects elements which it perceives as white references.

wild lines   Dialog that is recorded without the camera rolling.

wild sound   Sounds that are recorded without the camera rolling.

window burn-in   See *burn-in*.

workprint   Positive prints (workprint) of film created from the OCN. They usually consist of only the takes that the director orders printed. (Hence the director's on-location phrase "Print it!".) Workprint is disposable and used for editing. It gets cut, hung in a bin, spliced and unspliced together, cursed at, and abused. If destroyed, it can be reordered from the lab. If additional takes need to be printed, the editor can order them from the lab.

Y   Luma, or the value of luminance in the picture. Signal is made up of $0.59G + 0.3R + 0.11B$.

Y, R-Y, B-Y   The general set of CAV signals used in PAL and some NTSC video signals, where the first color difference signal is R-Y and the second color difference signal is B-Y.

YCbCr   The three nonlinear video component signals in which a signal is transformed into a luma channel and two color difference channels. Conventionally, Cb and Cr represent color difference channels in digital format with excursions values of 16–235.

yellow   One of the subtractive primaries, absorbs blue light and transmits green and yellow light.

YIQ   A less commonly used signal, most recently used with D2. YIQ was created on the basis that the human visual system has less special acuity for magenta to green transitions than it does for red to cyan. As a result, the I and Q signals are formed from a 123 degree rotation on the vectorscope of U and V signals in a YUV signal.

YPbPr   The three nonlinear video component signals in which a signal is transformed into a luma channel and two color difference channels. Conventionally, Pr and Pb represent color difference channels in analog format with excursions values between −350 mV and +350 mV.

YUV Component signal of Y, U, and V, YUV is exactly the same as Y, R-Y, B-Y. The derivation from RGB is precisely the same; however, YUV is an intermediate of composite video, not component.

Zone System A system of photographic reproduction developed by Ansel Adams during his involvement in the F64 group of photographers. Adams would use the system to practically eliminate the higher and lower ends of luminance in the picture, giving deference to a rich variety of textures and tones in the middle. Some describe a histogram of Adams' work as a bell-shaped curve, although histograms were nonexistent during his life.

Bibliography

Berns, Roy S., Fred W. Billmeyer, and Max Saltzman. 2000. *Billmeyer and Saltzman's Principles of Color Technology, 3rd Edition*, Wiley-Interscience: Hoboken, NJ. ISBN 047119459X.

Baker, Robert and Ansel E. Adams. 1995 (reprint). *The Negative, Ansel Adams Photography, Book 2*. Little Brown & Co.: Boston, MA. ISBN 0821221868.

Blazner, David and Bruce Fraser. 2001. *Real World Photoshop 6*. Peachpit Press: Berkeley, CA. ISBN 0201721996.

Eiseman, Leatrice. 2000. *Pantone Guide to Communicating with Color*. Indianapolis, IN. ISBN 0966638328.

Eismann, Katrin. 2001. *Photoshop Restoration & Retouching*. Que Books: Indianapolis. ISBN 07897231282.

Georgianni, Edward J., and Madden, Thomas E. 1997. *Digital Color Management Encoding Solutions*, Addison-Wesley: Reading, MA . ISBN 0201634260.

von Goethe, Johann Wolfgang. 1970. *Theory of Colours*. MIT Press: Cambridge, MA. ISBN 0262570211.

Itten, Johannes and Faber Birren. 1970. *The Elements of Color*. John Wiley & Sons: NewYork. ISBN 0471289299.

Itten, Johannes. 1977. *The Art of Color: The Subjective Experience and Objective Rationale of Color*. John Wiley & Sons: Hoboken, NJ. ISBN 0471289280.

Jack, Keith. 2001. *Video Demystified : A Handbook for the Digital Engineer* (3rd edition). LLH Technology Publishing: Eagle Rock, VA. ISBN 1878707566.

Luscher, Max. 1979. *Four Color Person*. Simon & Schuster: New York. ISBN 0671242326.

Scott, Ian A. 1969. *The Luscher Color Test*. Random House: New York. ISBN 0671731459.

Wyszecki, Gunter. 2000. *Color Science: Concepts and Methods, Quantitative Data and Formulae* (Wiley Series in Pure and Applied Optics). John Wiley & Sons: Hoboken, NJ. ISBN 0471399183.

Zwimpfer, Moritz. 1988. *Color Light Sight Sense*. Schiffer Publishing: West Chester, PA. ISBN 0887401392.

Index

Numerics

A

B

C

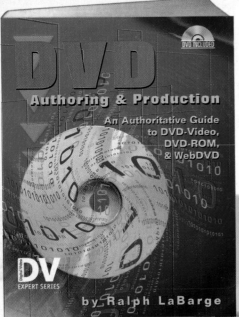

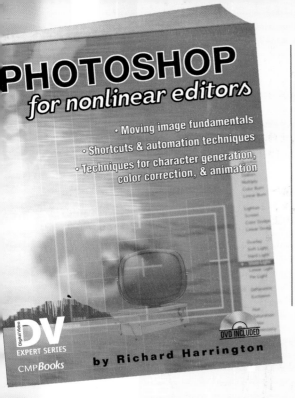

Photoshop for Nonlinear Editors
by Richard Harrington

Use Photoshop to generate characters, correct colors, and animate graphics for digital video. You'll grasp the fundamental concepts and master the complete range of Photoshop tools through lively discourse, full-color presentations, and hands-on tutorials. Includes a focus on shortcuts and automation and time-efficient techniques.

1-57820-209-4, $49.95
338 pp, 4-color, Trade paper with DVD

Compression for Great Digital Video
Power Tips, Techniques, & Common Sense
by Ben Waggoner

An essential reference for encoding digital video and audio for the Web, CD-ROM, DVD, and other media. You'll get a solid foundation in the fundamentals relevant to any compression software and discover the particulars of the most popular applications. Novices gain a clear introduction to the subject and advanced users enjoy the first cogent, accessible description of the elements of encoding.

1-57820-111-X, $49.95
447 pp, Trade paper with CD-ROM

Find CMP Books in your local bookstore
800-500-6875
cmp@rushorder.com
www.cmpbooks.com

What's on the CD-ROM?

The companion, hybrid CD-ROM for *Color Correction for Digital Video* includes

➤ graphic files for the tutorial projects,

➤ software tools and plug-ins from companies such as 3-Prong, Boris, Digital Film Tools, Discreet, Synthetic Aperture, and Tektronix, and

➤ full-length interviews with renowned experts.

For more information of the CD's contents and its copyrights, see the readme file on the disc.